REACHING INTO PLATO'S CAVE

Bringing the Bible into the 21st century

LUKE J. JANSSEN

REACHING INTO PLATO'S CAVE
Bringing the Bible into the 21st century.
By Luke J. Janssen

Cover images: *"Whisky Cave on Mull"* by Steven Deger (front cover) and *"Ancient Fingerprints"* from Forensic Outreach (back cover); full permission granted.

Illustrations: Luke Jeffrey Janssen; NASA

208 pages

ISBN 978-1503364462

CONTENTS

1. Introduction - Summarizes the conflict between faith and science and highlights the three target audiences of this book: (1) practicing theists struggling with this long-standing conflict, or the religious leaders to whom they turn for answers; (2) people who have given up any religious faith that they once had because of the cognitive dissonance engendered by their reading of the Bible; (3) people who are opposed to theistic thinking (atheists, agnostics, and adherents of other world religions).

2. The creation story - Presents several interpretations of Genesis chapters one and two (the origins of the universe, life and species), beginning with a traditional, literalist "Young Earth" (YE) view and then progressing through several more recent accommodative viewpoints which attempt to reconcile the Biblical texts with modern science. Conclusion: none of these fully explain the discrepancies, and we need further dialogue within the Christian community (chapter three) as well as between the theistic and atheistic viewpoints (chapter four).

3. The battle lines within the Christian community - Seven rebuttals frequently presented from the traditional, literalist YE viewpoint against the accommodative "Old Earth" re-interpretations, and the counter-arguments against those. Also presents a couple "messy problems" for the YE viewpoint. Conclusion: a YE-view is problematic; acceptance of some form of OE view is much needed.

4. Theists versus atheists - Atheists need to recognize that they also exercise a substantial amount of faith in their worldview. Theists need to be aware of three major pitfalls or errors when they argue with atheists. Conclusion: neither faith nor science need to be the points on which theists and atheists divide themselves.

5. The human family tree and our attempts to find God - Humans have been searching for some kind of "Great Being" for several hundred thousand years, leading to a wide diversity of world religions which attempt to explain that "Great Being". The impact that this has on traditional Christian thinking is explored in detail, particularly with respect to how Christians respond to other beliefs, as well as a re-interpretation of the Biblical "Adam".

6. The Fall and Original Sin - A central tenet of Christianity is that all people inherit sin simply by being descendants of the Biblical Adam and Eve (because of the "biting into the apple" story in Genesis three). I present a different way to view that Biblical story, and a re-definition of "Original Sin": the latter is symbolic of our natural tendency to be inwardly focused. Christianity calls us to fight against that selfish nature.   126

LIST OF FIGURES

1

Introduction

> Why write a book like this?
>
> Who is this book aimed at?
>
> What do other people think about the Creation story?
>
> Should I stop asking questions, or just believe?

WHY WRITE A BOOK LIKE THIS?

The very first book of the Bible — Genesis — has long made it difficult for me to be a believer, for two reasons.

First, it conflicted in a huge way with my love of science. I'd always been a science geek ... had a chemistry set as a pre-teen ... made a flying model airplane from balsa wood, and more than a few kites ... built my own Dobsonian telescope ... read hundreds of books on various scientific subjects ... loved shows like *Star Trek ... 2001: A Space Odyssey ... Hitch-hiker's Guide to the Galaxy.* At the same time, I went to Christian schools from grades 1 to 11. But as I continued the next two years in a public high school, then a few more years in a secular university and eventually made my way into a faculty position at that university, I found it increasingly difficult to reconcile my beliefs with my faith, especially when it came to the stories recorded in Genesis. Although I felt a responsibility to challenge so-called non-Christian teachings such as the Big Bang or evolution, I was intimidated and silenced by the overwhelming volume of the supporting evidence, and the paucity of evidence for my conservative Christian views.

Second, I was confused and bothered by the morality of some of the stories from this holy book. Some of these stories are almost humorous: Noah passing out drunk and naked, but putting a curse on his son for finding him that way (Genesis 9:20-25). But other stories are heinous. In an attempt to prevent the men of Sodom and Gomorrah from forcing homosexual relations on his guests, Lot offers his virgin daughters to them instead to *"do what you like with them"* (Genesis 19:5-8): a polite way to say *"go ahead and rape my little girls"*. (Judges 19 recounts a similar story committed by yet someone else, but that version comes to an even more disturbing end.) Later in Judges chapter 19, those daughters turn the table on Lot by conspiring to get him drunk and then become pregnant by him. The stories about the Israelites taking over the land of Canaan were particularly difficult to fit into my Christian theology. Here's a verbatim excerpt from my personal journal, dated June 8, 2012:

Today I'm reading an article in Maclean's magazine about a horrific slaughter in Syria. Apparently, government soldiers (Shia and Alawite Muslims) shelled a small town (Houla) populated mostly by another Muslim tribe (Sunni), then went in and slaughtered 108 people, including many women and children: kids had their throats slit or heads blown away. The world reacted in horror. Several nations, including Canada, Britain, France, Italy, Spain and Germany, expelled Syrian diplomats in protest. Even Syrian allies Russia and China condemned the attacks. If you were to ask ANYBODY on the street or at work what they thought of it, they'd say it was deplorable. Unbelievable. Despicable. No excuse for it. The soldiers are villains. Demons. Then it occurred to me: how is this different from some of the stories in the Old Testament describing the conquest of Canaan by Israelites? Although the Bible does spare us the details of exactly how they slaughtered the women and children — whether their throats were slit, or they were run through by swords, or stoned to death — it still says those defenceless people were killed by Israelite men much stronger and better armed than them (this makes them much worse than bullies). How would I answer someone who challenged me on those stories? Is it enough of an explanation to say: "God ordered those killings, so it must be OK"? Can I really believe that God ordered that? Or was it simply justified away and sanitized as "God's will" by an ancient, Semitic, patriarchal mind-set?

To be honest and blunt, Genesis presented God to me as someone with severe anger management issues: completely different from the image we receive in the life and ministry of Jesus Christ. I've often regretted the fact that Genesis is the first book of the Bible, and therefore the first thing that many non-believers read when they finally decide to *"check out Christianity"*, followed quickly by the never-ending lists of strange laws, penalties and sacrificial offerings described in Leviticus, Numbers and Deuteronomy (613 of them in the Pentateuch alone), and then the God-sanctioned genocides described in Joshua. In fact, when possible, I would advise scriptural neophytes to skip the Old Testament entirely, and steer them instead to the gospels. Some have hinted that this puts me in league with Marcion, who was a 1st / 2nd century theologian branded by the early church as a heretic because he taught an outright rejection of the Old Testament [1]. Before you judge me too quickly, ask yourself if you tend to avoid the Old Testament in your Bible readings or if you fully embrace all the passages, including those disturbing ones.

In the past I'd been content to think about my faith in pretty simple, comfortable, easily definable terms. But after being forced to think more seriously about things … to really think about what I believe about them ... I found I had to change my views.

The first big change in direction began with the whole creation / evolution debate, which unhinged my literal reading of Genesis. Actually, it unhinged my previous interpretation of the creation account in Genesis (this emphasis on the word 'interpretation' is an important point which I hope will become more clear by the end of this book).

Another major change in my thinking occurred after reading the Kite Runner [2], which I'll get into in more detail in chapter 4: this really challenged my previously held views about other religions.

Those new questions about world religions began to marinate in my new view about the origin of humans, and put a whole new light on our deep-rooted search for God (chapter 3).

Some of the answers to my questions began to crash with increasing force against my understanding of scripture, which sent me down a path of asking: What is scripture? Where did the book of Genesis in particular, and the Bible in general, come from (chapter 5 and 6)? What does it mean to say that writings are 'inspired' (chapter 6)?

Over the course of a few years with lots of reading, thinking and

---

[1] Eric Seibert. *Disturbing Divine Behaviour: Troubling Old Testament Images of God* (Minneapolis: Fortress Press, 2009)
[2] Khaled Hosseini. *The Kite Runner* (Riverhead Books, 2003)

talking to trusted friends and family, I found myself completely re-shaping what I believed. Discarding a number of ideas which were taught to me: ideas that were someone's interpretation of scripture rather than a straightforward understanding of the message and history of scripture. I nearly threw out the whole thing. But in the process of writing this book, I grappled many of my questions to the ground and really came to grips with what I myself believed, and now saw quite differently than a few years ago. I began to see a whole new breadth of God's care for humanity: not just the descendants of Abraham and the Christian church which was grafted onto that, but the various other lines of humanity existing at that time. In the process, I regained my faith, minus some human baggage.

In the end, I wrote this book because I still believed. I still love many aspects of the Christian faith. The old hymns. The community. The shared priority of reaching out to help our fellow man. I just want my Mondays-Fridays (who I am in the workplace) to be consistent with my Sundays (who I am at church). And I don't want any of the religion and churchiness that seemed to be wrapped up in believing. Finally, I want to help others learn from my experience.

WHAT'S THE BASIC MESSAGE OF THIS BOOK?

For the first half of my life, I'd struggled with my faith because I took the Bible to be purely a divine book: every word was precisely the word that God intended. It was only when I looked closely into how the Bible came to us that I saw how it is equally a human document. Humans were centrally involved in the writing, copying, interpretation, collection and distribution at every step along the way from individual books to collated canon (selection of which books would be become part of the Bible). Once I accepted that fact, it was easy to see that many of the issues I'd previously stumbled over could be attributed to that human involvement. Until then, the only explanations available made God somehow responsible, but that's what I found so unsettling.

So that's the main message of this book. I'm not at all trying to get people to throw out the Bible, and certainly not to give up their faith. Instead, I believe they can strengthen their faith and become more relevant to the 21st century by embracing the fact that the Bible is both human and divine (something they find easy to say about Jesus himself). The original title for this book was going to be *Interpretations*, because that's what I saw as the fundamental problem. I'd been shackled to certain interpretations, but now realized that other interpretations also treat the Bible as inspired by

God without being a literal transcript of his dictations.

For those of you who are interested in the scientific questions, you'll find chapters one to four will scratch that itch. I do my best to leave out the tedious details that only specialists will understand, but otherwise deal with those questions head on and with gloves off.

For those of you who find science overwhelming or uninteresting, you can easily skip straight to chapter five. Although that begins with a little bit more science, I very quickly get into general questions about Christianity and world religions, and from that point on till the end of the book I focus almost exclusively on more theological issues: the moral/ethical problems in the OT, how the Bible came to be, and how we can read it differently.

WHO AM I WRITING THIS BOOK FOR?

First and foremost, I'm writing this for those believers who come from a very conservative background like the one I grew up in, one that takes Genesis very literally, and to the clergy from whom those people seek spiritual guidance, in order to help both deal with a world of science that they don't understand.

The most recent (2014) Gallup poll showed that 42% of Americans believe in a literal interpretation of the biblical version of creation [3]; in fact, when they looked back at a dozen of such polls they've conducted since this question was first asked back in 1982, this number has hovered between 40-47%. The Associated Press found much the same in a poll they conducted in March 2014 [4]. Another poll done by Pew Research Center in 2013 found 33% of Americans believe that *"humans and other living things have existed in their present form since the beginning of time"* [5] (in other words, they reject the theory of evolution).

In 2012, a Christian think-tank organization conducted a survey among 743 pastors of churches *"big and small and from all Christian denominations"* across the USA. (I'll refer to this survey several times in

---

[3] Gallup, *In U.S., 42% Believe Creationist View of Human Origins* <*http://www.gallup.com/poll/170822/believe-creationist-view-human-origins.aspx*> (accessed Sept. 19, 2014)
[4] Associated Press, *AP-GfK Poll: Big Bang a big question for most Americans.* <http://ap-gfkpoll.com/featured/findings-from-our-latest-poll-2 >
[5] Pew Research, *Public's Views on Human Evolution,* <http://www.pewforum.org/2013/12/30/publics-views-on-human-evolution/> (accessed April 13, 2014)

this book as the 'Biologos survey'). They found 54% of respondents most closely identified with the view that God "*created life in its present form in six 24-hour days*" [6]. That same survey found that 66% of pastors holding to a traditional / literal interpretation of creation, and 61% of those accepting less traditional interpretations (which I'll describe in more detail in chapter 2), agreed with the statement that "*younger adults today are more concerned than ever about whether faith and science are compatible*". There was also concern among the pastors themselves: 58% of the literal interpretationist pastors agreed that "*If you publicly admitted your own doubts about human origins, you feel you would have a lot to lose in your ministry*" (there was much less of this concern among the pastors from other creationist viewpoints). A vast majority of all those 743 pastors felt it was important to address science issues in the local community (72%) and on the national and global stages (89%).

The same polling research group which conducted the study summarized above also ran another 5-year study of 1,296 respondents in which the main question being asked was why people who were regular church-goers during their teen years had disconnected with the church since age 15 [7]. Seven reasons were given, none of which seemed to dominate over the others. One of these reasons was the tension between churches and science, with the following sentiments being indicated: "*churches are out of step with the scientific world we live in*" (29%); "*Christianity is anti-science*" (25%); and "*been turned off by the creation-versus-evolution debate*" (23%).

In yet another survey conducted on-line in 2013 [8], respondents were asked two questions: (1) *if you left the Christian faith, what was your greatest reason for doing so?* (2) *what do you consider to be the greatest obstacle to belief in the Christian God?* This survey wasn't conducted by a recognized statistician, and does not have the level of recognition of standards like Gallup or Pew, but it's very instructive just the same. Of the 2,020 people who participated, 74% claimed to have been Christians at some point in their lives, but 96% defined themselves as non-Christian at the time of the survey.

---

[6] Biologos Foundation, *A Survey of Clergy and Their Views on Origins*, <http://biologos.org/blog/a-survey-of-clergy-and-their-views-on-origins> (accessed June 2, 2013)

[7] <https://www.barna.org/barna-update/teens-nextgen/528-six-reasons-young-christians-leave-church>

[8] Reddit, *Reasons For the Decline in Christianity According to Ex-Christians and non-Christians*, <http://www.reddit.com/r/TrueAtheism/comments/1j7lup/the_results_of_the_survey_are_in_reasons_for_the/> (accessed November 29, 2013)

Among the respondents who had left the Christian faith, the most popular reason for doing so was *"Christian teachings that conflict with findings of modern science"* (shared by 54%). All the other reasons given were far less consistent or popular, each being shared by 6% or fewer of the faith-rejecting respondents; interestingly, from the point of view of the book I've written, their third most popular answer was *"acts of violence attributed to God in the bible"* (the answer given by 4% of the faith-rejectors).

With respect to the second question — the greatest obstacle to belief in the Christian God — the top answer given was once again *"Christian teachings that conflict with findings of modern science"*: this was the top answer for 42% of those who had rejected the faith, for 39% of those who had never accepted the faith, and for 14% of those who were currently Christians. The second top answer was *"Non-falsifiable claims"* (29%, 29% and 5%, respectively). The third most popular answer was *"Acts of violence attributed to God in the bible"* (4%, 3% and 14%, respectively).

All of these surveys, and many others which I don't recount here, echo the sentiment that today's society is hugely concerned with the perceived conflict between Science and the Bible, and the perceived offensive nature of stories found in the Old Testament. At least, that seems to be the case in North America, particularly the U.S.. There seems to be less dogmatism and division on this point among Christians in Europe and Asia. It's worth adding here that the conflict between creationism and evolution, and the resulting denial of the authority of science, is also becoming an issue among members of the Muslim community around the world.

Some believers will be very comfortable clinging to the literal interpretationist viewpoint, but a lot of others will, like myself, be privately struggling with it. Do I base my life on fact or faith? Science or scripture? Darwinism or design? Will God really send good people to hell? What is sin? Why is God always judging people and destroying things? What should I believe? I've pondered questions like these for several decades, partly out of personal interest but also because I want to be able to defend what I believe to non-Christians. I'm no longer content to stop at those easy answers that Christians will circulate among themselves but which hold no currency whatsoever in conversations with non-believers. If you have no problems with these questions or with the traditional interpretations of Genesis, then maybe you need to consider how other people are responding to that theology, especially the non-believers who you've been called to reach. But if you do wrestle with these things, I'm hoping you find alternative explanations in here that let you keep your head and your heart together. I think one can still believe in God, and in Jesus Christ as his best example of how to live, and the Bible as a partial record of our interactions with him, his hopes for us, and the faith journeys and life lessons from many believers before us. I hope my book causes you to evaluate what exactly you believe, and encourages you to distinguish that which is human interpretation from that which would be God's actual teaching to us.

I'm also writing to those who once believed, held the Bible as sacred, but have let their faith grow cold or even rejected it entirely because it was all too hard intellectually to hang on to. Who found it too hard to integrate their Biblical faith with contemporary scientific teachings and modern society. Who were repulsed by the way the Bible deals with women, homosexuals, slaves, Canaanites, et cetera, and decided it must all be worthless tripe. Who've thrown out the baby with the bath-water. I'm hoping you can come back to it and put it into a context — it was written by humans of a specific gender from a very tightly racially-focussed point of view — and sift out the truth and the valuable from the rest.

Third, I'm writing to those who are absolutely opposed to the Christian faith — atheists on the one hand, and those who subscribe to other world religions on the other hand. But let me be clear, this is not simply a polemic: I don't intend to debate you here, or present you with reams and reams of evidence and arguments in favour of a theistic creation or the existence of God, or to otherwise change your mind on which religion is the only right one. Instead, I want this book to discourage antagonism between groups, and promote discussion: between Christianity and other religions, or between theists and atheists. To reach this goal, Christians will need to become more open-minded about the good in other people, religious or not, and what we can learn from them. At the same time, we should realize that all of us, including ourselves, have got it wrong in one way or another; none of us have it all together, nor have the monopoly on truth. As for atheists, they need to realize that much of what they hold as fact is really faith. Both groups (Christians and atheists) have to stop seeing the creation/evolution debate as an either/or situation. That's a false dichotomy: there's a wide spectrum of people in between the two extremes of conservative fundamentalist Christianity and secular atheism ... creationists who do accept Big Bang cosmology and Evolutionary Theory, as well as atheists who unwittingly hold varying degrees of beliefs. The latter group need to know that not all Christians ignore the data that are out there, and also need to be challenged to critically evaluate their own 'beliefs'. That's right: most atheists are not aware of the amount of faith in much of their world views (you'll see what I mean by this statement in chapter 4).

THE REACTION I EXPECT TO GET

I fully expect this book will get a defensive or even hostile reaction from both sides of the theological fence, but probably the most emotive one from the Christian side. The view I'll try to present is not a typical fundamentalist one. As I began to question all the things I had once believed — that I had simply grown up believing because I was taught, without having to digest them — there were moments of fear in which I wondered if I should just stop questioning and simply believe. And I'm sure there are people — family members or close friends that I might confide in and share these doubts with — who would tell me to do just that: to simply believe. That it's wrong to doubt or question. But then I realize that Jesus didn't ask people to *"simply believe"*. He gave the parable of the person who should *"count the cost"* before committing to following him (Luke 14:28). To people who needed physical evidence and hard facts, the Bible says he gave signs and miracles. He invited Thomas to gather his own evidence: to put his fingers in Jesus's hands to feel the nail holes, and his hand into Jesus's side to feel where the spear was thrust in (John 20:27). To people who needed to reason their way through faith, he *"<u>explained</u> to them what was said in all the Scriptures concerning himself"* (Luke 24:27; emphasis added). To the unconvinced: *"Taste and see that the Lord is good"* (Psalm 34:8). Even Abram (later re-named Abraham), who Paul holds up as a paragon of faith in the fourth chapter of Romans, needed a sign: when God promised Abram an uncountable number of descendants, the text says *"Abram believed the LORD, and he credited it to him as righteousness"* (Genesis 15:6), but two verses later when God promises Canaan to him, Abram says *"how can I know that I will gain possession of it?"* Apparently Abram needed some kind of evidence. Faith in the fact that *"God said it"* simply wasn't enough for him, so God participates with Abram in an elaborate covenant ceremony which was common in Ancient Mesopotamia.

For these reasons, I have to fully disagree with those who say I need to have a simple blind faith: what I believe has to make sense and stand up to scrutiny. *"Always be prepared to give an answer to everyone who asks you to give the reason for the hope that you have"* (1 Peter 3:15).

Nonetheless, I still expect many Christians won't like the questions I ask of the Bible, or more specifically, when I question the layers of meaning and interpretation which have been added by humans to the Bible, especially the book of Genesis. They'll accuse me of rejecting the Bible, and that that's the beginning of a slippery slope. *"It's no wonder he's rejecting so many of the fundamental, undeniable truths of the Christian faith, if he doesn't accept the Bible as inerrant and infallible!?"* Yes I'm now putting question marks around certain parts of the Bible. God's word and God's creation shouldn't tell two different stories, nor should the images of God in the Old Testament and of Jesus in the New Testament be so totally and dramatically different, so I'm re-evaluating my previous assumptions and explanations, and just following the data to where they lead. But if at any point in reading the ideas and questions raised in this book you become so offended that you decide not to finish it, I ask you to first read the very last section of the book, the one in chapter 9 entitled 'Conclusion: what have I still hung on to?'. If that doesn't change your mind about writing me off, then please go ahead and throw this book away.

I also wonder if some readers will be overly sensitive or reflexive when I refer to the cultural context for some of my problems with scripture. Let me be absolutely clear on this point: I am not anti-Semitic. But I am honest enough to hold up for scrutiny the fact that Genesis (and of course the rest of the Old Testament) was written by an extremely narrowly-defined group of people: men with a patriarchal, Ancient Near Eastern viewpoint. And that is going to influence the words they wrote and the interpretations that come out of their writings. I would have said the same thing if all the writers had been Chinese or Inuit or Italian, or if they were all female, or every one of them teenagers who went to Woodstock in the 1960s; any compilation of dozens of books written by any single one of these groups of people will also have a very narrowly focussed viewpoint. Please don't deflect the message of my book by raising the red herring of racism.

Lastly, I'm anticipating a response from certain atheists who become emotionally charged when questions are asked about Darwinian evolution, and especially whenever Intelligent Design is even alluded to. In both cases, I would just ask those readers to relax, and simply consider the arguments made or the questions raised. Don't immediately react. Think. Evaluate. Critically. Let's together take an evidence-based approach and see what we find. Let's not deflect the dialogue just because we think we see where it's going and we don't like the destination. Socrates: *"The unexamined life is not worth living"*. Carl Sagan: *"It is far better to grasp the universe as it really is than to persist in delusion, however satisfying and reassuring"*.

Irrespective of where you're coming from, I would greatly appreciate your feedback on the points I make in this narrative of my journey. Did it help you in your own? Answer any questions you've struggled long against? Or did it make you question your own faith? Make you angry? If you think I'm wrong on any point, please let me know. My theology has been evolving constantly, and I'm open to revising it yet more.

I've set up a dedicated email account for all those comments (lukejjanssen@gmail.com) as well as a blog page which continues my thoughts on these questions (http:/lukejjanssen.wordpress.com).

MATTERS OF BUSINESS

When I quote from the Bible, I'll use the New International Version (NIV) unless specifically indicated otherwise, in which case I'll say whether I'm using the King James version (KJV), the New American Standard Bible (NASB) or the Aramaic version in Plain English because their wording better helps me make my point.

Second, I may use some abbreviations which aren't familiar to all readers. In particular, YE and OE for 'Young Earth' and 'Old Earth' respectively; you'll know what I mean by those terms once you read chapter 2. Of course, a book on the topic of the conflict between science and the Bible would be incomplete without a section on Intelligent Design or ID (chapter 4). Readers of the Bible should be familiar with the abbreviation OT for the Old Testament. For dates, I'm going to use the well-worn abbreviations BC (for 'before Christ') and AD (for 'Anno Domini'; Latin for 'Year of the Lord'), respectively, rather than pander to political correctness by using the newer terms CE (Christian era, or common era) and BCE (before CE). 'YHWH' is one way to represent the Hebrew name for God, "Yahweh"; some refer to this as 'the tetragrammaton' (the four letters) or 'the Name'. Other abbreviations are in such common use that I don't feel a need to define them: NASA; DNA; GPS; CPR; USA.

Finally, and most importantly for this section of the chapter, are the credits. I'd like to acknowledge and thank many people for their many, many discussions of the questions raised in this book and for taking the time to give me feedback on excerpts of it. There are so many. I'd like to particularly mention friends and colleagues with whom I went on a medical mission trip to Bolivia in 2013, and in the process had many long talks about these matters, and it was those very discussions which finally moved me to put all these thoughts to paper in the form of this book: Dr. John Harvey, Rev. Peter Cowley, Dr. David Burk. Also a host of other friends with whom I've had many coffee chats: Rev. Lane Fusilier, Rev. John Wilton, Jimmy Rushton, Don Corry, Harold Laser, Rick Bradford, Marcus Verbrugge, Dr. Nabeel Ghayur, George Wright. I feel I owe a huge debt of gratitude to Justin Brierley and the podcast / radio show that he hosts called "*Unbelievable*", which gave me innumerable insights into many of the questions addressed in this book; I highly recommend all readers to check out the diverse list of podcasts available on their website. Also in this group are my whole family, who are a feisty bunch with no end of diverse opinions and a long history exploring who God is: my son Ryan, my parents Harry and Grace, and siblings Allan (who helped immensely with text editing), Margot, Renee and Ivan. Of course, my wife, Miriam, who has heard me carry on at great length at many of the discussions alluded to above, and on our many walks through the country-side. Finally, there's such a long list of hugely influential authors of books which I've read on this subject, and I've done my best to cite them in my footnotes. I'm likely forgetting many others, and I apologize to them if I've done so.

2

The Creation story

How do I reconcile the Genesis account of creation with the theories of the Big Bang and Darwinian evolution?

Why does it look like things evolved slowly, but the Bible describes a very different process and time-line?

Should I read the Bible like a science book and/or history book?

Is the Bible meant to be a science textbook?

Faith versus fact? Scripture versus science? Darwinism or Design?

I grew up with the stories of Genesis presented in big picture story books at home and on flannel boards in Sunday School. All through childhood, the stories were presented to me 'as is': it all happened exactly as they're written. The stories were toned down somewhat; sanitized with respect to their more difficult aspects. For example, the pictures of Noah's Ark always showed happy, smiley people and animals with a rainbow in the sky and lots of colorful trees and flowers, but didn't show the dead bodies or arms and legs sticking out of the mud, or the scratches on the sides of the Ark from hundreds of desperate fingernails. It was all so clean and straightforward then. But that was about to change.

THE YOUNG EARTH VERSION OF CREATION

In general, Christians have long held that the world is only a few thousand years old (though this view was not universal). For example, even as far back as the fourth century AD, Augustine wrote: "*They say what they think, not what they know. They are deceived too, by those highly mendacious documents which profess to give the history of many thousand years, though, reckoning by the sacred writings, we find that not 6,000 years have yet passed*[9]. However, the issue of exactly how old the universe and the earth are wasn't a divisive one in the Christian community until well over a millennium later.

In the mid-1600s, a number of people sought to come up with an answer to the question *"when did creation happen?"* Some collated the various genealogies provided in the Old Testament (OT) — for example, Genesis chapters 5 and 11, but there are several others — and then placed them in context with known recorded world history. That is, once they had mapped out the full family tree for key individuals such as Abraham, Moses and David, as well as their ancestors and descendants, they assigned dates to those individuals based on Biblical accounts of their interactions with historical figures and cultures. The latter included: the Pharaohs of Egypt; the Queen of Sheba; kings of other surrounding city states or countries; rulers of Babylonian or Persian empires.

In 1642, Cambridge University Vice Chancellor John Lightfoot came up with an answer: Sept. 17, 3928 BC. In 1650, Anglican Archbishop of Ireland's James Ussher calculated it to be Oct. 23, 4004 BC [10]. I have to admit, I at first found it humorous that they nailed it down to a specific date. And even more so when I found out that they announced the specific time of day: Lightfoot claimed it happened at 9:00 am, while Ussher said it happened in the evening. I at first supposed that this enhanced precision was intended simply to convey a greater sense of accuracy. But precision and accuracy are not at all the same thing: the former gets at how exact a measurement might be, while the latter gets at how correct the measurement is. For example, when telling my friends about my latest fishing trip, I could say I caught a 15 pound bass, or be more precise and say it was 14 pounds and 8.73 ounces, or be more accurate (and honest) and say it was a 2 pound bass.

I've since learned that Ussher got to a specific date and time not by adding up the genealogies in the scriptural texts (which at best might give you the year when the patriarchal ball started rolling) but by using a form of (then) contemporary science. That is, he used the Roman calendar system and historical documents, constructed an extensive series of solar and lunar cycles and correlated them together with ancient Egyptian and Hebrew historical documents, eventually falling on the year 4004 BC (again, not by adding up genealogies, but by looking at how those cycles interacted and

[9] Augustine, "Of the Falseness of the History Which Allots Many Thousand Years to the World's Past" in *The City of God.*
[10] James Ussher, *Annales Veteris Testamenti, A Prima Mundi Origine Deducti* ("Annals of the Old Testament, deduced from the first origins of the world.")

converged). He then assumed that Creation took place in the fall, apparently because fruit and vegetables would be ripe and ready for Adam and Eve to eat. He then consulted astronomical tables to find out what day the autumnal equinox fell in that year, presumably because the number of daylight and night-time hours would be equal, given that God would have divided them up equally. Finally, he then factored in the ideas that creation would have begun on the first day of the week, and that the Hebrews saw the evening as the beginning of a new day, and thereby concluded that it all happened on the evening of October 23, 4004 BC.

Many other people have come up with other dates and years, but they generally agree that the day of creation occurred somewhere around the year 4000-6000 BC. One reason they came up with different dates is that some used Masoretic texts (Hebrew), while others used the Septuagint (a later Greek translation of the Bible), which differs in some places. It may also be in part because the ancients saw nothing wrong in pruning an individual or two from a family tree for the sake of numerology and symbology (a family tree with very symmetrical branching looked more well-kept, perhaps more ordained by YHWH) or to emphasize the importance of certain ancestors. It's worth noting that the Hebrew words for father ('ab) and son (ben) can also mean forefather and descendant.

Irrespective of these minor differences, many Christians generally agreed that the world was created around the year 4000 BC, and Ussher is usually named as the originator of this idea (even though Augustine referred to it as a mistaken idea over a millennium before Ussher).   More recently, some creationists have extended this time-line to 10,000 years in order to accommodate historical records from ancient civilizations such as the Mesopotamian or Chinese, or even 50,000 – 100,000 years to account for paleontological findings of Neanderthal and other hominid artifacts, but this doesn't really change the picture too much. The fact remains that these Creationist timelines crystalized the growing tension between two groups. On the one hand, those that emphasize a literal reading of the book of Genesis and therefore see the earth and universe as being less than a few tens of thousands of years old: the Young Earth believers. And on the other hand, those that 'read' the physical universe all around, which was also 'written' by God, and see something much, much older: who are then often referred to as the Old Earth or OE proponents. But as Sir Francis Bacon first put it: 'The book of God's words' should say the same thing as 'The book of God's works'. This dichotomy sets the stage for one of the first turning points I had in my own faith journey.

GOD, THE GREAT COSMIC CON-MAN?

Like many people with a Christian background and who went to Sunday school, I was taught and grew up with a YE world-view. Every now and then I'd be confronted with a little factoid that was inconsistent with this: a certain dinosaur having reportedly lived 125 million years ago, or that a certain star was 100,000 light years away. For many years, I would basically just dismiss those claims. Not necessarily think or say that they were false: I just buried my head in the sand and tried to ignore them. As I got older, and then went to university, those inconsistencies confronted me more and more, becoming more bothersome and compelling. Eventually, the cognitive dissonance overwhelmed me, and I had to come to terms with this question: how can I hold a YE viewpoint in the face of all this evidence for a much older universe?

Somewhere along the line, I came across the idea of 'apparent age' [11]. I've since come to learn that this theory was first introduced in 1857 by the British biologist and preacher Henry Philip Gosse [12] in order to explain how the universe could look much older than it was believed (by some) to be. When scripture described the creation of Adam and Eve, it never implied that God made them as fetuses or infants that had to be bottle-fed and cared for until they were old enough to care for themselves. Instead, it seems he created them as full-grown adults: scriptures don't indicate if they were teenagers or in middle age, but they were old enough to take care of the garden and to *"be fruitful and multiply"*. In other words, even on their first day of existence, they looked like they had been around for decades ... 'apparent age'. And so in theory we could say the same thing about the rest of creation. When God created the star that looks like it's 100,000 light years away, God created not only the star, but the light beam(s) between that star and earth that would have otherwise been emitted 100,000 years ago. Why not? Then we could see it, right? And the evidence for the evolution of life forms down through the millennia, including the various fossils that have been found, he embedded within the rocks and soils. Using this idea of apparent age, it was now very easy to hold onto the traditional YE hypothesis and the discoveries of modern science which would otherwise contradict it.

---

[11] John MacArthur, *The Battle for the Beginning: Creation, Evolution, and the Bible*, (Nelson Books, 2001)

[12] Philip Gosse, *Omphalos: An Attempt To Untie The Geological Knot.* (London: J. Van Voorst, 1857) (note: Gosse's book is entitled 'Omphalos', which is the Greek word for 'navel', because a central argument in his book is whether or not Adam had a belly button, given that he never had an umbilical cord attached to a mother)

But as time went on, some of the discoveries became harder to reconcile because doing so raised a much bigger question: why would God do that? Sometimes it was easy to answer that question. It made sense that God would create Adam and Eve to be old enough to take care of themselves and to propagate the species. And it made sense that he would create light beams from very distant stars in order for us to see the stars and appreciate the grandeur of his creation. But there were other signs of apparent age which made me question God's motives for doing it that way.

For example, Richard Dawkins wrote [13] about a nerve that he dissected in a giraffe neck called the recurrent laryngeal nerve, or the 10th cranial nerve. This nerve travelled all the way down the giraffe's neck to the main artery coming off the heart (the aorta), looped around that artery and then headed back up the neck several feet to the voice box (larynx). Dawkins explained that other animals with shorter necks also have this same nerve which also loops under the same artery, but the final destination of that nerve — the larynx – in those shorter-necked animals is only a few centimeters away. It's not too hard to explain why this nerve took a short detour before reaching its destination within short-necked animals, Nerves don't always take the shortest, most direct route to their target. Perhaps a bit inefficient, but not shocking. However, to see that same nerve travel down the neck of the giraffe, passing within centimeters of its ultimate target, continue on for another meter or so, and then loop back to intersect with its final target was indeed quite surprising: it didn't make sense that God would make the nerve do that. The most sensible explanation might seem to be that, as the predecessors of the giraffe grew slightly longer and longer necks over the millennia, their laryngeal nerve had to travel progressively yet another fraction of a millimeter with every few generations: something that is entirely conceivable for a nerve to do over millions of years. Or maybe God just made it look that way ... created that nerve in the giraffe neck 6,000 years ago, making it follow a path which was just plain nonsensical (outside of an explanation which involved a slow evolution). But why?

Or, more recently, I read about 'pseudogenes': genes which are functional in other animals but which are mutated in the human genome such that they no longer function. We have approximately 12,000 of these in our genome (our personal collection of genes). For example, one of these is the gene for the enzyme L-gulono-γ-lactone oxidase (GLO, or GULO), the enzyme which is necessary to make vitamin C. Most non-human species have a functional GLO gene and can make their own vitamin C. But it's become damaged and non-functional in humans and some other primates

---

[13] Richard Dawkins, *The Greatest Show on Earth*, pp. 360–362 (New York: Free Press, 2010)

and in guinea-pigs, which is why we need to continually eat citrus fruits like oranges to remain healthy (in ancient times, sailors would come down with scurvy if they went too long without citrus fruits like limes ... hence some called them 'limeys'). In humans, the GLO gene is non-functional because of mutations within its coding sequence: what's particularly interesting is that many of the mutations are the same in the human and primate pseudogenes, but quite different in the guinea-pig genome. This is exactly what one would expect if the mutation occurred soon after our evolutionary tree branched, leading to humans and primates on one side and guinea pigs on the other.

Another example would be the genes which in egg-laying animals produces the major protein in egg yolk (vitellin), or the ones that make tails in the fetus of many mammals: those are still present in the human genome, but they're switched off. One interpretation is that we inherited our genes from our predecessors, but some of them have since been mutated or otherwise turned off and yet we continue to pass them on (common descent). The alternative is that God just made it look that way (common design). But why?

Somewhat similar to pseudogenes, there are bits and pieces of dead viruses within our human DNA sequence [14] [15] [16]. When certain viruses infect us, they insert a string of genetic information into our DNA and then use our own cells to make other viruses. Some of those inserted bits of information remain in our DNA and can even be passed down to our offspring. The interesting thing is that there are such remnants — called proviral gene sequences — in both human and chimpanzee DNA. In this way, or so it seemed, we can still see the evidence of certain disease epidemics which attacked the common ancestors of both humans and chimpanzees, and which those ancestors fought off and survived, albeit with some genetic scars to tell the story. Or maybe God just placed those viral (diseased) sequences in human and chimpanzee DNA on the fifth and sixth days of Creation to make it look like both species fought off the same infection? But why?

While we're on the subject of genes, we could also talk about "alleles". For any given gene in our body, we inherit two versions: one

---

[14] W. E. Johnson and J.M. Coffin. "Constructing primate phylogenies from ancient retrovirus sequences", *Proceedings of the National Academy of Science* 96, no.18 (1999): 10254-10260
[15] N. Wolfe, *The Viral Storm: the Dawn of a New Pandemic Age*. (New York: Times Books, Henry Holt and Company, 2011)
[16] Robert Belshaw, Vini Perelra, Aris Katzourakis, et al. "Long-term Reinfection of the Human Genome by Endogenous Retroviruses". *Proceedings of the National Academy of Science* 101, no.14 (2004):4894-4899

from our father and the other from our mother. But the allele we inherited from our father was one of two that he possessed, and the one from our mother was one of two that she had, and all four of those could be different versions of the particular gene. Those four versions of the given gene are referred to as "alleles" of that gene. One example that most people have heard about is blood type, for which there are three alleles: A, B and O. Here's where the science and the YE theology collide: if we all began from two individuals (Adam and Eve), and that only a few thousand years ago, then there should only be at most four alleles for any given gene in the human genome (and some could even argue that we should only have two alleles per gene, if Eve was actually created from Adam's rib, which would contain his X-chromosome that was then duplicated to make the XX female). And yet many genes have many more than four alleles: in fact, there are fifty-nine different alleles in one gene called the human leukocyte antigen complex (has to do with our immune system). It might be conceivable for a species to go from 4 alleles to a couple dozen in the course of thousands of generations with a normal background degree of mutation, but not within only three to four hundred generations (the approximate equivalent of 6,000 years), unless you posit some unbelievably high degree of mutation in the human genome between then and now.

Genes, pseudogenes and alleles are all organized into very large strings called chromosomes. Many animals have pairs of chromosomes, one set inherited from their father and one from their mother, but the number of pairs can vary considerably between species. Many primates (chimp, gorilla, orangutang) have 24 pairs of chromosomes, but humans have only 23. This difference seemed to shoot a whole in the boat of evolutionary theory: it implied that the evolution of humans from primates involved the loss of a whole pair of chromosomes, an incredible amount of genetic material and information that evolution, if it had a mind, would not tolerate. In fact, the difference seemed to be more consistent with the interpretation that we are indeed created uniquely and separately from the primates. But a closer look at our chromosomes brought the story back to the evolutionary camp. All chromosomes have a unique central region called a centromere which the cell uses as a kind of handle to pull the pairs of chromosomes around within the cell (a hugely important function when the cell is undergoing division and has to divide the chromosomes evenly between the two daughter cells). The chromosomes also have unique structures at each of their tips called telomeres, which help keep the chromosome "healthy". Geneticists have special stains which differentially colorize the centromeres and telomeres, as well as the gene-coding regions in between each. Using those stains, all chromosomes appear under the microscope like multi-

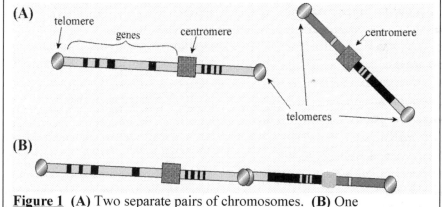

Figure 1 **(A)** Two separate pairs of chromosomes. **(B)** One chromosome formed by a head-to-tail fusion of the chromosomes shown in (A).

banded snakes, with a telomere at each end, and one centromere somewhere around the middle, and many bands of varying color and thickness in between (see Figure 1). When the human chromosomes are stained in this way, not only does a simple counting show that we are missing one pair compared to the other primates, but also that one of our chromosome pairs has a very strange banding pattern [17]: in addition to a telomere at either end and a central centromere, it also has the remnants of a second centromere as well as a third telomere band in between the two centromeres. When geneticists looked more closely at the banding pattern of the genes in that strange human chromosome, they realized that it is in fact a head-to-head fusion of two different chromosomes in the primate genome: essentially, the A-to-Z banding pattern from one primate chromosome, and the a-to-z banding pattern from another primate chromosome matched up nicely with an A-to-Z-to-z-to-a banding pattern in the human chromosome. The two best explanations are that two chromosomes in one of our primate ancestors fused head-to-head, or that God made it look like they did.

Another set of observations that make me wonder *"why would God do it that way?"* relate to the fact that he gave us the tiny remains of a tail, or buried just the remnants of the pelvis and hind limbs deep within the body of a whale, all of which seem to have no function at all within a YE scenario but look like they might have served a purpose in a much more distant evolutionary past. Or put functionless eyes on animals that live their whole lives underground or in subterranean caves and are therefore blind (for example, the olm, or proteus fish): those could either be the degenerated

---

[17] that 23rd chromosome is actually referred to as chromosome #2, because chromosomes are numbered from largest to smallest, and it's the 2nd largest of our chromosomes

remains of functional eyes from ancestors long ago, or those modern animals were intentionally created that way. But why?

There's also evidence outside of biology which demands a much longer time-line than just 6,000 years. Layers of sediments at the bottom of Lake Suigetsu in Japan go back 50,000 years [18]. Ice cores from Greenland reveal layers in the ice documenting annual snowfalls going back 100,000 years [19], including layers speckled with the dust from known volcanic events like the Krakatoa and Vesuvius eruptions, as well as variations which reflect the predicted wobbles in earth's orbit that reappear at intervals of hundreds of thousands of years. The size of the deposits of coal and oil around the world: even if all the sunlight striking the earth was converted by plants to hydrocarbons at 100% efficiency, it would still take a minimum of several hundred thousand years to generate those tremendous deposits (or millions of years if you make less demanding assumptions). Astronomers can provide images and measurements of stars which appear to be at the middle or even the end of their stellar lifetimes, which in turn are measured on the order of billions of years.

There are just so many other similar examples of scientific discoveries which require us to really stretch the concept of apparent age. In each case, it's entirely possible that God might choose to do it that way ... to make things look ancient, and/or make it look like they required processes that moved slowly over millions and billions of years. But I kept asking *"Why? Why would God do that?"*

The only explanation which seemed available to me was that he did that to test our faith. To force people to make a choice: him or science? Faith or fact?

That explanation might have been satisfactory very briefly. Except for the fact that it required me to also believe something very deeply disturbing about God.

I imagined a very unsettling scenario: myself testing my wife's love for me and trust in me by making it look like I was having an affair. In this scenario, I would write a letter from someone other than her, leave it in one of my shirt pockets and then intentionally put that shirt in the laundry for her to discover. My credit card bills would show expenses for tickets to movies and theater presentations that my wife had never been to, or receipts for jewelry that she never received. When I would come home from trips overseas, she might find something in my luggage that clearly didn't belong

---

[18] CB Ramsey, RA Staff, CL Bryant, et al. "A Complete Terrestrial Radiocarbon Record for 11.2 to 52.8 kyr B.P." *Science* 338 (2012) :370-374
[19] Christopher Readinger, *Ice Core Proxy Methods for Tracking Climate Change*, <http://www.csa.com/discoveryguides/icecore/review.php> (accessed January 23, 2014)

to me. The list could go on, but you get my point. Eventually the evidence would accumulate to such an extent that my wife would confront me. And my response would be an emphatic: *"Look, I'm not having an affair. It might look like I am. But I'm telling you: I'm not. You're going to have to trust me on this. And if you can't trust me, then you're not good enough for me"*.

In my mind's eye, I stood there with my mouth hanging open. What kind of husband would that make me? But I found I had to ask the same question of a God who bends the truth, plants false clues and sets up a false scenario — who makes everything look like it's been around for billions of years and evolved slowly when in fact it's only 6,000 years old — all just to test our faith. Set it up so that a critical scientific mind would have to suspend all logic and reasoning, just to trust him. And if such a logical person couldn't make the leap of faith, then that person wasn't good enough for God. Once I looked at it that way, I could no longer embrace the concept of apparent age and the YE hypothesis.

HAVING THEIR CAKE AND EATING IT TOO

Later I heard of another attempt to hang onto a YE version of creation while at the same time explain how some things are nonetheless very old. This idea took root in the 18th century when a growing mountain of geological data challenged the idea that the world was only 6,000 years old, and was widely popularized when it was cited within the study notes of the Scofield Study Bible. Briefly, it was proposed that, fifteen billion years before the creation event recorded in the first three chapters of Genesis, there was an earlier creation event in which God created all kinds of animals including the dinosaurs, and left Lucifer in charge. Lucifer then rebelled, chaos ensued, and God destroyed the earth. The proponents of this idea say that Genesis 1:1 has been mistranslated. Instead of *"Now the earth was formless and empty"*, it should have been translated to *"Now the earth became chaotic and in confusion"*, in order to explain this early, unrecorded destruction of the world. God then presumably left the rubble and debris and dinosaur bones lying around for fifteen billion years until, approximately 6,000 years ago, he then started all over again with the six calendar day creation event described in the opening chapters of Genesis. For the advocates of this 'Gap Theory', this earlier creation/destruction event was enough to explain the old age of the universe and the fossil record. Of course, it does nothing to explain the genetic evidence of a long and gradual evolution, or the fossil evidence of humans going back hundreds of thousands of years, or many other lines of scientific evidence. Not to mention that the scriptural evidence for this idea is microscopically thin, to say the least. Personally, I find this theory ludicrous, and I debated back and forth on whether to mention it here. For the sake of being complete, I opted to keep it in.

HARMONIZING GENESIS WITH BIG BANG COSMOLOGY AND EVOLUTIONARY THEORY

More recently, I came across another explanation which allowed me to more easily reconcile the creation story with the many, many lines of scientific evidence for a very old universe and continuously evolving living forms. This explanation originated out of discussions and writings between a diverse group of Hebrew linguists, theologians and scientists in the mid- to late-1900s. I read about it in a book authored by Dr. Hugh Ross, who gave an excellent version of this new approach to understanding the Genesis account [20]. It seems you can get a whole new imagery, from the very same written words in the book of Genesis, if you just take a slightly different perspective on the creation event itself.

First, imagine the writer of the Genesis story describing a series of visions, or a single vision with a series of scenes. This is much like how many of the Biblical prophets described being taken from one place to another and writing what they see: for example, Ezekiel being led from one room to another in his vision of the Temple (Ezekiel chapter 40), or the author of the book of Revelation being presented with one scene after another of events taking place in heaven and earth, either past, present or future. In the same way, the writer of Genesis could have been receiving a series of visions or intermittent vignettes and images of creation as it unfolded over the course of millennia. In this way, 'morning' and 'evening' could be metaphors for the curtains rising and falling, or the spotlights coming on and off, on the different 'days' (in chapter three, I'll return to this issue of taking the words 'morning', 'evening' and 'day' literally or not).

But here's the second and most important part of the new perspective from which to re-interpret the Genesis account: the place from which the writer and the readers view the unfolding story. Rather than imagining yourself hanging in space looking down on creation, watching from a distance the dramatic changes as the stars, planets and life-forms suddenly appear in front of you, he suggests taking the vantage point of

---

[20] Hugh Ross, *Creation and Time*. (NavPress, 1994)

someone actually sitting on earth's surface and now looking up and out from inside that creation as the story unfolds. That is, rather than being in a seat in the audience looking at the stage as the spotlights come on and off, you're actually sitting on the stage itself and watching the actors and stage props move all around you.

From this viewpoint, the different creation 'days' can fit neatly into the sequence of events called for by the Big Bang story and the processes of naturalistic evolution:

"In the beginning God created the heavens and the earth. Now the earth was formless and empty, darkness was over the surface of the deep ..." (Genesis 1:1,2)   The cosmic explosion we call the Big Bang marks the beginning of everything, producing all the energy and matter which now makes up all the stars and planets and living things that we know of (actually the matter was almost entirely hydrogen and helium: the other elements were produced when those two elements were baked in the nuclear furnaces of stars).   However, at first, all this matter was formless: it was merely a tremendous cloud of atoms, high energy particles and lots of energy.   Of course, from the point of view of the writer sitting on the stage, all he could bear witness to was the formlessness of the immediate 'stuff' within the sphere of his physical reach, and which therefore represented to him 'the earth' that he was hovering on (can't say 'sitting on' because it wasn't solid just yet).   According to Big Bang cosmology, as that cloud of gas and energy expanded and cooled down, the atoms began to aggregate and eventually accumulate into chunks of matter which in turn coalesced into larger and larger bodies of matter.   Deep within one of those billows of dust in the high energy plasma sits our author of Genesis (it's a good thing this is only a vision, because otherwise he'd vaporise in a nanosecond from the heat!).   From his perch, however, deep within the cloud of dust which would eventually become the earth, he can't discern anything distinct: all he sees is a formless opaqueness of gases and dust particles all around him.   At the same time, the gravitational forces of that cosmic cloud of debris have also produced the star we now call the sun, and pulled that matter together so tightly that the sun ignited and began to produce light energy.   But for a long time that light would be invisible from the spot at which our author is watching and taking notes: the intensity of the solar energy is just not strong enough to penetrate the dust particles and gases which will eventually become earth and its atmosphere.

"And God said, 'Let there be light', and there was light ..." (Genesis 1:3).   This is not the light from the explosion of the Big Bang per se.   The Big Bang event would seem to fit better into verses one and two of Genesis chapter one, and was followed by the slow aggregation of the cloud of dust

into the sun, planets, stars and galaxies described in the paragraph above. Eventually, as the dust and particles began to clear from earth's atmosphere, the sun's light began to leak through: *"... and there was light ..."*. At first, this would be a very diffuse light, much like what we see on a very cloudy, foggy day. From the relative brightness of the day, it might be obvious that it's noon or midnight; but early morning and late evening would be hard to distinguish. The actual position of the sun in the sky is absolutely indiscernible: the author can't even tell if it's off to his right or to his left (assuming he knew there was such a cosmic body out there to begin with).

"And God said, 'Let there be an expanse between the waters to separate water from water. So God made the expanse and separated the water under the expanse from the water above it ..." (Genesis 1:6). Earth begins to cool even further: to the point that water vapour can now condense around the dust particles in the atmosphere and form rain droplets which fall toward the surface. At first, this rain would re-evaporate on its way down or shortly after hitting the still scorching hot surface of the planet. Nonetheless, the author of Genesis notices the beginning of a stable water cycle, and puts up his umbrella as he continues to take notes. Not that there's much to see: it's still so hazy he can barely see his hand in front of his face.

"And God said, 'Let the water under the sky be gathered to one place, and let dry ground appear..." (Genesis 1:9). Eventually, once the earth cooled sufficiently, rain could accumulate into shallow pools, which became lakes and ultimately seas and oceans. The author looked out across the ocean from his front row seat on the continent's shore, and noticed the sky grow dim yet once again. He still can't make out the sun through the dense clouds of water vapour and dust particles in the atmosphere, any more than someone on Jupiter's 'surface' today would be able to. But he does note the passing of yet another day into night, as has happened many times before.

"Then God said, 'Let the land produce vegetation ..." (Genesis 1:11) With these stable bodies of water and a continuous input of light energy from the sun (even though the sun's disk itself might still not yet be visible through the clouds and haze), the stage is now set for the beginning of life. Naturalistic evolutionary theory predicts one possible incubator for life would be the shallow pools of water; others point to deep hydrothermal vents in the ocean, where life forms could obtain their energy from the heat and chemicals put out by bubbling volcanic vents. Of course, the expectation would be that the first life forms would be single-celled species — too small to be seen by the human eye unaided by microscopes (in other words, our observant but nonetheless scientifically-challenged OT author of

Genesis strolling past that shallow pool) — but would eventually evolve into larger multicellular life. He'd take a little slip on some of the algae growing out of shallow pools. And he'd eventually notice, because the atmosphere was clearing up more and more (getting less 'foggy'), that plants were moving out of the pools and invading the continents.

"*And God said, "Let there be lights in the expanse of the sky ...*" (Genesis 1:14). Finally, the atmosphere clears sufficiently that the sun, moon and stars can now be seen. They'd been there all along throughout the past many millennia, but the author just couldn't perceive them through the haze as he lounged by the water's edge. Now they poke through in all their glory, and the author is presented with visions of the first beautiful sun-rise ... the first glorious sun-set ... the first comet racing past the now visible constellation of Orion.

"*And God said, "Let the water teem with living creatures, and let birds fly above the earth ...*" (Genesis 1:20). Life continues to bloom, producing all kinds of strange and beautiful forms, both plant and animal. It's interesting that the Genesis story begins with aquatic animals before referring to land-based animals (next paragraph). Naturalistic evolutionary theory, based on a lot of fossil evidence, says the first animal life consisted of aquatic creatures, which eventually crawled out onto land, and in turn eventually took to the skies.

"*And God said, "Let the land produce living creatures ... Then God said, "Let us make man ...*" (Genesis 1:24-26). Evolution continues, and the writer of Genesis sees the appearance of all kinds of land animals and eventually humans. As an aside, if any reader absolutely denies any involvement of naturalistic evolution in the creation story, I would point out an interesting choice of wording here: "*Let the land produce ...*" versus "*Let there be ...*". It would definitely seem that the land itself played some important role in the appearance of plant (verse 11) and animal (verse 24) life forms. Interestingly, later on, God says "*Let us make man ...*", and does so from the dust of the earth (and later yet is said to create Eve from Adam), again emphasizing the importance of the earth in producing people, while at the same time reserving a distinct role for God in that part of creation (which I'll come back to in chapters four and five of this book).

So I learned that it's possible to take the same words of Genesis and line them up reasonably well with what one would see from the vantage point of a lounge chair on the face of the earth as the various processes of nature discovered by science acted on the matter produced by the Big Bang. Which is not to say that God had no hand whatsoever in the creation of the universe or of life. He still could have started the whole thing off with the Big Bang ... created that first cosmic egg that produced all the mass and energy that eventually re-organized into a universe full of life. There's still no way to explain that seminal event from an atheistic point of view. Likewise for the initial creation of life: the leap from inanimate chemicals to a living cell is so huge as to be insurmountable based on what we know right now about molecular biology and biochemistry. I'll discuss both of these points in more detail later in chapter four.

This alternative interpretation of Genesis satisfied me for a number of years. My opinion now is that, if you feel it's necessary to use the Genesis accounts to understand the origin of everything ... to reconcile the scriptural account with the scientific data ... this might be the best way to do so. How is this alternative viewpoint received among other Christians? The Biologos survey (of 743 pastors) [21] found 54% best identified with a YE theology while 18% accepted theistic evolution (*"God created life, used a natural process like evolution ... natural selection can explain the rise of new species"*) and 15% gave varying support to progressive creation (*"God created life in its present form over a period of time, but not via evolution"*); 12% of those pastors were uncertain (couldn't best identify with one of those three positions, or chose not to).

But this new interpretation of Genesis doesn't match up perfectly with the scientific evidence currently at hand. In particular, it has birds appearing on day five, before land-dwelling animals on day six, while the fossil evidence has the ordering of their appearances the other way around (the latter says birds evolved from reptiles). This may seem like a very minor picky point. And as far as it pertains to the order of the creation events, it is. But it has huge impact on how we view the inerrancy and inspiration/authorship of Scripture (a topic which I'll take up in chapter 8). Anyone who claims that the sequence of events outlined in Genesis chapter one is an accurate historical description of the way things actually happened has to come up with an explanation for that minor discrepancy. Theists will naturally shy away from blaming God for getting the story wrong, so they might feel compelled to bend science to fit scripture by insisting that the paleontological evidence and/or its interpretation are flawed. However, they're fighting against an exceedingly large (and growing) body of evidence, and I find that kind of head-in-the-sand rationalization is inexcusable.

But another — and I think better — explanation points the finger at the human author(s) of Genesis: maybe the discrepancy is somehow a

---

[21] Biologos Foundation, *A Survey of Clergy and Their Views on Origins*, <http://biologos.org/blog/a-survey-of-clergy-and-their-views-on-origins> (accessed June 2, 2013)

human error.   The scientist in me has to point out that the alternative interpretation of Genesis outlined immediately above requires some initial assumptions. Scientists prefer to have theories that don't have any 'a priori' assumptions, but which are just based on the facts as they present themselves.   What are 'a priori assumptions'?   They're assumptions you hold in mind before you consider the data.   Let me use an analogy to explain: a shopkeeper with several employees found that some of the money in the cash register regularly disappeared over the lunch break, and one day he enters the shop in the middle of lunch to find his daughter standing behind the counter with her hand in the open cash register stammering that she was simply returning a coin she found on the shop floor.   The facts themselves simply state that she is likely the culprit behind the disappearing money. But the shopkeeper might maintain the a priori assumption that it just cannot be her because she's his daughter and *"she's too honest and devoted"*, and as a result would reject any explanation that put the blame on her: he would then have to keep looking for some other explanation of how the money keeps disappearing, perhaps even bending the available evidence to fit an alternative (but erroneous) explanation.

When it comes to the creation account, one of the a priori assumptions is that the writer of Genesis was told in some way by an irrefutable authority (God) how it happened, so that their version of the creation account has at least some ring of truth. But it's entirely possible that God was directly involved in creation but didn't tell anyone exactly how he did it, and we humans have been trying to guess at the process and fit the available evidence to our theories. I dared to ask the question of whether the Genesis account might be a myth, a fiction constructed by ancient Near Eastern humans bringing their world view to bear on this question of origins, and that therefore none of the details in that account need to be matched up with any kind of naturalistic explanation whatsoever for the origin of all things.   As I continued my search for what I truly believe, which now included a look at the origin of Scripture (chapter eight), I needed to look into the possibility that the writer of Genesis borrowed extensively from previous Mesopotamian stories.

CONCLUSION

In this chapter, I've opened the curtains on the conflict between the written words of the book of Genesis and the continuously accumulating mountain of scientific evidence which seriously challenges the traditional, literalistic, YE interpretation of those written words. How do we reconcile that conflict? I've recounted a few naïve attempts at trying to rationalize the two, and my realizations that those explanations were not the most satisfactory: they eventually failed when put up beside certain scientific observations. In chapter five I'll continue to describe my journey through this theological/scientific conundrum, but first I want to tease out some loose threads that have unravelled at this point, since I think some readers will still be hovering at this fork-in-the-road for a while yet.

Some will find it hard to let go of a YE viewpoint, hard to continue on the path that leads to an OE explanation.

Others will have decided to take that second path, but will need to understand why it might be a hard decision for YE'ers to do the same. So we need some dialogue within the Christian community (chapter three).

Other readers will wonder why we need to even hang on to a theological explanation at all: why not accept the fact that Genesis just hasn't been able to explain anything well at all, jettison the whole Bible thing, and embrace science exclusively? So we also need some dialogue between theist and atheist viewpoints (chapter four).

3

The battle lines within the Christian community

How do I reconcile the Genesis account of creation with the theories of the Big Bang and Darwinian evolution?

Should I read the Bible like a science book and/or history book?

What happened at t=0?

Would God use naturalistic processes?

Does a naturalistic explanation diminish God?

Was there death before the Fall?

Were there 6 creation days lasting 24 hours each?

Should science be used to help interpret the Bible?

What about incest?

YE ARGUMENTS AGAINST THIS ALTERNATIVE "OLD EARTH" INTERPRETATION

Even though it seems that taking an OE perspective makes it possible to reconcile the words of scripture with seemingly contradictory discoveries from science, and thereby resolve this unnecessary tension between faith and fact, some YE proponents might still have a number of objections to an OE interpretation [22]. Let me address some of the ones I've already heard or can anticipate.

(1) God would not use naturalistic processes Some readers might not like this idea that God used natural processes like the Big Bang and Evolution to bring creation into being. They might feel that it lessens God: it obviously takes a bigger God to just speak things into a sudden existence, than to slowly build them up over time, right? I actually think the opposite. To illustrate why I think that, let me describe two very different gardeners who want to decorate a backyard hill with plants.

One gardener goes out every spring to the local greenhouse and buys armloads of seedlings: dozens of varieties of flowers of different colors and various sizes. After a little bit of work, he or she has a garden that puts out a beautiful display for a few months until fall and winter come, at which point the gardener would clean it all up and prepare new ideas for yet another attempt the next spring. There's nothing wrong with that approach. It might take six days of hard effort ... preparing the soil, digging the holes, placing the seedlings and watering them ... but it can produce some of the most beautiful gardens imaginable.

The other gardener, on the other hand, does it quite differently. With a vast experience working with plants and an encyclopedic knowledge of their various characteristics, this gardener could choose bulbs that poke their blooms out as soon as the first patches of dirt appear in the spring, even when the ground is still partially frozen and there are mounds of snow here and there. After carefully placing those bulbs in strategic places, she plants perennials that bloom later in the spring, and yet others that bloom at other times of the year: from early summer to late summer and even into the autumn. Such a gardener would take into consideration the different heights of the plants (so that some plants don't hide the others from view), their various needs for sun versus shade, how the anticipated colors might blend with the other plants, whether they would attract butterflies or hummingbirds. In the end, what this gardener has done, through a very detailed knowledge of those plants — their needs, abilities, life cycles, et cetera — is to create a garden that unfurls itself every spring all on its own. With very little intervention on the part of the gardener (other than a bit of fertilizing and pruning), the garden re-appears every year seemingly all on its own, re-seeding itself every summer and fall as it prepares itself for the next round of winter and spring. Such a garden would proclaim loudly the

---

[22] John MacArthur *The Battle for the Beginning: Creation, Evolution, and the Bible*, (Nelson Books, 2001)

skill and creativity and ability of the gardener. I would even say that such a self-renewing perennial garden says more about the gardener than one which is quickly dropped into place from trays of annuals into a bare patch of soil, all within a few days every spring.

And so I can imagine God taking a ball of nothingness, rolling it around in the palm of his hands, molding it and folding it around, implanting it with the various laws of nature (for example, the laws of space-time dimensionality, gravity, electromagnetism, mass-energy, thermodynamics, genetic evolution, natural selection), getting it ready for the big reveal. He then gently places it on the marbled floor in the courts of heaven, and says to the angels and heavenly host: "*OK, stand back and watch this!*" Then there's a sudden flash as this cosmic egg explodes and expands and morphs into the visible universe and all of life, in obedience to the laws of nature and his will which he imprinted onto and into it as he was massaging that ball of nothingness in his hands.

Some readers might still be unsettled by the idea of God using natural processes that aren't described in the Bible. In fact they would say "*a plain reading of Scripture*" describes instead a very direct involvement on God's part. But this would not be the only instance in which scripture describes God as being physically involved in accomplishing something, while we modern, 21st century readers interpret that same scripture as mere allegory and acknowledge that he in fact actually uses naturalistic processes. For example, the writer of Psalm 139 says: "*For you created my inmost being; you knit me together in my mother's womb ...*" (verse 13). Job acknowledges that God formed him the way a potter forms something out of clay (Job 10:8-9). In the opening chapter of Jeremiah, God says "*Before I formed you in the womb I knew you ...*" (verse 5). We now know that embryogenesis — the development of a fetus — is a pre-programmed sequence of biochemical events which can be repeated and sustained in a test tube. Most contemporary readers of the Bible will admit that the allusions to knitting needles and clay are just poetic devices rather than scientific explanations.

In the 37th chapter of Job, God portrays Himself as being directly involved in controlling all the aspects of weather: unleashing and scattering lightning (v.3, 11); vocalizing thunder (verses 4 and 5), telling the snow and rain to fall (verse 6); breathing out ice (verse 10); controlling the clouds (verse 15) by hanging them in the sky (verse 16) and loading them with moisture (verse 11). The 38th chapter refers to his storehouses of snow and other storehouses for hail (verse 22); him dispersing the lightning (verses 24 and 35); cutting channels for the rain and paths for thunderstorms (verse 25); him fathering drops of dew (verse 28) and birthing the ice and frost (verse 29). Today, most Christians have no problem attributing all these meteorological events to solar energy being injected into the planet's atmosphere and surface, and then being redistributed by the winds and the water cycle.

In the Genesis story of the destruction of Sodom and Gomorrah (Genesis 19), he appeared to use a volcanic eruption (raining down burning sulfur upon the city) rather than simply blinking it out of existence through the power of his will.

When God tells the Israelites how he'll clear space for them in the Promised Land (Deuteronomy 7), he doesn't say it will happen instantaneously by the snap of his fingers, but instead it will be a long hard process in which he'll use the Israelites themselves (to drive out the original inhabitants by means of war) and *will send the hornet among them until even the survivors who hide from you have perished ...*" (Deuteronomy 7:20). And in verse 22 of that chapter, the text says something really interesting about God limiting himself by naturalistic processes: "*The Lord your God will drive out those nations before you, little by little. You will not be allowed to eliminate them all at once, or the wild animals will multiply around you*". I'd like to believe that if he created the universe out of nothing by the words of his mouth, then he could easily control the wild animals so that they weren't a threat to the Israelites.

Some people use Colossians 1:16 to argue for specific acts of creation: "*For in him all things were created: things in heaven and on earth, visible and invisible, whether thrones or powers or rulers or authorities; all things have been created through him and for him.*" But I can use this same verse to argue for creation involving naturalistic processes. Was there a specific instantaneous creation event in which I myself was 'created', or did God use existing processes (my parents and embryogenesis) to bring me into existence? What about the space shuttle or computers, which are also within the universal set of objects referred to as 'all things': did God create those machines, or use existing people and processes (scientists; engineers; astronomers; governments; mining companies; et cetera)? What about the Progressive Citizens' Party of Liechtenstein (since the book of Colossians refers to powers, rulers and authorities): is that political group a specific act of creation on God's part, or did he simply allow certain people of Liechtenstein to elect and empower its members? [note: some might insist that the phrase "*powers and principalities*" refers only to spiritual things like angels and demons, but nothing in the wording of that text precludes earthly powers and principalities.]

Even the narratives of some of Jesus's creative miracles have him working with physical material and processes. When he sought to feed an audience of 5,000 people in the desert, rather than waving his hands and having lunchboxes appearing instantaneously in all their laps, he first asked for whatever starting material they had on hand — the proverbial five loaves and two fishes — and then multiplied that (Matthew 14:13-21) [23]. When he healed one blind man, he first created some mud using his own saliva and the dust of the earth and applied that to the man's eyes to give him his sight back (John 9:1-7). All of these stories not only illustrate the point that Jesus often used the natural to accomplish supernatural goals, but they also share interesting parallels with the creation story itself: all these stories have some starting material being turned into something bigger and better ... the few loaves and fish providing enough to feed *"about 5,000 men, besides women and children"* and fill up twelve baskets of leftovers ... the mud restoring sight to blind eyes ... the land producing vegetation and living animals ... the dust of the earth being used to create Adam, and a rib from Adam being used to create Eve.

Some theists will be reasonably comfortable with the idea of God using evolution on a very small scale, but not a large one. They'll be quick to distinguish between 'microevolution' versus 'macroevolution'. The poster child for the former is the peppered moth, which can exhibit a variety of colorations, some much darker than others. British biologists in the 19th century noted that most peppered moths were quite lightly colored before the Industrial Revolution, but that the darker colored variety outnumbered the lighter ones after the Industrial Revolution. The explanation was that the lightly colored moths were previously better camouflaged when they rested on the lightly colored trees and lichens, but when pollution from coal-burning started depositing excessive amounts of soot everywhere, that the lighter ones now stood out much more clearly and birds found it easier to spot them and eat them. The darker colored moths on the other hand, had previously stood out for the birds but now benefitted from the darker surroundings. So the peppered moth evolved to better suit the change in its environment. Again, many theists will be okay with such a small evolutionary change within a species, but not with much larger changes between two different species. This is an overly simplistic distinction. The fact is that the accumulation of many such small changes can lead to a whole new organism. *"A journey of a thousand miles begins with a single step"* (Lao-tzu; Chinese philosopher and founder of Taoism). (That having been said, I should also add that evolution doesn't only involve small and subtle changes, but can sometimes be the result of a sudden and dramatic large-scale change).

---

[23] a second similar but distinct anecdote is given in Matthew 15:29-38

Yet other theists may be able to accept that God uses certain naturalistic processes, but become uncomfortable about those processes that have a certain degree of randomness in their nature, which includes classical Darwinian evolution. They don't like the idea that God would bring you and me and everything else into being through a long series of undirected chemical collisions and genetic mutations. They would say theism is not compatible with random processes. They feel there has to be some kind of intentionally planned series of events, especially when it comes to the creation of people. But what those people don't realize is that many things in life that they take for granted as predictable, fixed and unchanging — perhaps even God-ordained — in fact involve random processes.

For example, a couple can decide to have a baby, but the specific individual(s) that is born is completely unpredictable: the average human female produces several hundred thousand eggs in her lifetime and the average male puts out 40 million to 1.2 billion sperm cells each time he contributes to the cause, each one having the potential to produce an entirely different person, but only one of those can ultimately fertilize the egg from the female. The chances of producing specifically the one individual that is 'you' are astronomical: in fact, approximately 100,000 (number of eggs) multiplied by 1 billion (number of sperm), or 1 out of 100,000,000,000,000. If that doesn't blow you mind, consider the odds this way: the chances were 99,999,999,999,999 times greater that your parents' new baby could have instead been a different sister or a different brother rather than you! The odds are actually much greater than that, because we haven't also taken into account that the genes from the two parents are actually shuffled around through an event known as 'cross-over between homologous chromosomes', very much like two kids trading hockey cards or stamps. So altogether, you are indeed 'lucky' to have been born, and yet you might maintain the view that your existence was pre-ordained and inevitable.

When the brain of the couple's baby develops, 100 billion nerve cells organize themselves into very specific brain regions with particular jobs and even preprogrammed instincts and activities (like how to breathe, or suckle from the mother). And yet if you could put a flag on any one of those cells before the development process begins, and use that flag to follow where that one nerve cell goes as the brain develops, you would be unable to predict the exact spot it would end up when all the construction was finally finished. Each one of those nerve cells is given a very fuzzy set of instructions of where to go, but they otherwise randomly take up one of hundreds (in some cases even thousands or millions) of positions in that general brain area, and then begin to randomly make connections to the other nerve cells around them. No combination of nerve cell placements and cell-to-cell connections is the same from one individual to the other (which is in part why our IQ scores can vary so much). And yet the final brain structure is entirely predictable.

Radioactive compounds decay at a known rate, and scientists measure that decay in 'half-lives': the time it takes for 50% of the compound to break down radioactively. For example, carbon-14 has a half-life of 5730 years, and is extremely useful in determining the age of long-dead materials (we call that 'carbon-dating'). If you're given a lump of carbon-14, there's absolutely no way to predict which molecule in that lump will be the next to undergo radioactive decay, nor which ones will have decayed in the next 1000 years, but you can be absolutely sure that half of them will have done so within the next 5730 years.

Likewise, we can't predict exactly what the weather will be three weeks from now, particularly when it comes to cloud cover and precipitation, since that's determined by all kinds of meteorological inputs that can affect each other in seemingly random ways. But we know for a fact that it we'll be wearing shorts and T-shirts in July but will need long pants and thick coats in January (at least in the Northern parts of the globe) … what time of year we can expect the bulk of the year's rainfall, or even the average amount of rain we'll get in a given month … what the average temperature or hours of sunshine will be on a monthly basis. Many different factors contribute to the weather we experience on any given day, and there are a lot of uncertainties in each of them, and yet there's an amazing amount of regularity and predictability in that weather.

The same is true for the growth of a snowflake, a crystal, an ant colony, a solar system, or a thousand other things. There are many examples of completely predictable outcomes (at the macroscopic level) arising from completely random events (at the microscopic or quantum levels) governed by fundamental laws. I personally feel God could delight in randomness producing his intended purpose. Just like certain card tricks based on mathematical relationships, in which a certain card is chosen but then shuffled through the deck and through various manipulations — carefully orchestrated reorganizations of piles of cards, et cetera — the card handler is always able to retrieve the chosen card. In both cases, randomness is present (shuffling in the case of the card trick; mutation in the case of evolution), but scientific and mathematical laws and processes are built in to ensure the desired outcome.

So there should be no reason to reject the idea that God would use naturalistic processes like the Big Bang, gravity, chemical reactions, random genetic mutation and natural selection in the process of unfolding his creation.

(2) Science shouldn't trump scripture   One perceived danger of OE theology is that it contradicts scripture solely in order to accommodate advances in science. That it's nothing more than a compromise; and don't fundamentalists hate that word.   However, whatever tension there is between scripture and science exists only because the former is taken unnecessarily literally. We all use wording that we don't mean precisely and literally. *"I've told you a million times to ..."*, when in fact you might have said it 68 times. *"I've been waiting all morning for you"*, when in fact you might have been waiting an hour and a half. *"I was scared to death"*. *"I'm your biggest fan"*. We can start to get really silly if we start insisting on absolutely precise meanings of every word we choose to use.

But it's more than simply using hyperbole and embellishment to add color to what we're trying to say: I don't think the Bible was ever meant to be taken as a science book. And the church has certainly looked pretty silly when it tried to do exactly that.

One humorous story involves Andreas Vesalius (1514-1564), a Belgian anatomist and physician at the University of Padua who overturned many ideas about human anatomy which had till then held strong for over a thousand years (from the teachings of the Greek-speaking Roman physician Galen). One of those ideas he overturned: he showed irrefutably that men had the same number of ribs as did women [24]. This stoked a storm of controversy because certain religious leaders were adamant that men had one fewer rib, given the account in Genesis in which God took one of Adam's ribs to make Eve. Although many words were spoken and written, the religious leaders didn't actually physically mistreat Galen for poking this hole in their balloon. But they were much less forgiving of other scientists [astronomers] just a few years later.

I'd be surprised that any readers haven't heard about the 'geocentric theory', although they may not know it by that name. Ptolemy — a Greco-Roman mathematician, astronomer, geographer, and astrologer — proposed in the 2nd century AD that the sun and planets revolved around the earth (hence, 'geo' for earth, and 'centric'; Figure 2). For centuries, the early church insisted on this idea (and even that the earth was the centre of the universe), despite an ever increasing body of evidence to the contrary from physicists and astronomers. This mistaken belief justified an arrogant need for people to be seen as the centerpoint of all God's attention, but it was also rooted in the repeated appearance in sctadporipture of phrases like "... *the rising of the sun* ...", sometimes followed by "... *to the going down of the*

---

[24] Andreas Vesalius, *De Humani Corporis Fabrica* in 1543

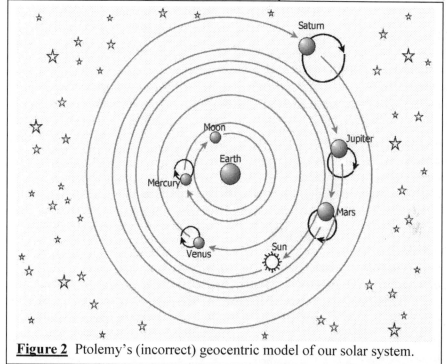

Figure 2 Ptolemy's (incorrect) geocentric model of our solar system.

same ..." (Genesis 32:31; Numbers 2:3; Joshua 8:29; Joshua 10:12,27; Psalm 50:1; Psalm 113:3; Isaiah 45:6; Isaiah 59:19; Malachi 1:11; Mark 16:2). The "Teacher" in Ecclesiastes actually refers to the orbit of the sun: "*The sun rises and the sun sets, and hurries back to where it rises*" (Ecclesiastes 1:5). There were also the interesting passages in which the sun was said to have "*stopped in the middle of the sky and delayed going down about a full day*" at Joshua's command (Joshua 10:13), and another one in which the sun was said to have gone "*ten degrees backwards*" as a miraculous sign for King Ahaz (Isaiah 38:8). Scripture seemed to be absolutely clear that it was **the sun** doing the rising, setting, stopping and reversing, and who was going to suggest that God didn't realize it was actually the earth spinning on its axis around a sun that wasn't changing its position relative to the rest of the solar system? I don't think there's any need here to repeat all the details of this story: how the church leaders insisted on this false idea for centuries, and persecuted people who sided on scientific evidence to the contrary ... the roles that Galileo and Copernicus played in changing our thinking on that controversy ... the long overdue apology from the church about how they handled this fiasco. We now fully accept the 'heliocentric model' ('helio' is the Greek word for 'sun').

As an aside, there has been a very long running story that NASA scientists were using their computers to make predictions about the orbits of the sun, moon and earth, in order to make key decisions about launching satellites and rockets, and came upon a perplexing problem when they ran the program backwards a few thousand years. The story has it that the simulations stopped abruptly at a point in time a few thousand years ago, and could only be resumed if they introduced some fudge factors — adding an extra day here, and a brief reversal of the sun's orbit there — apparently at the suggestion of one scientist who vaguely recalled the stories of Joshua and Ahaz from Sunday school classes. This story has stoked the conviction of many YE Christians, but it doesn't stand up to investigation: there are many factual errors in the story, but the biggest one is simply that NASA never ran such a simulation (those who promote this story have not explained why NASA would decide to run the program backwards). For any interested reader who wants to look more into this, I'd suggest a quick look at Snopes.com [25].

Another hoax which has circulated within the YE community pertained to a fear on NASA's part that the astronauts they sent to the moon would be buried under tens of feet of cosmic/lunar dust, and that NASA's discovery that the moon in fact has less than a few inches of dust was confirmation that the moon is only 6,000 years old. Neither of those two points is correct. When they fired off Apollo 11 (the first to land humans on the moon), NASA had crude measurements which predicted only a few inches of accumulation: otherwise, why would they drop their guys into a possible death trap on live television? Also, more recent measurements (using more refined and accurate techniques) of the rate of cosmic dust settling out on earth [26] when applied to the moon also predict an accumulation of just over one inch even after 4.5 billion years (some will be quick to point out, correctly, that this extrapolation assumes that the rate of dust accumulation has been constant for that whole period of time). Needless to say, informed YE'ers are no longer talking about accumulation of lunar dust in their apologetic arguments.

[25] Snopes.com, *The Lost Day,* <http://www.snopes.com/religion/lostday.asp> (accessed March 9, 2014)
[26] S. G. Love and D. E. Brownlee, "A Direct Measurement of the Terrestrial Mass Accretion Rate of Cosmic Dust". *Science* 262: 550–53, 1993.

Figure 3 "Earth-rise" over the lunar horizon, taken in 1968 by William Anders. Used by permission from NASA.

Perhaps a little bit less at the forefront of our collective memories is the story of the 'flat earthers': people who were convinced that the earth was in fact a large flat plane, rather than the sphere that we now know it to be. This belief was based in part on a few other phrases which are also repeated in scripture: "... *the four corners of the earth ...*" (Isaiah 11:12; Ezekiel 7:2; Revelation 7:1; Revelation 20:8) and "*... the ends of the earth ...*" (Job 37:3; Acts 1:8), and "*... the edge of the earth ...*" (Job 38:13). Once again, the conclusion was that God was omniscient and clearly could see and knew that the earth had edges. I'm not aware that anyone was persecuted for believing otherwise, as was the case for the geocentric versus heliocentric controversy I talked about above, but I have picked up somewhere along the way that mariners were cautious about getting too close to the edges of their maps out of fear of sailing right off the edge of the earth. Humans have long since sailed off far into the horizon, circumnavigating the globe and even going out into space and taking a look back at the earth, finding that, in fact, it is round. Most readers will have seen the famous picture taken by astronaut William Anders during the Apollo 8 mission of the so-called 'earth-rise' [27] over the moon's horizon (Figure 3).

---

[27] A note for astronomer geeks: the 'earth-rise' seen when you're standing on the moon is very different from the moon-rise we see on earth, because the moon rotates on its axis in such a way that it always shows the same face towards the earth (this is called 'tidal lock', and gives a clue for one theory about the origin of the moon: it broke off the earth after an impact 4.5 billion years ago with a Mars-sized rock which some hypothesize had been another planet we've since named Theia). So the earth, when viewed from the moon, would otherwise always be in the exact same spot in the sky, except for the fact that the moon wobbles on its axis very slightly (just a few degrees) and very slowly (one back-and-forth cycle takes 27 days), a process called 'libration'. For this reason, if you stand at certain places on the moon's surface where the earth is positioned low in the sky, right on the horizon in fact, you'll see the earth dip and fall just a few degrees above and below the horizon once every 27 days.

Don't forget those verses in the book of Job that refer to God's storerooms in the sky which hold either the snow or the rain or the lightning. Are we going to insist that those are also literally true? Should we push for a reformation of our university courses in meteorology?

All of these examples speak loudly about the dangers of putting the specific words of scriptural writers in authority over the actual discoveries of science. Sometimes it just makes us look silly. In the Biologos survey (of 743 pastors), a large majority (including just over half of the YE'ers) agreed with the statement *"Just as scripture should influence human interpretation of science, science should also inform our understanding of scripture"* [28].

(3) Scripture specifically says there were six individual 'days'   Many theological debates have been framed around the alternative meanings of any given word which appeared originally in ancient Near Eastern texts, but was then translated from Hebrew into Greek or Latin and then into other modern languages before they reached our eyes in the form of English. I'm not sufficiently equipped nor interested in getting into most of these: I'd rather refer you to other writers and books [29]. But three words that are worth talking a bit about in this context are those that we see translated as 'morning', 'evening' and 'day' in the first couple of chapters of Genesis.

One of the main arguments for the YE hypothesis is the specific use of these words many times in the Genesis account. This specificity has led many to insist on distinct 24-hour periods of time. But 'day' doesn't have to mean only a 24-hour period. It can also mean 'era' or 'epoch': the word is used in this sense when it appears in Genesis 2:4 ... *"These are the generations of the heavens and of the earth when they were created, **in the day** that the Lord God made the earth and the heavens"* [KJV; emphasis added]. Note that it doesn't say *"... in the six days that the Lord God made the earth and the heavens..."*. Today, we might say: *"back in my grandfather's day ..."* and be referring to his entire lifetime, or to the era to which he belonged, not a 24-hour period.

I've heard it said several times by ardent YE defenders that everywhere else in the Bible in which the word that we translate as 'day' (in Hebrew, this is 'yom') is accompanied by an ordinal number, then it always means a 24-hour period. This isn't actually correct: Hosea 6:2 has the phrases "after two days" and "on the third day", but is clearly not meaning

---

[28] Biologos Foundation, *A Survey of Clergy and Their Views on Origins*, <http://biologos.org/blog/a-survey-of-clergy-and-their-views-on-origins> (accessed June 2, 2013)

[29] Hugh Ross, *Creation and Time*; chapters 1, 2 and 3. (NavPress, 1994)

them as 24-hour periods (whoever is being talked about in those verses was not restored after 48 hours, nor *"living in his presence"* by 72 hours). Zechariah 14:7 offers another exception to this 'rule'.

But ignoring these exceptions for the moment, even if it happened to be true that every occurrence in the Bible of the word 'yom' with an ordinal number was referring to a 24-hour period, this doesn't make it a hard and fast grammatical rule. When used as a noun, the English word 'arm' refers to the limbs attached to your shoulders. It can also mean literally a gun (as in the weapon a modern soldier takes into battle) or a sub-division of people or power (as in a legal arm of the military, or the diplomatic arm of a government), and metaphorically mean strength or ability (as in 'by the arm of Pharaoh …'). Every time the Bible uses the word 'arm' in the context of people, it means 'the limb that your hand is attached to'. So when the Bible uses the word 'arm' elsewhere in the context of God – as in *"to whom has the arm of the Lord been revealed"* (Isaiah 53:1, and John 12:38) – do we have to then necessarily translate the phrase as *"God's biceps and triceps with elbow, four fingers and a thumb"*? I think the reader can see how silly things can become when one starts making strict grammatical rules like these.

I have another reason against being too literal about the appearances of the words 'morning', 'evening' and 'day' in Genesis and equating them to the 24-hour periods with which we're all generally familiar. All three words can only have such meanings in a context which takes into account earth's orientation relative to the sun. That is, 'morning' is defined by a certain point in earth's spin on its axis when the sun appears to be rising from the horizon, while 'evening' is defined by that point in its spin when the sun appears to be setting into the horizon. Whenever it's morning in North America, it's simultaneously afternoon in Europe and evening in Asia. A space probe that NASA launches from the Florida coast on a given morning experiences no further mornings or evenings for several years as it travels through space, until it reaches some destination like a neighbouring planet or a planetary moon and begins to take up orbit. The very minute it does that, we can re-introduce the idea of a 'day' again, and the length of that 'day' depends on the celestial body that the space probe is orbiting: within our own solar system it can range from just short of ten Earth hours if you're geostationary around (or standing on) Jupiter, to just over 243 Earth days if you're doing so around Venus. Given that you can really only define 'morning', 'evening' and 'day' from the context of one's orientation with respect to the sun and horizon, let alone the fact that you need the sun to supply the very light itself that is synonymous with 'day', how does a YE'er interpret the first few appearances of these words several times before the sun was even said to have been created on the fourth 'day' (Genesis 1:14-19) (to be fair, I'm not the first to hang this argument on the fact that the sun wasn't created until the fourth day ... even as far back as a few centuries after Christ, St. Augustine stumbled over this paradox [30]).

There's another point to be made on this matter of the order of the Creation 'days' [31]. There are two versions of the Creation story in Genesis. In the 1st chapter of Genesis, God creates the plants on day three and man on day six. The 2nd chapter of Genesis, however, states: *"Now no shrub had yet appeared on the earth and no plant had yet sprung up, for the Lord God had not sent rain on the earth and there was no one to work the ground ... Then the Lord God formed a man from the dust of the ground and breathed into his nostrils the breath of life, and the man became a living being. Now the Lord God had planted a garden in the east, in Eden ..."* (Genesis 2:5-8). The second version implies that the plants weren't created until there were humans, both male and female, around to *"work the ground"*, which contradicts Genesis chapter one (in which the creation order is plants, then man and then woman). But even if you ignore the contradiction in the order of creation of man/people versus plants and still want to hang onto a six-day Creation time-line, one has to wonder why the Bible says God couldn't or wouldn't create plants until there were humans around to work the ground, given that it would only be three more days until man was put on the scene. How often don't we ourselves plant a garden and then leave it on its own for a few weeks before we come back to it? These two versions of the same event don't make sense together. But since the writer(s) of Genesis gave us those two divergent versions back-to-back, perhaps that's the first clue that they didn't expect the stories to be taken literally.

The church has long wrestled with this question of the age of the universe. Even some of the earliest writings from the 1st and 2nd centuries by authors such as Josephus, Origen and Irenaeus acknowledged that the earth and the universe looked much older than a literal reading of scripture might suggest, and many early church writings questioned whether the 'days' of creation refer to 24-hour periods. Some have naively pointed to 2nd Peter 3:8 — *"With the Lord a day is like a thousand years, and a thousand years are like a day"* — to deal with this. This is NOT the same as saying *"With the Lord a day is equal to a thousand years ..."*, as if we can simply scale up the time-line mathematically (and doing so would be completely ineffective in making the creation narrative match scientific

[30] St. Augustine of Hippo, *De Genesi ad Litteram*, 415 AD

[31] Tim Keller, *Creation, Evolution, and Christian Laypeople*. pp.1-14, The Biologos Foundation. <www.BioLogos.org/projects/scholar-essays> (accessed Jan. 23, 2014)

evidence, anyway). That verse in 2nd Peter is just emphasizing how God is not limited by time.

(4) There couldn't have been any death before the Fall Another argument that YE proponents have made against incorporating evolutionary theory into their theology pertains to death as the penalty for Adam and Eve's sin in the Garden of Eden, and this becomes a major point in Paul's theology of the redeeming work of Jesus Christ [32]. As they rightly point out, natural selection is a fundamental component of evolutionary theory: random mutations occur in each generation of a given species, some of which eventually confer an advantage on holders of those mutations during some kind of environmental change or stress. Those advantaged individuals are slightly more likely to survive and pass on their new genetic information, while those without the mutations are more likely to die off. Survival of the fittest. So death becomes one of the sieves that separates out the fit from the unfit. And it takes thousands of generations — that is, thousands of rounds of dying — to see even a few changes in one animal species, let alone all the species that have ever existed.

However, some insist that death did not exist until after the creation story, based on Genesis 2:17 ... *"but from the tree of the knowledge of good and evil you shall not eat, for in the day that you eat of it you shall surely die"* [NASB]. And if there was no death, there could not have been millions of generations of individuals gradually gaining selective advantages over other generations. I disagree completely, and will give three arguments from scripture, and two others from biology, supporting the idea that biological death had to have existed before the fall.

First, God could not have been referring to physical death, because God's warning was that *"... in the day that you eat of it you shall surely die"*, yet the scriptures go on to tell of how Adam and Eve do in fact eat from that tree and live physically to see another day. In fact, a very great many number of days: according to the scripture, they go on to live long enough to produce numerous generations of children, including Cain, Abel (murdered by Cain) and Seth (who, according to Genesis 5:3, was born when Adam was 130 years old). And it wasn't a mental, emotional or intellectual death, because the text says they went on to be fearful of God himself (Genesis 3:10), or of other people (Genesis 4:13-14), and to be ashamed of their nakedness (Genesis 3:10), and angry (Genesis 4:5), and murderous (Genesis 4:8), et cetera. Instead, another interpretation of Genesis 2:16 is that the day they ate of the fruit they died spiritually. I don't

---

[32] Romans 5:12

think anyone would contest the latter idea: many, many scriptural writings talk about it in one way or another. Confusing biological life/death with spiritual life/death is the same mistake that Nicodemus made when Jesus taught him about the need to be born again (John 3:1-21). Nicodemus couldn't understand, saying that a man *"cannot enter his mother's womb and be born a second time, can he?"* Jesus corrected him by distinguishing between being born of the flesh versus being born of the Spirit. If Genesis 2:16 is referring solely to a spiritual death, then there's no problem with the idea that physical, biological death was indeed a fact of life before the Fall.

The second point is a bit related to the first one. Some use scriptural passages like Romans 5:12, which says *"… sin entered the world through one man, and death through sin, and in this way death came to all people, because all sinned"*, as evidence that there could not have been millions of generations of plants and animals dying over the billions of years of evolutionary history. But to be precise, that verse in Romans only refers to death in humans: it says nothing about death being absent in the plants and animals before that event in human history. Likewise, God's warning of fatal consequences in Genesis was directed at Adam and Eve alone, not at the whole living world in general. To put this point in a modern perspective: our own various levels of government impose all kinds of laws and taxes on people, but those are not enforced upon our pets or plants.

Third, Genesis describes two specific trees in the garden of Eden, one of them being 'the tree of life' (Genesis 2:9), and also records God giving them permission to eat from that tree (Genesis 2:16-17); but then later, after the story of the Fall, God is quick to say that Adam *"must not be allowed to reach out his hand and take also from the tree of life and eat, and live forever"* (Genesis 3:22). Unless you assume (without scriptural support) that the Fall happened so soon after Adam and Eve were created that they hadn't yet gotten around to eating from that tree of life, even though it was *"in the middle of the garden"* (Genesis 2:9), it's entirely reasonable that they would have already eaten from that tree more than once. This leads some [33] to conclude that people were subject to the processes of death even before the Fall, but that eating from the tree of life reversed or prevented those processes. This idea that the tree of life was necessary as a tonic against the ravages of death reappears in the book of Revelation 22:2 when it describes a river of life flowing out of the new Jerusalem: *"On each side of the river stood the tree of life, bearing twelve crops of fruit, yielding its fruit every month. And the leaves of the tree are for the healing of the nations."*

---

[33] John H. Walton, *The Lost World of Genesis One*, pp 99-100 (Intervarsity Press, 2009)

Then there's also a perfectly logical reason from biology to say that God would have actually <u>wanted</u> to incorporate physical/biological death as a necessary process into his original creation, especially if there was the possibility that creation would carry on for more than a few seasons before someone took a bite from the proverbial apple. At the very least, there would have been a lot of dying of plants in order to feed all the animals and people that he had created. But more importantly, the scriptures have God issuing commands to every living creature, including humans, to "*be fruitful and multiply*" and to fill all the earth. With all those animals being fruitful and multiplying but not dying, the earth would very quickly just be overrun with a seething mass of flesh that choked the skies, the land and the seas, and which the earth's plant life just could not possibly sustain. It would have been an irresponsible act on God's part.

Finally, we also know today that many normal biological events <u>require</u> death. The transformation of a caterpillar to a butterfly involves a whole cellular reorganization, and some of the caterpillar's cells must die in order to accomplish the feat. Likewise, in normal fetal development, some cells serve merely to act as signal lights and guides for other cells which need to shuttle from one part of the growing fetus to the other, or which have to grow in a very specific direction to some particular target (for example, a nerve fiber growing from the brain all the way down to the toe), after which those guide cells must die to make room for other cells and/or to stop consuming precious metabolic resources. Inflammation, immunity and tissue healing all involve certain cells 'choosing' to die in order to protect and rebuild the body. Death is actually programmed into our genes! Scientists are actively studying all of these diverse forms of 'programmed cell death', which they have given the Greek name 'apoptosis'. At the cell level, life without death is cancer.

Altogether, then, to say that physical/biological death could not have been part of the original creation absolutely demands a reconsideration of what God meant when he said "... *for in that day* ...", as well as a complete head-in-the-sand approach to the advances in our understanding of normal cellular biology.

(5) God wouldn't create a world with "evil" built-in   To some, the Garden of Eden was a place where everything was blissful. No carnivores. No predator-prey relationships. No thorns or thistles. No pain. And for those reasons, God could not, or would not, use classical Darwinian evolution because of all the suffering that it entails, including the fact that 99% of all the species to have ever appeared on earth would go extinct along the way. *"Nature, red in tooth and claw"* [34]. All of these things, it is said, were introduced after the Fall, and the massive extinctions were due to the Flood.

Much of that thinking is based on what God says as he pronounces judgement on Adam, Eve and the serpent in the story of the Fall. But more importantly, it's based on a number of assumptions which deserve more careful consideration.

To begin with, it assumes that the Garden of Eden was initially the only place on earth that harboured life. But let's look more closely at what Genesis says about that Garden. I've already referred above to the two different versions of creation recorded in the first and second chapters of Genesis. These describe two very different scenarios. One scenario – Genesis 1 – describes the creation of the entire universe and life on earth, and has plants appearing before people. The second scenario – Genesis 2 – describes the planting of a garden, and requires a human gardener to be present before the plants can be introduced. One way to reconcile these two anecdotes is to consider Genesis 1 as describing the general creation story, including all life forms, and Genesis 2 as describing the making of a little garden somewhere within that Creation. This distinction would help explain Genesis 2:15 ... *"The LORD God took the man and put him in the Garden of Eden to work it and take care of it"* ... it would be unreasonable to think that God created Adam to take care of more than a few acres, let alone the entire world. (note: I'm not espousing either literalist view, but simply showing that other interpretations are equally valid; my view now is that this story is more metaphorical than literal). Inside the walls of this little garden is indeed a violence-free existence. Outside of the walls surrounding the garden, life carries on exactly as it does today, with lions ripping into a gazelle with a broken leg and bacteria overwhelming the immune defenses of a sick lion. Numerous times I've heard YE'ers insist that carnivores lived on vegetation before the Fall, and claim that it's still possible for them to do so today. To buttress that claim, they will quote Isaiah's prophetic description of what the Afterlife will look like: *"... and the lion will eat straw like the ox ..."* (Isaiah 11:7), ignoring the fact that the very same author will a few chapters later give another description of that place and say *"... no lion will be there ..."* (Isaiah 35:9). They will also ignore scientific evidence that lions can't survive on straw (their intestinal tract is too short), but may cite stories like one in which lions in London zoo were said to have been fed grass and cabbages during World War II. Those stories are fabricated. Here's an excerpt from the press office of the

---

[34] Alfred, Lord Tennyson, *In Memoriam A. H. H.* (1849)

Zoological Society of London: "*In fact, the lions and other carnivores were not put on a vegetarian diet. In his article 'The History of London Zoo' (The World of London Zoo, p.74), John Edwards writes: '...the carnivores were kept alive with comparative ease, because the Zoo was sent a lot of condemned meat from bomb-damaged buildings, as well as the corpses of dogs from Battersea Dogs' Home.' Lions cannot live on grass. Like domestic cats, they would only eat grass as an emetic.*"   (An emetic is something that makes you vomit – cats often eat grass to help them clear their guts of hairballs). Likewise, contrary to certain outrageous claims, *T. rex* did not live on mangoes (I've actually heard this claim). Fossils of carnivorous animals, and bite marks on the bones of their prey, predate the fossils of hominids by millions of years.

Another assumption often held is that everything was blissful in the Garden of Eden, including the absence of any pain. But recall that one of God's judgments on Eve was to "*… greatly increase your pains in childbearing…*" (Genesis 3:16). It doesn't say "*give you pains'*, but rather "*increase your pains*", and it specifically refers to pain in childbirth, not pain in general. Pain is a useful physiological message: ask anyone who has leprosy … they suffer all kinds of injuries because they feel no pain. Pain co-ordinates the immune system, strengthens bones, causes aversion to dangerous situations/stimuli/foods. And to Adam God says that the ground "*…will produce thorns and thistles…*" (Genesis 3:18). The text doesn't say anything like "*… for the first time ever the ground will produce thorns and thistles….*"   Instead, it's equally possible that God is speaking to his personal gardener, who up until that point had been working inside that protected little garden and was easily able to maintain a very neat and tidy garden free of the weeds, thorns and thistles that were invasive everywhere beyond the Garden's walls right from the very beginning, and says "*… but now, despite your best efforts and hard work, you won't be able to keep back the thorns and thistles …*". Thistles are simply another species of plant life and play a key role in many ecosystems, and thorns are merely deterrents to predation by herbivores; why would it be perfectly OK for an animal to eat the plant but not OK for the plant to defend itself? So pain, thorns and thistles are not intrinsically 'evil', and the only reason one might label them 'curses' is because humans don't like them.

Finally, there's the assumption – or maybe I should call this an interpretation – that predation – animals turning against each other and eating each other – only started to happen after the Fall. That before this event, all animals were herbivores … again, lions eating grass and cabbages, and *T. rex* eating mangoes. Why are carnivores considered to be 'evil' when they take down their prey, but not herbivores when they nibble a young sapling down to its roots? Those carnivores perform a function that's critical to the maintenance of a healthy ecosystem. A perfect example of this has been documented in Yellowstone National Park [35]. During the late 1800s and early 1900s, wolves were progressively exterminated from that area. By 1970, there was no evidence of any wolf population at all. Which was great for farmers and hikers. But what the Park Rangers and farmers also noticed was that the elk population went out of control, and was getting increasingly unhealthy, with more and more elk exhibiting obvious signs of sickness and injuries. What's more, the groves of aspen, willow and poplar were being nibbled down to the ground because there were too many elk browsing on them, and those elk no longer had fear of forests and brush (where wolves could more easily catch them). The loss of those trees removed nesting places for songbirds as well as a food source for beavers, and the beaver population began to dwindle. And with fewer beaver dams being built and repaired, the whole aquatic ecosystem was changing: water was rushing through the area and eroding the river banks, and marsh-life was disappearing. Then in the 1970s, the Forestry Service began re-introducing wolves, against much public opposition, and saw the reversal of all the changes mentioned above. The exact same sequence of events were noted in Zion National Park (Utah), Wind Cave National Park (South Dakota), Yosemite National Park (California), Olympic National Park (Washington) and Jasper National Park (Alberta) when the top predators (wolf, cougar, lynx) were decimated or eliminated, and then reintroduced [36]. Ecologists refer to these top predators as 'keystone species' referring to the keystone of a stone archway that holds all the other stones in place: remove that keystone, and the arch comes tumbling down.

A similar destructive outcome – a complete imbalance in population numbers – results when animals are introduced into an environment that lacks their natural predators: jack rabbits in Australia in the 1700s, Asian carp in the Mississippi River watershed in the 1970s, zebra mussels in the Great Lakes in the late 1980s, purple loose strife in North America … this list is a very long one. Ecologists refer to these as 'invasive species', and their solution to this devastating problem is often to introduce a predator to control it.

So is it more evil to abolish predation, or to welcome it? Are predators themselves evil, or an essential component of the health, balance and beauty of God's creation?

---

[35] Yellowstone National Park Service, *Wolf Restoration*,
<http://www.nps.gov/yell/naturescience/wolfrest.htm>
[36] Will Stolzenburg. *Lords of Nature: Life in a Land of Great Predators*. Directed by Karen Anspacher-Meyer. 2009

(6) God would have made it complete all at once Some don't like the idea
that God would make something incomplete but then have to continuously
step in to re-direct it, revise it, add to it, improve it, et cetera. I found this
puzzling in several ways. First: the traditional interpretation of the creation
account has God doing exactly that: stepping in six times to add to or revise
his previous creation. And as I pondered this rebuttal a bit more, I thought
of the entire Bible and how God had to continually step in to fix things. He
creates Adam, but then notices that *"It is not good for the man to be alone. I
will make a helper suitable for him"* (Genesis 2:18), almost as if this is an
oversight on his part, and creates Eve. Later on, Adam and Eve rebel and
God has to quickly cut off their access to the tree of life or he'll have a
bigger problem (Genesis 3:22-24). Cain kills his brother Abel and God has
to step in to put a mark on Cain so that other people won't take revenge on
him (Genesis 4:15).   God sees that humanity has become completely
immoral and *"regretted that he had made human beings on the earth, and
his heart was deeply troubled"* (Genesis 6:6-7), so he destroys it in a flood;
if anyone else made something but soon regretted having done so and
destroyed it, you would say they made a mistake. God seems to get nervous
about people building the Tower of Babel and decides he has to quickly
come down and disrupt things or they'll get out of hand (Genesis 11).
Sodom and Gomorrah become so uniquely wicked that he has to come down
and fix that problem too (Genesis 19). He covenants with the nation of
Israel and sets up the temple practice of offering animal sacrifices for sin,
but then does away with all of that in a new and better covenant that
involves the death of Jesus Christ on the cross. There's a long list of
examples of God having to come in and fix or revise what he first created
and ordained as good. I'll agree that the reason he has to do so is basically
because of humanity messing things up, but that doesn't take away from my
point here: YE'ers can't criticize OE theology on the grounds that God
would have made it all complete in one single step.

(7) Evolution is godless and leads to immorality I've heard Christians say
that a world-view that includes classical Darwinism inevitably leads to
moral decay. If biological evolution is true, then we're just animals driven
by our genes and instincts, and this gives people an excuse to live as they
want without any accountability for their actions other than the laws of the
land. This is just too simplistic. It's no more valid than the antinomian
viewpoint that we should *"go on sinning so that grace may increase"*
(Romans 6:1), or another theistic line of thinking that: *"I'm sinful at heart,
God made me, so he's responsible and I can't be held accountable for*

acting on the impulses that he created in me".

As Robert Pennock put it: "*It is misleading for creationists to characterize science in general and to define evolution in particular as 'godless'. Science is godless in the same way that plumbing is godless. Evolutionary biology is no more or less based on a 'dogmatic philosophy' of naturalism than are medicine and farming"* [37]. Evolution is like a tool: morally and ethically neutral. It only matters how that tool is used. It is a biological process, not a world-view or accountability system. No matter which society we come from, nor what kind of parents raised us, each of us are accountable according to the knowledge and values that we each possess. As we learn more about life ... about ethics, morals and values ... about God himself ... more will be expected of us. Some theists will point fingers at the horrendous outcomes of societies that rejected religion and embraced evolutionary theory: Nazi Germany and its eugenics program, Stalinist Russia, and Communist China. In response, I would also point fingers at societies that embraced religion and rejected empirical science: the ones that gave us the Inquisition, the Crusades, witch-burnings, Jihad and the Twin Towers.

SOME MESSY PROBLEMS FOR THE YE HYPOTHESIS

I've already pointed out above one moral problem that's raised for anyone who insists that the universe is approximately 6,000 years old but has been made to look so much older ('apparent age'). For me, this turns God into an incredibly deceitful being who maintains a ruse — a lie, actually — just to see who's willing to put their brain on the shelf or who, for whatever reason, hasn't taken the time to really think about what they believe or why. Or it makes them invent stories that aren't in scripture: such as God creating a proto-earth fifteen billion years ago, then destroying it, and rebuilding the current earth from the ashes 6,000 years ago.

But here's another problem with taking the traditional interpretation of the Genesis account. Scripture makes it very clear what God thinks about incest: it's completely abhorrent to Him. Leviticus 18 begins with "*No one is to approach any close relative to have sexual relations*" (Leviticus 18:6), but in case the reader missed the point, it then goes on for several verses through a long list of the relatives who are off limits: mother, sister, grand-daughter, cousin, aunt, uncle's wife, son's daughter, sister-in-law, and a few

[37] Robert Pennock, *Tower of Babel: The Evidence Against the New Creationism*, ch. 6, p. 282 (Bradford Books, 2000)

others. And yet God must have foreseen that, by creating only one single couple, he was absolutely forcing their descendants to start off the whole human race solely through incest. The Bible never tells us anything about the 'wives' of Cain, Abel and Seth, but the YE view requires that the people with whom they had children would have been their sisters, nieces and grand-daughters. Unless one proposes that God went through a few more rounds of special creation in order to provide genetically unrelated wives for them the way he did for Adam (actually, one could argue that Eve was genetically-related, given that Genesis says she was created from Adam's rib), but there's absolutely no scriptural support for that. I can't think of any theological reason why God couldn't have created two couples, or several for that matter, in order to avoid this absolutely messy problem. But by setting up a scenario in which the only way for the human race to expand would be through incest, that either makes God short-sighted (he didn't anticipate this problem) or ultimately responsible for a form of sin that he later spoke so harshly against. As an aside, the story of Noah puts a bandage over this problem by presenting a whole new group of three brothers — Ham, Shem and Japheth — from whom *"came the people who were scattered over the earth"* (Genesis 9:19), but this time with wives who didn't have to be their genetic siblings (they're never named, nor are their genealogies ever given, so we don't know how genetically related these four couples were).

Several times I've heard Christians dismiss this concern by pointing out that incest wasn't an issue in the beginning. Their explanation is that Adam and Eve's DNA was initially perfect, but was corrupted following the Fall; as genetic mutations began to accumulate to such an extent that inbreeding became dangerous, God had to issue the prohibition against incest within the laws given to Moses 2,500 years later. In other words, God hadn't yet issued the command to Adam and Eve that incest was forbidden, and therefore it was OK. I have to admit, I cringe every time I hear this. I won't get into the dubious morality of this view, except to say that the Genesis account also doesn't say God specifically commanded Adam and Eve to not murder, lie, steal, covet, or many other things which were specifically mentioned in those 613 laws given to Moses a couple millennia later, yet we'd still say those activities were wrong right from the beginning. But let's look at it from an intellectual point of view: this argument assumes that the genome was flawless at first, but we know of so many flaws which appear to have been present in our genome right from primordial times (for example, the proviral sequences and pseudogenes I talked about above).

CONCLUSION

I'm not on an anti-YE crusade. I don't have an agenda to disprove that hypothesis. I do believe that it's conceivable for God to have created the universe in six days roughly 6,000 years ago. And if one is happy to hold that view, so be it. However, YE proponents need to realize that holding such a view does have some implications that give pause for concern. It raises intellectual problems. Scientific and historical problems. Ethical problems. Even theological problems. Especially if one hopes to share their faith and the Gospel with non-believers, then they need to consider the implications of that viewpoint. Preaching a theology that's only half thought out and then having the holes in your theology pointed out in front of those non-believers actually accomplishes the opposite of what we've been commanded to do: rather than going out and making disciples, we go out and make scoffers and immunize people against the truth. It's an indictment against the church whenever the gospel story is presented and non-believers walk away snickering or shaking their heads saying *"that stuff's just not for me"*. So believe firmly what you believe, but *"always be prepared to give an answer to everyone who asks you to give the reason for the hope that you have."* (1st Peter 3:15). Even as far back as the 4th century AD, St. Augustine of Hippo in 415 AD wrote: *"be on guard against giving interpretations of scripture that are farfetched or opposed to science, and so exposing the Word of God to the ridicule of unbelievers"* [38]. In the Biologos survey, *"72% of pastors with [YE Creationist] views and 73% of pastors with [Theistic Evolution] views agree with the statement that 'the Christian community needs to take a serious look at its understanding of science and human origins in order to maintain its witness in the world.'"* [39]. 85% of the YE pastors agreed with the statement *"Christian disagreement on matters of creation and evolution is compromising our witness to the world"*. Although 63% of pastors believing that God could have used naturalistic processes like evolution disagreed with this statement, the same percentage of them did agree that *"The church's posture toward science prevents many non-Christians from accepting Christianity"*. That was also the overwhelming conclusion from the on-line survey I referred to earlier

---

[38] St. Augustine of Hippo, *De Genesi ad litteram*, 415 AD
[39] Biologos Foundation, *A Survey of Clergy and Their Views on Origins*,
<http://biologos.org/blog/a-survey-of-clergy-and-their-views-on-origins> (accessed June 2, 2013

asking over 2,000 people why they gave up on Christianity [40]

.

[40] Reddit, *Reasons For the Decline in Christianity According to Ex-Christians and non-Christians,*
<http://www.reddit.com/r/TrueAtheism/comments/1j7lup/the_results_of_the_survey_are_in_reasons_for_the/> (accessed November 29, 2013)

4

Theists versus atheists

Faith versus fact? Scripture versus science? Darwinism or Design?

How do you explain the origin of the universe? of life? of species?

Do theists base their view solely on faith, while atheists base theirs solely on fact?

If science can't explain it, then it must be God, right?

Can the incredible complexity of things be an accident?

How can you be a scientist and a believer?

COMPARING THEISTIC AND ATHEISTIC FAITHS REGARDING ORIGINS

Some people with whom I've talked about this creation/evolution question are puzzled that I'm a scientist and yet could believe in a creator. As I see it, though, the more I learn about the complexity of things around me, the harder I find it to believe that everything arose by accident, all on its own. And I end up having to ask *"How could I not believe in a creator, given the evidence?"* Even more, I start seeing that my atheistic colleagues are also leaning on a belief system, despite their self-deception that they're relying solely on facts. Let me give a few examples of this.

(1) origin of the universe Big Bang Theory and gravitational forces can explain a lot. They explain the extremely low level of background radiation that fills the universe in a very splotchy kind of way. You can imagine this to be like the billows of smoke and the ringing in your ears a few seconds after there's been an explosion. (Although I should point out that the term

'Big Bang' is a bit of a misnomer because in the vacuum of space you can't have any sound, and the phenomenon was not so much an 'explosion' as it was a dramatic unfolding of the dimensions of space and time ... so the "Big Bang" was actually more of a 'Silent Expansion'). Big Bang Theory and gravitational forces explain the distributions of galaxies. They've predicted black holes, which would never have been observed except that the equations which were used to understand the Big Bang predicted such singularities, and when we looked, we found them! (We don't actually 'see' them, but rather the gravitational effects they have on other cosmic bodies and even light itself). And one might be naive enough to think that it would be possible to take those equations and 'run them in reverse' to figure out exactly when the Big Bang happened, and even what things looked like before the cosmic fuse was lit. However, those equations don't allow that. We can inch our way closer and closer to that initial moment in time, but the equations just don't work when t=0 ('t' being the abbreviation for time). In fact, Stephen Hawking and James Hartle, in 1983, said it was impossible to get any closer than 10^{-43} seconds after the Big Bang (for perspective, one thousandth of a second is 10^{-3} seconds, one millionth of a second is 10^{-6}, one billionth = 10^{-9}, one trillionth = 10^{-12}, ... so 10^{-43} seconds is a really, really brief period of time).

Naturally, some people find that frustrating. But other people find it reassuring: it means that one never needs to explain the actual origin of energy and matter in the universe. It shields us from paying the penalty for breaking the First Law of Thermodynamics, which says that energy/matter can neither be created nor destroyed. Although it may not be obvious to a non-physicist, energy and matter are the same thing: they're interchangeable through Einstein's famous equation $E=mc^2$, where 'E' is energy, 'm' is mass, and c is the speed of light (how bizarre a relationship is that!?). It may be mathematically or theoretically true that we don't have to answer the question "what happened at t=0?", but it's not satisfying. Intuitively, there can only be two options: (1) the sum total of matter and energy has always existed; or (2) matter and energy came into existence at some point in time. I suppose a third possibility is that neither matter nor energy have ever existed: they're both just a figment of imagination within my non-corporeal consciousness, or 'Boltzmann brain'. But that's just too metaphysical and abstract to be satisfying to me, and so I discount it (which I'm allowed to do in this third possibility if my mind is the only thing that exists).

The first option doesn't make any sense. Not only is it incomprehensible that everything just always existed all through eternity, but it contradicts the Second Law of Thermodynamics: everything eventually decays down to complete disorder. So it can't have 'always existed', or we wouldn't be here: the entire universe would have by now dissipated into a uniform haze of dispersed dust and evenly distributed energy: you wouldn't have the splotchiness of the background radiation I referred to above. One can simply choose to believe that the universe has always existed and yet there's still some order around (you and me, life, the solar system), but there's absolutely no way in the practical sense nor through mathematics to prove it. So let's be honest: this atheistic view is nonetheless a faith system.

What about the second option: that everything did have an origin somehow. How do you get everything from nothing? One answer I've heard to this conundrum is: through the spontaneous creation of anti-matter. This will be easier to understand if you consider an analogy. Imagine taking a molecule with no net electrical charge and extracting a positively charged piece from it (for example, a proton), instantaneously leaving you with a negatively charged molecule in one hand and a positively charged molecule in the other: so you've suddenly 'created' charge from no charge. By the way, it cost you energy to do that: the energy of physically separating two opposite charges that really 'want' to be together.

In the same way, quantum mechanics theory tells us that fluctuations of energy in empty space can cause a small piece of anti-matter to spring into existence out of nothing, leaving behind it a mirror-imaged piece of matter, plus a pretty hefty energy bill. However, this generally occurs on such small scales that the piece of matter and anti-matter immediately collide and annihilate each other, repaying that energy bill. But if some way were found to immediately move the matter and anti-matter a sufficient distance apart, they wouldn't eliminate each other. And if this event repeated continuously over a sufficiently long period of time, you could eventually create a universe of matter and another one with the same mass made up entirely of anti-matter! Voila: the spontaneous creation of something from nothing! ... without God! But here's the thing. The closer those pieces of matter and anti-matter are to each other, the more likely they'll eventually find each other and fuse explosively back into nothing. So you need to separate them a nearly infinite distance apart, or somehow make the anti-matter disappear. And you need to do that for all the matter and anti-matter in the universe. To separate them physically takes an incredible amount of energy. You have a sense of how much energy it takes to throw a large rock into a lake, or to launch a rocket into orbit around the earth: imagine how much energy it takes to move all the matter in the universe a nearly infinite distance? (And the direction in which all the matter is moved needs to be diametrically opposite to that in which the anti-matter is moved in order to avoid any future annihilation events, so there's the question of exactly how all this moving of stuff around is orchestrated) Don't forget the incredible amount of energy that was needed to separate matter from anti-matter in the first place. Altogether, it's an absolutely mind-boggling amount of energy that's required. Of course, the Big Bang would have provided an immeasurable amount of energy. One author [41] suggested that positive energy was channeled into matter while an equal quantity of negative energy went into the gravitational field to produce the 10^{50} tons of matter which make up our own universe (and presumably the same happened for other universes in the "multi-verse"). I was struck by this word "channeled", which to me implies an agent, direction and purpose.

The current idea is that immediately after the Big Bang, the universe consisted of a massive ocean of different kinds of subatomic particles at incredibly high temperatures. All of those particles do not have any mass, except for one particular type referred to by physicists as the Higgs particle or Higgs boson, but many people call it 'the God particle'. When the other particles cooled sufficiently — approximately one trillionth of a second after the Big Bang— they interacted with the Higgs boson and became quarks, and in the process acquired the property of 'mass'. This process applies to both matter and anti-matter, but some have proposed, without any shred of physical data, that it happened slightly more frequently or more easily with matter than with anti-matter. At this stage in our understanding of particle physics, it's completely unknown how matter was selectively produced out of the ocean of particles and how or why anti-matter did not.

So from an atheistic point of view, you just have to believe that it happened. Somehow. Quite a miracle if you think about it: the appearance of all the matter in the universe from nothing, by no one, for no reason. On the other hand, you can choose to believe that God was behind it all (right now, some readers are screaming 'God-of-the-gaps!?' ... I'll come to that problem at the end of this chapter). But either way, with respect to the question of where did 'stuff' come from, you have a faith system: you simply have to believe it one way or the other. Atheists can stop trumpeting that they place fact over faith.

Before I move on, I need to address the counter-challenge that's so often put up when someone announces that they choose to believe that the universe was created by some greater being. The usual rebuttal is something like *"then who created God?"* or *"when did God begin?"*, and the lack of an answer to questions like those is generally interpreted to mean that the theistic view has no more credibility than the atheistic one. I don't agree:

---

[41] Paul Davies, *The Fifth Miracle: the Search for the Origin and Meaning of Life*. (New York: Simon and Schuster, 1998)

any naturalistic explanation must by definition operate within the laws of science, but a supernatural explanation, also by definition, doesn't have to. It's hypocritical (or naive or inconsistent) to claim to operate solely within the laws of science but to continue to believe things that contradict those laws. But it's not hypocritical (or naive or inconsistent) to claim a belief in someone else who operates beyond the laws of science and can accomplish things that are otherwise limited by those laws.

I know that that defence will not satisfy atheists, but I'd challenge them to mull the previous two sentences over a few times and show me how the sentences are wrong logically, and how atheists themselves might not be living in a state of cognitive dissonance. I particularly like the way G. K. Chesterton made this point: *"It is absurd for the Evolutionist to complain that it is unthinkable for an admittedly unthinkable God to make everything out of nothing, and then pretend that it is more thinkable that nothing should turn itself into everything"* (you might need to read that a couple more times as well). Some atheists will be quite dismissive and ridiculing of an argument that God is outside the laws of science, exclaiming that if the idea can't be tested scientifically (that is, within the laws of science), then it's not worth considering. However, those same people have no problems holding other ideas that are impossible to test directly, such as multiverse theory (I'll describe this theory in more detail in a few more pages, as well as why it's impossible to get hard evidence for it), or the idea that the universe has gone through a series of Big Bang events, each followed by an expansion and then a contraction (can't be tested unless we can go back in time, step outside of the contracting universe as it collapses, and then get out of the way as it re-explodes).

I would also appeal to Edwin Abbott's *"Flatland"* [42] to explain how a Being beyond our dimensions of space and time can do things that we can't possibly understand or explain. In his fictional story, *"Flatland"* is a world of only two spatial dimensions: forward-backward and left-right. In Flatland, there is no such thing as up-down. The people in Flatland live within a thin flat universe much like a page in a book, although the edges of the page go on in both directions into infinity. With that image in your mind, you can consider the other pages in the book as parallel but distinct universes: the people in one page would have no concept or understanding — theoretical or in practice — of people in the adjacent pages. They're completely isolated in space and time from those other universes, because they're limited in their thinking within their own two spatial dimensions. The only way to move around in Flatland is to go left or right or forward or

---

[42] Edwin Abbott, *Flatland : A Romance of Many Dimensions* (Seely & Co., 1884)

backward, but always within the page itself. But along comes something from an entirely different dimension: in Abbott's story, it's a three-dimensional sphere, but I'd like to instead personalize this and make it my own hand. In addition to the two dimensions that Flatlanders are aware of, I am fully able to operate in a 3rd dimension — the up-down dimension — something that the Flatlanders are just not possibly capable of understanding: the up-down dimension just doesn't exist in their world. Imagine I extend my finger down 'out of the heaven' into Flatland: all of a sudden my finger appears in Flatland like a little circle that grows in circumference as I extend my finger deeper through the page (Figure 4B). Out of thin air, I just suddenly appeared to them, albeit only in the form of an expanding circle. And when I pull my finger back, I become a shrinking circle and then just as suddenly disappear. Next I re-extend all four fingers and my thumb into Flatland, and from their perspective, I suddenly re-appear, but now there are five of me that suddenly appear out of thin air in Flatland! And though they appear as five distinct and completely separate manifestations of me (Figure 4C), they know somehow that all five are the same person. Five persons in one — a "quintity"? I could belabor this analogy, but I hope by now you get the point. From my three spatial dimension experience, I can do things that Flatlanders can't comprehend. Think of the possibilities if there were a Being who could operate in all the dimensions of the universe, when physicists tell us there are at least 10 dimensions!

Figure 4 A layer of oil on top of water simulates a two-dimensional "Flatland". Inhabitants within that oil layer would only be aware of the parts of my 3-d hand that invade their "2-d" universe (compare B and C).

On the other hand, to the creationists I would say: a supernatural explanation for the origin of the universe may be satisfactory on an individual and personal level to those who believe in the Judeo-Christian God, but that explanation cannot be imposed on others who may not share that view (for example, by forcing it into a public school's curriculum). Otherwise, by insisting that equal treatment be given to 'both' sides, you need to also give equal treatment to all other creationist explanations: Muslim, Mayan, Hindu, Aboriginal, Inuit, Raëlian, et cetera. As Robert Pennock points out, this is not merely a two-sided debate [43].

(2) origin of life Francis Collins, geneticist and at one time the head of the Human Genome Project, wrote: "*Four billion years ago, the conditions on this planet were completely inhospitable to life as we know it; 3.85 billion years ago, life was teeming. That is a very short period — 150 million years — for the assembly of macromolecules into a self-replicating form. I think even the most bold and optimistic proposals for the origin of life fall well short of achieving any real probability for that kind of event having occurred*" [44].

The more I learn about how cells work, the more I am amazed. Cells are incredibly complex pieces of machinery. Way beyond anything that we ourselves might attempt to create, despite all that we've learned about molecular biology, biochemistry, engineering, physics, electronics, et cetera. It's way beyond the scope of this book to even begin to summarize how bewilderingly sophisticated cells are. A number of years ago, I came across a very thought-provoking book by Dr. Michael Behe entitled "Darwin's Black Box" [45], which introduced me to the compelling idea he called 'irreducible complexity'. Let me illustrate this point using a car. It doesn't matter what make or model or manufacturer we're talking about, so long as we begin with a car that works, by which I mean you have to be able to drive it down the road. This is a fairly complex machine. But there's lots of redundancy and 'bells and whistles' that aren't necessary for its ultimate function. In theory, you could remove parts of its computer control system which optimizes its fuel economy, its anti-lock braking system, its GPS system, and other such electronics: you'd make it a much less complex car but you'd still have something that you can drive down the road. And you

---

[43] Robert T. Pennock, *Tower of Babel: The Evidence Against the New Creationism*. (The MIT Press, Cambridge, 2000), ch. 4.

[44] FS Collins, *Faith and the Human Genome*. Perspectives on Science and Christian Faith 55, no.3 (2004):152

[45] Michael Behe, *Darwin's Black Box: The Biochemical Challenge to Evolution*. (New York, The Free Press, 1996)

could also remove other physical items that aren't absolutely necessary for this minimalist function ... the mirrors ... the horn ... the seats ... the body ... a couple of the spark plugs ... all but one of the forward gears ... and a thousand other parts ... even one or two of its tires (and certainly the spare tire) ... even the entire braking system (since the only function we're interested in is 'being able to drive down the road on its own'). But eventually, you'd reach a point where every single remaining piece was absolutely essential to get that car moving on its own power a short stretch down the road. A point at which you couldn't remove another single piece of the car — even a bolt or nut — without rendering it immoveable on its own. At that point, you would have reached irreducible complexity.

Behe makes the same point using a mouse trap composed of five parts: the base, the 'hammer' that actually falls down on the mouse, the spring that drives that hammer down forcefully, a latch that holds the hammer back, and some form of trigger (on which you place the cheese) that trips the latch. That little piece of machinery is irreducibly complex. You can't remove any single one of those five parts without making the mouse trap incapable of accomplishing its ultimate function (to trap mice all on its own).

This concept of irreducible complexity is indeed a compelling one. Many antagonists, however, will say that it has been defeated: that the examples which have been rolled out as key pieces of evidence for this idea have since been explained in evolutionary terms.

The most frequently cited piece of evidence in this debate is the bacterial flagellum, which is essentially a whip or hair that a bacterium can use to paddle itself through the water. It's a very complex little piece of machinery with dozens of unique parts, and the argument was that removing even a single part would render it completely non-functional. And if it were non-functional, there would be no reason for cells to waste so much energy for millions of years making it until that last part appeared on the scene to give it a function. But it was later shown that after removing approximately 40 of its 50 parts you have a completely different machine, a form of syringe needle that bacteria use to inject their genetic material into their target hosts. So the flagellum is metaphorically a mixed bag of re-purposed parts. We know that the cell is literally just a bag stuffed full of its various bits and pieces, and those pieces either self-assemble into bigger pieces or their assembly is helped by enzymes which are also floating around inside that bag. An entirely plausible explanation is that at some point in time, certain parts from one machine mixed with certain parts from another machine or two and produced something completely new and different, and which now gave the cell a huge selective advantage in the fight for survival. In theory, each of those other machines could have arisen by a repurposing of parts from yet other little machines and left-over pieces.

Another piece of evidence often used to support irreducible complexity is the biochemical system in our blood which prevents us from bleeding to death. The clotting system is a complex and integrated series of biochemical reactions, each one triggering the next one down the line, much like a carefully stacked string of dominoes: step A produces molecule B, which itself is useless for clot formation but does produce molecule C, which again could not make a clot but does produce molecule D, and so on down the line. Eventually, after enough of these dominoes have fallen, the stage is finally set for clot formation. Again, it was argued that this cascade would be non-functional if you removed even one of these dominoes. But then the evolutionists pointed to the blood system of whales and dolphins which do in fact lack one of these key steps, and the blood system of the puffer fish which is missing several of them: all three of those species have blood which clots just fine.

So the concept of irreducible complexity is an intriguing one, but its track record in the origins debate isn't perfect, at least when it comes to individual parts of a cell. But the debate isn't over: let's talk about the first living cell. Just like the car above, you could start removing all kinds of pieces ... organelles ... enzyme pathways ... receptors on the cell membrane ... its cilia ... many of its genes ... and a million other components. In theory, you could keep doing this until you finally got to an irreducibly complex cell: one which has the fewest and simplest components remaining that allow it to continue to achieve its most essential of functions ... to live long enough and gather together enough biological material to reproduce at least one daughter cell and thereby perpetuate the species. Here's the amazing thing: even that irreducibly complex cell would be so astoundingly complex that it makes the space shuttle look like a paper airplane!

And yet some people insist on <u>believing</u> that that first complex little machine could arise spontaneously from the self-organization of inanimate chemicals in the prebiotic soup or a hydrothermal vent. They will point to scientific evidence that this or that particular cellular process or structure can arise entirely spontaneously given the right conditions. For example, oils in water can form 'micelles', which are basically water-filled balloons in which the walls of the balloon are made of those oils, and they resemble a cell and its membrane (although very crudely). Or a few of the several dozen amino acids forming when you pass an electrical spark through a warmed and bubbling mixture of certain simple gases and liquids [46]. Small proteins which can assemble themselves into chains of a few dozen amino acids given the right chemical conditions (ignoring the fact that the vast majority of functional proteins in a cell are made up of many hundreds of amino acids).

So as time goes on, we're learning that many of the millions of steps which lead to a functional, reproducing cell can happen all by themselves, given the right conditions (which is itself a pretty dubious caveat, given that the 'right conditions' for one crucial step are completely in conflict with the conditions needed for other crucial steps). In this context, some maintain the faith (key word here!) that in time we'll see how the whole thing happened spontaneously from start to finish. And it's easy to convince the average person of this idea because they and/or their listeners just don't understand the science behind it all. But let me use another analogy that they might better understand. Let me warn you, though: you might think this analogy is stretched pretty thin, but from my point of view as a scientist studying cellular processes for three decades, this is a twin to the arguments I often hear about naturalistic explanations for the origin of life. Here's the analogy:

During a walk in the woods, a couple hikers come across a perfectly functioning, beautifully-decorated cottage, complete with plumbing, wiring and heating/AC. It's perfectly obvious to one of them that someone built it there, even though there's absolutely no sign of anyone having ever been present. But his walking partner is 'more enlightened' and points out that…

"… the copper plumbing is easily explained, because they've found deposits of nearly pure copper in one hillside, and in another hillside they found hollow tubes cut into the rock by water flowing through cracks over millions of years. Generally, those tubes have varying diameters and meander in all different directions, but in certain places they can go more or less straight and with uniform diameter for a distance of a few feet. Eventually, we'll learn how cracks also formed in the copper deposits and the water flowing through them eventually formed tubes with a wall thickness of $1/8^{th}$ of an inch and a uniform diameter of exactly ½ inch, for distances of up to 40 or 50 feet. Unlikely, indeed, but given enough time it could possibly happen. By chance, those natural tubes with only the appearance of design will line up and connect in interesting patterns leading to taps

---

[46] Stanley L. Miller, Harold C. Urey, "Organic Compound Synthesis on the Primitive Earth". *Science* **130** no. 3370 (July 1959): 245–51.

which regulate the flow of the water through them, some of which also seems to line up with a heating source that we'll call the water heater. But that shouldn't be too surprising, since I happened to have also visited Yellowstone Park and saw geysers which can heat water, and spew that water out at intervals through complex networks of channels, which is an admittedly crude form of flow regulation. Come to think of it, the bathtub in this cottage looks very much like, and functions exactly like, the hot spring I visited in a local resort. As for the water heater in the cottage: sure it's got a propane-fired heating element, but there too, I've seen examples of naturally-occurring methane flares in the Karakum desert. And the copper wiring? Again, remember the copper deposits I told you about? Sometimes, if you purify the copper a little more (some deposits are exceptionally pure) and exert tensile forces in exactly the right way, you can stretch them out into long filaments or wires. Although I will say it's remarkable, but not impossible, that in this case they're all stretched out into long filaments of exactly $1/8^{th}$ inch diameter. The color coding on those wires --- some black, some white, some red --- is easily explained by different species of lichens or fungus growing on that copper filament ... just like the species of fungus growing over the tree branches on the ground over there ... see how they change the color of the branches? The electrical current? We see that all the time in nature: ever heard of lightning? You can also make a battery out of simple acids and certain metals, both of which you can find almost anywhere, or generate electricity using an oscillating magnetic field. In fact, that oscillating field may explain why the current in the cottage is an alternating current rather than a simple direct current like that which batteries produce. The square beams in the cottage? They're just trees which have been worn down against the rocks, maybe through some kind of back-and-forth tidal action. And the fancy decorated gables on the face of the cottage? Ever seen a snowflake? You know what they say: 'no two are exactly the same'. OK, sure, we haven't worked out all the precise details just yet, but the basic principles are there: give us more time and research funding, and, wow, will we ever surprise you".

I could continue this analogy ad nauseum, or go through the exact same exercise to explain Stonehenge, which one could argue is not man-made but is instead nothing more than a natural occurrence of interestingly-shaped rocks which happen to be arranged in some peculiar pattern with a truly remarkable correspondence to the sun and the seasons (*"perhaps certain astronomical events were responsible for the formation and organization of these naturally-formed stones?"*).   But by now my point should be clear. As absurd as those explanations sound to a non-scientific reader, the same is my response as a scientist when I hear or read of some of the atheistic explanations for the spontaneous appearance of life. It's one thing to show how certain raw materials and simple synthetic events can appear all by themselves, but it's an entirely different thing to conclude that those can on their own produce precisely-defined, functional structures like cottages, Stonehenge or cells, even if we continue to make newer discoveries to fill in some of the gaps.   There are gaps, and then there are Gaps! Creationists are often accused of having a God-of-the-gaps mentality (which I'll discuss further below), but I feel the naturalists are also susceptible to promoting a naturalism-of-the-gaps mentality when they say things like *"we haven't worked out all the precise details just yet, but give us more time"*.

There are already many books which go into great lengths explaining how exceedingly improbable it is for biochemical processes to spontaneously produce a living cell. Perhaps the very best book I've read on this question of the improbability of life springing from inanimate chemicals is '*Signature In The Cell: DNA And The Evidence For Intelligent Design*', by Stephen C. Meyer [47].   In this book, he very easily and capably applies a number of scientific disciplines (for example, mathematics, physics, and information theory) to dispel the idea that living systems could arise spontaneously.   I can't recommend it enough: it's a must read for theists and atheists alike who are interested in exploring this question.

The bottom line is this: the mechanism underlying the origin of life is still very unclear, and whatever explanation you might have is simply something that you have to believe in.   One can choose to believe that it happened all by itself, but at this point there's absolutely no way for science to prove that, let alone re-create it (which is one of the essential measuring sticks for scientific theories).   Or one can choose to believe that God was involved in some way.   Either way, it's a matter of faith.

(3) origin of species   This is a third example of an origins question in which atheists have to exercise faith in their favorite answer, whether consciously or otherwise.   I'm not going to challenge Darwin's theory. I can see and accept an abundance of evidence that many species present and

---

[47] Stephen C. Meyer. *Signature in the cell: DNA and the Evidence for Intelligent Design.* (Harper One, 2009)

past seem to have arisen by a gradual evolution from previous common ancestors. It's my choice – a position of faith – that God was involved in that evolutionary process. I myself am a tinkerer and thoroughly enjoy building things, and I can imagine God doing that with living things. And again, that's a choice I might make as a theist.

One of the biggest criticisms of this theory is summed up in two words: "*missing links*". These two words and this criticism have been seriously misused and abused, and really need to be properly understood.

Darwin himself pointed out that his theory suffered from an absence of some crucial pieces of evidence: the fact that there were lots of missing pieces in the fossil record. Darwin: "*Why, if species have descended from other species by insensibly fine gradations, do we not everywhere see innumerable transitional forms?*" [48]. There were lots of fossil specimens and fragments of this animal or that animal, but not a spectrum of intermediate forms that linked the one animal to some other predecessor.

From the Creationist point of view, the situation is analogous to 25th century archaeologists digging through the post-apocalyptic ruins of North America and finding thousands of pennies, nickels, dimes and quarters, and occasionally some really old fifty cent pieces; interestingly, when they dug around in the northern parts of North America, they also found coins with a face value of $1 and $2 (Canadians call these 'looneys' and 'twoneys'). With this data set consisting of lots of coins denominated in values of either 1, 5, 10, 25, 50, 100 or 200 cents, they might choose to propose that 21st century North Americans used at least 200 different coins, each denominated in incrementing values of one, thinking that eventually archaeologists would uncover the missing coins or gaps ... the 13 cent coin, the 49 cent coin, the 81 cent coin, et cetera. But proponents of that idea would be wrong. Or they could choose to stick with the data set that they had in hand, and propose a different coin system which was designed with big gaps, and they'd be right.

But people who claim that the fossil record for vertebrates (animals with a backbone) has too many "missing links" just haven't done enough homework; they may even be simply parroting what they've heard other people say without doing any researching for themselves at all. There is in fact an abundance of these transitional forms. And we keep finding more every year.

To explain in part why the fossil record looks like it skips and jumps, imagine watching a sunflower seed planted in your backyard garden beside a pond with frog's eggs. You know that the seed slowly unfurls itself

---

[48] Charles Darwin, *Origin of Species*. (Gramercy Publishing; New edition, 1995)

into a seven foot tall plant, and that the eggs produce tadpoles that gradually morph into frogs. But now imagine that you set up a camera to take pictures of the seed and tadpoles as they develop, but you set it up so that a snapshot is triggered only when a lightning bolt strikes. For every lightning flash you add another frame to the movie. Sometimes you have to wait three weeks before the next set of shots are taken, and on that night you get two dozen pictures. Then another two weeks go by before twenty or thirty more pictures are taken. And so on till the end of summer. What are you left with? A series of snapshots that accurately capture the changes in these two organisms, but does so in fits and starts as you re-play the movie. The same thing happens with fossilization. Most dead bodies rot away within a matter of weeks. But every now and then ... very rarely ... you get exactly the right conditions for dead bodies to become fossilized and last millions of years.

At this point, I want to return to my coin analogy and explain how it's not a good one, before creationists begin using it naively to promote creationism, and before evolutionists write me off as a 'gapist' or a 'link denier'. The problem with my coin analogy is that it's linear: it's easy to see how the 18 cent coin follows after the 17 coin, and is followed in turn by the 19 cent coin, et cetera. The evolutionary tree, however, is branched, not linear. Humans are believed to have evolved from a common ancestor of the monkeys, not from monkeys themselves. Humans and monkeys have long ago diverged from each other on that evolutionary tree and headed down different paths. As such, the images one often sees of a crawling monkey on the left side and a fully erect human on the right side, and several intermediates in between, are actually completely misleading. While both species may continue to evolve over the next million years, there's absolutely no requirement that the monkey's descendants must first pass through a human stage: those descendants will most likely look completely different than either monkeys or humans. The so-called 'missing link' is not a strange animal that looks a little bit like one modern species, and a little bit like another modern species.   Let me give another simple analogy for this crucial point. Figure 5 shows a hypothetical evolution of the letters of the alphabet. Starting with the letter 'o' which gains or loses a small section to produce the letters 'a' and 'c', respectively, one can carry on to produce all the other letters of the alphabet through relatively minor changes (of course, each letter is meant here to represent a different animal species, whether it be still living or long ago extinct and fossilized). With this example, you can see that the letters 'w' and 's' have a common ancestor ... the letter 'v' ... and that we don't have to look for some intermediate that looks like some strange combination between a 'w' and an 's'. More importantly, if the letter 'v' were to continue to evolve, it doesn't have to become a 'w' or an 's'; it can become any one of several other letters. This concept of evolution producing branched trees rather than linear chains is crucial, and creationists should get this idea straightened in their heads before they speak in public about the evolutionary tree.

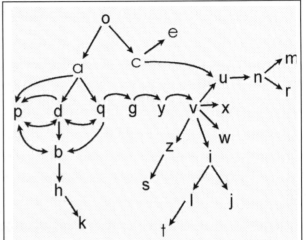

Figure 5 Evolution of letter 'o' into all the other letters by small cumulative changes. Those little changes can include a simple:
- addition of a small section ('o' → 'a')
- loss of a small section ('o' → 'c')
- lengthening of the added section ('a' → 'd')
- sliding of a section ('d' → 'q', or 'v' → 'x')
- 180 degree rotation ('d' → 'p')
- mirror reversal ('d' → 'b')
- duplication of part of the letter ('n' → 'm')

As such, the Darwinian notion that humans share an evolutionary heritage with other primates that have a long tail does not require that we should find some humanoid fossils with a tail half as long. Likewise, the idea that whales and hippopotamuses have a common ancestor does not require that there should be fossils that look a bit like both. In both cases (and many others), the two species went in different evolutionary directions from their common ancestor, just like the letters 'm' and 't' did in my analogy above. This is the answer to the question some creationists hurl at evolutionists: *"you don't see monkeys turning into humans anymore, do you? Nor dogs becoming cats?"*

So as time goes on, living organisms accumulate more and more genetic changes. A single gene mutation can lead to a minor change or a major change (the latter is especially true if the gene in question kicks in early in the development of a fetus). Whole genes or groups of genes can become accidentally duplicated in a single step, allowing the one copy to carry out the normal function while the other one accumulates mutations and eventually leads to an entirely different function.

Sometimes, circumstances can prevent two groups of a particular species from intermingling and mixing up those genetic differences. For example, the two groups can be trapped on different islands or in different lakes ... migrate to different continents ... get separated by a mini Ice Age that cuts across a continent ... find themselves in completely different ecosystems ... or any one of dozens of other possibilities. When this happens, those two groups can continue to evolve in different directions until they become so different that they can no longer inter-breed. At that point they become two different species, and will continue to become more and more different.

Some people can accept this explanation for the origin of very closely related and similar organisms like Darwin's finches, but not very different organisms like humans and chimps: *"the latter two are miles apart"* some would say. But look at the diversity of dogs, which are one single species: from the tremendously-sized Great Dane to the tiny Chihuahua ... from the burly, hairy and lumbering Saint Bernard to the sleek and speedy Greyhound ... dachshund, poodle, Shitzu, spaniel, pit-bull. Those are all truly very different animals! When you look at the astounding range of possibilities even within that singular species of canines, is it really too big a leap to say that the primates and humans are 'similar'? Sure we're very different in some respects, not the least of which is our relative cognitive abilities, but we're also very similar in so many ways, not the least of which is our respective genetic codes.

But after warning theists against making too much of this matter of 'missing links', I want to also explore the question from the other side and show how it becomes problematic for atheists. And let me start by returning to my coin analogy.

First, I want to emphasize the need for scientists to stick to the data they actually have in hand, and tread very lightly when they interpolate within that data set, or worse, extrapolate outside of it. In the hypothetical archeological coin record, there would always be huge gaps because the fact is no archaeologist would ever find a seventeen cent coin: they were never made. And the same would be true of many other coins. So one completely legitimate interpretation of the data actually in hand is that the coins were made in discrete steps and there were no intermediate forms. An alternative interpretation is that the intermediate forms exist but just hadn't yet been found. As it turns out, in this coin analogy, the first interpretation would be correct and the second one false.

This coin analogy has been really useful to pull out two key ideas: one for the theists (branched versus linear chains) and one for scientists (sticking with the data at hand). But now I'd like to use it to draw out yet a third important concept for those who subscribe to the idea that big changes can be the product of multiple little steps. This is a key aspect of naturalistic evolution, a mechanism proposed to explain entirely new things through incredibly small incremental changes.   The key words here will be 'variations on a theme' versus 'completely different themes'.

Consider that the coin system evolved out of an earlier bartering system, in which you paid for things with other things: your sack of flour pays for 4 chickens. Or perhaps with services: a house is paid for by the promise to clear a forest and help turn it into a field. These are variations on a common theme: substituting one thing of value for another thing of intrinsic value. In some countries, this bartering system still flourishes.

Also consider that from that bartering system you had a "branching" occur leading to an entirely new monetary system (an entirely different theme): substituting things of actual value with things of representative value.   For example, monetary systems developed around the world in which rocks or shells or other physical objects were used as money substitutes to pay for goods and services. One variation on this new theme would be the coins themselves, which only represent value: you can't eat gold, or use it to plough a field or defend yourself against a predator.

And that from the coin system there was a branching event in which metal coins were replaced with a series of paper bills, and then from both of those monetary systems there branched off an entirely different one based solely on electrons and magnetic strips (internet banking and credit/debit cards).

Within each of those major themes, you can have minor variations. The coins can have different sizes ... be made of different combinations of metal (content of gold or silver, alloyed with nickel, molybdenum, et cetera) ... have different inscriptions on either face (with each changing ruling monarch, or major world event to be celebrated) ... different edging (smooth, rippled, corners). But in the end, they're all still just variations on the common theme of 'round and metallic'. The paper bills and electronic strips, on the other hand, are entirely different themes from the coins, as well as from each other. We don't expect the hypothetical 25th century archaeologists to ever find money which is a hybrid or transitional form between round/metallic and rectangular/paper, and it's entirely possible for a society to transition immediately from the bartering system to an electronic one, avoiding entirely any system involving those coins or paper bills.

There are many other examples of minor variations on a single theme. The invention of the wheel led to the chariot, followed by all kinds of variations on a theme like wagons, horse-drawn carriages, baby strollers, bicycles, and conveyor belts. But an entirely new theme arose from the invention of the combustion engine --- the automobile --- and the world was very quickly filled with variations on that theme. Not simply cars with different colors, shapes and sizes, nor different bells and whistles like radios, automatic transmission, power locks, et cetera, but more drastic variations on the theme like trucks, trains, tractors, tanks and snow mobiles. The invention of the air foil led to yet another entirely new theme, beginning first with all the different shapes and sizes of gliders and airplanes, but then later other variations on this theme such as helicopters, fans, hovercrafts, gliding parachutes, and the spoilers on the back of high-performance race-cars which keep the rear wheels in firm contact with the ground.

The point is, it's extremely important to distinguish between variations on a theme from entirely new categories of things. And an honest and critical thinker will realize that a mechanism involving small, gradual and incremental changes can explain variations on a theme, but not the quantum leaps into whole new categories of things that seem to come out of nowhere. The invention of radio can explain televisions and walkie-talkies and telephones, but not the computer and its variations, or lasers and their variations.

So to now return to my point that evolutionists exercise faith when explaining the sudden appearance of new themes in the fossil record. Stephen Jay Gould, a Harvard paleontologist and hugely influential thinker in this area acknowledged this problem: "*The extreme rarity of transitional forms in the fossil record persists as the trade secret of paleontology. The evolutionary trees that adorn our textbooks have data only at the tips and nodes of their branches; the rest is inference, however reasonable, not the evidence of fossils*" [49]. Gould focussed on a particularly egregious example of absent transitional forms, one occurring during a prehistoric period known as the Cambrian period (roughly 530 to 545 million years ago [50] [51]). Fossils of relatively simple animals — mostly single-celled organisms — were found in older (deeper) soil layers and rocks, but the Cambrian period was marked by a sudden appearance of many completely new animal forms: the majority of phyla appeared in a geological blink of an eye – within five to ten million years – and without any trace of intermediate transitional forms [52] [53] [54]. It's important to get a clear picture of the dramatic event we're talking about here. This is much, much bigger than the gradual

[49] Jay Gould, *Evolution's Erratic Pace*, Natural History, 86, no. 5 (May 1977), pp112-116
[50] Marcello Barbieri. *The Genetic Codes: An Introduction to Semantic Biology*. (Cambridge University Press, 2003)
[51] Stephen Jay Gould. "Of it, not above it" *Nature* 377 (1995): 681-682
[52] Marcello Barbieri. *The Genetic Codes: An Introduction to Semantic Biology*. (Cambridge University Press, 2003)
[53] William A. Dembski, Sean McDowell. *Understanding Intelligent Design* (Harvest House Publishers, 2008)
[54] Stephen C. Meyer. *Darwin's Doubt.* (HarperOne, 2013), p. 71

evolution (over hundreds of millions of years) of all those organisms with a general body plan comprising four limbs, a head and a tail. That general category of body plan includes variations on a theme like horses, dogs, cats, crocodiles, dinosaurs, birds, humans, dolphins, fish and even whales and snakes (the latter two have remnants of limbs buried in their bodies). And the gradual kind of evolution within that single body plan to produce those very different animals amounts to little more than relatively fine adjustments on a central theme (a head and a tail, and four limbs [two of which can later be gradually lost in the case of snakes and whales]). Instead, the Cambrian explosion involves the sudden appearance within only five to ten million years of completely different body plans, including the arthropods (which give rise to six-legged insects, eight-legged spiders, the many-legged millipedes and centipedes, lobsters, et cetera), the mollusks, the jellyfish, sponges, and others, as well as the four-limbed animals referred to immediately above. Each of those diverse body plans (scientists call these 'phyla', the singular being 'phylum') requires an entirely new developmental set of blueprints once the egg is fertilized. One estimate [55] has it that 20 of the 26 phyla present in the known fossil record made their first appearance within those 5-10 million years, and no new phylum has since appeared over the subsequent 530 million years leading up to the present. And it isn't just that the various animal forms suddenly appeared: immediately after their sudden appearance in the fossil record, we see evidence of a complete ecology, with complex inter-organismal relationships. To his chagrin, Richard Dawkins is often quoted as saying *"... the Cambrian strata of rocks, vintage about 600 million years, are the oldest ones in which we find most of the major invertebrate groups. And we find many of them already in an advanced state of evolution, the very first time they appear. It is as though they were just planted there, without any evolutionary history."* [56]. It's all an incredibly dramatic change in such a short period of time. Standard Darwinian evolutionism predicts a long series of small incremental changes – subtle variations on a theme – which eventually accumulate until you have a whole new kind of organism. But we see the exact opposite happening in the Cambrian explosion: the sudden appearance of entirely different kinds of animals, followed after that by a steady series of variations on those new themes.

And here's where the story gets really interesting. Gould and his colleague Niles Eldredge imaginatively proposed a scientific theory which is now widely accepted as fact, but is based on the absence of data. I need to

---

[55] Stephen C. Meyer. *Darwin's Doubt* HarperOne, 2013), p. 31
[56] Richard Dawkins, *The Blind Watchmaker*. (Penguin: London, 1986), p. 229

repeat that last point, because it may not have struck you the first time, especially if you're not a scientist. Unlike other scientific theories which are based on hard evidence and can be tested, this one is based on the absence of evidence and which cannot be tested. Actually, the only test it has to stand up to is that we continue to <u>not</u> find evidence which would contradict it. According to their 'punctuated equilibrium' theory, animals had been evolving relatively slowly before and after the transition between the Proterozoic and the Cambrian periods, but in the geological equivalent of a blink of an eye the rate of evolution suddenly went into high gear — in fact, a gear that was off the scale — and nearly instantaneously (again, in the geological sense of time) produced many entirely new animal forms and types. Then this suddenly accelerated rate of mutation fell back down to baseline levels and life/evolution continued on slowly as it had been doing for millennia before.

Please don't think I'm denying that the Cambrian explosion happened: clearly the fossil record shows a sudden, explosive appearance of many diverse forms of life in a very short period of time. I'm just pointing out that the mechanism posited to explain it is based on the absence of data, and the mechanism (a sudden, and very brief, and stratospheric acceleration in genetic mutation rates) is something that atheists have to believe happened and have in no way reproduced in the laboratory. If one was not the type to a priori rule out the existence of a designer, then the data are equally consistent with the Cambrian explosion reflecting a point in time when the designer was having particular fun trying out new ideas. The only reason that explanation isn't acceptable to many other people, though, is that it involves some higher intelligence or designer, which then demands the question of who that designer might be, and some people just don't want to go down that road [57]. Neither of those two explanations can be tested, and just need to be believed.

In addition to failing to explain the sudden appearance of entirely new biological body design plans (types of animals, or phyla), standard Darwinian theory is also often inadequate for explaining very complex all-or-none biological process like metamorphosis, in which a caterpillar essentially entombs itself within a silk cocoon, partially digests its body and

---

[57] Scientists struggled with a similar conflict-of-interest when astronomers discovered that our universe is expanding in all directions, leading to the Big Bang Theory. Prior to that, they could insist that the universe just always existed, never had a beginning. But the discovery that the universe did indeed seem to have a beginning brought on huge theological implications, and for that reason alone many atheistic scientists vigorously resisted Big Bang Theory for a while. But open minds prevailed and now the theory is widely accepted and huge advances have been made.

then completely reorganizes its basic structure, eventually crawling out of that coffin as an entirely different kind of animal: a butterfly. Try to imagine how that process might evolve in small incremental steps. Adamant die-hard Darwinists have to just believe that it did.

While on the subject of butterflies, let's talk about another marvel of nature that is hard to explain by any mechanism that involves the accumulation of small, subtle changes: the migration of the Monarch butterfly. (This discovery is particularly meaningful to me: it was made by two fellow scientists from Southern Ontario, Fred and Norah Urquhart) Many species of birds make comparable trans-continental migrations, but make their first complete round-trip excursion together with other relatives who made the same trip one or more times in previous years (in other words, each generation might be learning from previous ones). The Monarchs, on the other hand, break up their round-trip journey across three or four distinct generations, each one taking a different leg of the journey using a flight path they've never been on before for a destination that they've never seen, and never with the accompaniment of a generation that has made the trip before. One generation leaves their wintering grounds in Mexico and heads north to the Gulf States, where they settle in, feed on milkweed plants and reproduce. The second generation starts from there and flies further north into the mid-US states, and does the same. The third generation embarks from there to various regions in Canada to birth the fourth generation of Monarchs, who in turn fly the entire distance from Canada to Mexico (it is in fact, this same fourth generation who then start the journey from Mexico to the Gulf States the following spring). How is it that the relatively simple little brains of these insects could have these 4 distinct flight paths hard-wired in? It's easy to say with a casual shrug of the shoulders that it 'just evolved', but how could this kind of complex behaviour evolve in small increments?

The zombie wasp is another fascinating example of a behavioral feature that's hard to explain in small incremental steps, and I highly recommend the interested reader check it out, but here's the short version of its story. The zombie wasp stings a roach which is tremendously bigger than itself, but the sting doesn't kill the prey. Instead, the wasp injects a highly developed neurotoxin into one specific region of the roach's brain to pacify it, and then a second neurotoxin into another brain region which allows the wasp guide the roach towards its underground lair. Once there, the wasp lays an egg next to the roach and seals up the lair. The roach simply rests paralyzed in the underground burrow until the egg hatches, at which point the larva feeds on the internal organs of the roach until it is mature and flies off as a zombie wasp. This complex parasitic relationship can't develop in small incremental steps. The venom in the sting of the primordial zombie wasp couldn't be so strong as to kill the prey because then its eggs wouldn't have a long-lasting food supply, nor could its venom be merely diluted to the point that it just paralyzed the prey, because the immobilized roach would soon become 'road-kill' to feed all kinds of other insects and larger animals. So the venom had to be carefully calibrated to be harmless enough to allow the prey to continue to move itself under the wasp's direction, but not so harmless that the wasp would be unable to wrestle control over the roach, which is far too big for the wasp to carry. The ability of that venom to give the wasp steering control over the prey provides a really neat twist on the story too.

These and many other behavioural features, predator-prey relationships, and even beneficial symbiotic relationships are poorly explained by a mechanism that involves small incremental changes.

DO ATHEISTS EXERCISE FAITH?

I hope an honest atheist will admit that those three origins questions illustrate how they exercise faith. Current scientific understanding can't easily or fully explain them, and one just has to believe that it happened somehow. (Please be assured, I'll get to the "*God-of-the-gaps*" on the next page).

There are other examples of scientific ideas which atheists are perfectly comfortable accepting or believing without any proof. For example, multiverse theory, in which there isn't just our own universe, but many. An infinite number in fact. There's the one that we're in now in which I'm right-handed, but another in which I'm left-handed. This one in which I chose to be a scientist, but another in which I'm the president of Antarctica. Actually it gets stranger than that: universes in which physical constants like gravitational strengths or the speed of light are different. But my point is, there are people who can accept the theory that there are multiple universes even though there's no hard evidence for them. In fact, there never can be hard evidence because by definition we can't leave our own universe to get the evidence. I don't mean simply that we don't yet have a fast enough rocket or alternative mode of transport, like warp drive or the transporter on Star Trek. Instead, I do mean that any point in space and time that we might in theory be able to reach is, by definition, within our own universe. So there's absolutely no way we can get outside of our universe to collect direct hard evidence of alternative ones.

Or superstring theory. You may know that 'stuff' is made up of atoms, which in turn are made up of protons, neutrons and electrons. But superstring theory tells us that protons, neutrons and electrons (and other things which we can barely detect) are made up of even smaller things known as quarks or strings or strings attached to membranes. These are incredibly small: less than 10^{-33} cm, on the scale of Planck's constant, which is the smallest meaningful size possible. Right now it's impossible to 'see' these things or collect direct evidence of their existence, but we believe they exist. I'm not denying their existence, and I'm sure everyone agrees that we might not have the details about these things quite right yet. I'm just emphasizing our choice to believe string theory in the absence of good hard data.

Another widely accepted 'fact' for which evidence is hard to come by: superstring theory predicts that we live in a universe with more dimensions than just the three spatial dimensions (up/down, front/back, left/right) and one of time that we're familiar with. Superstring theorists say there may be at least ten dimensions! But try putting that in a test tube. Again, I'm not saying this isn't truth: but rather that it's so inconceivable and incomprehensible that you just have to take it on faith in the mathematical equations or the scientists promoting the idea.

Theists and atheists alike hold their world views with one foot firmly planted on faith. Atheists cannot claim that they consistently and without bias reject any claims which are not backed up by hard evidence and data, and can no longer accuse theists of having the monopoly on belief.

SOME PROBLEMS FOR THEISTIC EXPLANATIONS OF ORIGINS

(1) God-of-the-gaps This is a real problem for theists and creationists, and they need to be careful not to so easily succumb to it. In the section above, we looked at some of the biggest questions of all time — the origins of the universe, matter, life, species. And it's pretty easy for Christians to say that, since atheistic scientists can't answer those questions satisfactorily, then the only other answer is that God did it miraculously. Jared Diamond, in *The World Until Yesterday* [2], surmised on the various functions of religion, trying to explain why religion has been so prevalent throughout human societies past and present. He proposed one of those functions was to explain things and thereby *"defuse our anxiety over problems and dangers beyond our control"* [58]. [By the way, I would say the same thing about science]. I have heard so many Christian apologists give examples of a

---

[58] Jared Diamond, *The World Until Yesterday*. (Penguin Group, 2012), p. 344

biological observation that seems very hard (they'll often use the word 'impossible') to explain from an evolutionary viewpoint, and thereby claim it as proof for creationism and evidence that evolution is false. The danger is that it's too easy to say that if we don't understand it (at this point in time), then it can only be explained as a miraculous intervention of God. For millennia, only God could make people fly ... until Orville and Wilbur Wright flew the first plane across the dunes of Kittyhawk, North Carolina. Only God could look down on the 'four corners of the earth' ... until we sent astronauts around the moon and they watched the first 'earth rise' (Fig. 3). Conception and fetal development were once the sole domain of God ... until we learned how to do things like take cheek cells and fertilize them or turn them into stem cells (which can reproduce every cell type in the body), and sustain zygotes in test tubes, and do *in utero* surgery on fetuses. Only God could restore life to a dead body ... until we invented CPR and a variety of machines and powerful drugs. Only God could create matter ... until we built the Large Hadron Collider and started smashing atoms together at near light-speed and creating anti-matter (with matter being a by-product).

The problem with attributing the gaps in our understanding of the world to God is that those gaps keep getting smaller and smaller: and each time God shrinks a little bit more and becomes a little less relevant. Henry Drummond, a 19th century Scottish theologian credited for being the first to recognize (and criticize) the God-of-the-gaps approach to explaining things, said that *"God should be found in human knowledge not in human ignorance"*. The absence of a scientific explanation is not proof of God; conversely, scientific discoveries are not the antidote to God. Apologetics are a very ineffective way to evangelize. As I said above, rather than making disciples, we risk making cynics and immunizing people to the truth.

One danger in taking the God-of-the-gaps approach to explain the unknown is that it can't be tested or proven, and therefore is no better than other explanations that can't be proven. On that level, the Christian version is no more convincing to someone who isn't a theist than the Hindu version, or the Mayan version, or the Inuit version. Rather than testing the various explanations to look for the evidence that supports it, one person simply endorses the Christian explanation because they hold Christian beliefs, while another person endorses the Krishna version because of their spiritual paradigm.

In addition to this ambiguity between religious explanations for a scientific problem, another danger of the God-of-the-gaps approach is that it has the potential to stifle further searching for natural answers. When we come to a scientific problem that can't be explained — such as the origin of the universe or the origin of life — it might be too easy to say *"God did it"* and stop looking for exactly how he might have done it. If a natural explanation does exist, we'll likely never find it if we just satisfy ourselves with the unquestioned acceptance of the explanation *"God did it"*.

That having been said, we shouldn't let the pendulum swing all the way to the other side by stifling any and all comments that even hint of a God-of-the-gaps sentiment. It's one thing to arrive at a difficult problem and all too quickly resolve our ignorance by stating *"God did it"* and stopping there. But it's an entirely different thing to continue looking for other explanations while still leaving the possibility that *"God did it"* on the table. Sir Isaac Newton was an ardent theist (I'm told he wrote more about theological matters, some of them quite strange actually, than he did about scientific questions). When he became curious about gravity or the nature of light, he didn't just stop at *"God did it"*. He pursued **how** God did it. Many great scientists and philosophers had religious tendencies or were even outright theists: Plato, Aristotle, Socrates, Galileo Galilei, Johannes Kepler, Thomas Aquinas, René Descartes, Johannes Gutenberg, Christopher Columbus, Leonardo da Vinci, Nicholas Copernicus, Sir Francis Bacon, Blaise Pascal, Robert Boyle, Carolus Linnaeus, Gregor Mendel, Michael Faraday, Louise Pasteur, William Harvey, Max Planck, Werner Heisenberg, Albert Einstein, Alexander Graham Bell, Raymond Damadian (inventor of MRI), Francis Collins (former head of Human Genome Project), and hundreds of others. Many of the greatest institutions of higher learning were founded by religious groups: Yale, Harvard, Oxford, Princeton, Stanford, Columbia. Please don't misunderstand me here. I'm not saying that all of the people mentioned above had theological viewpoints with which I would agree, nor am I saying that those institutions are still religiously oriented. Instead, I'm just saying that to argue that theism is necessarily a 'science-stopper' is patently false.

So there's a big difference between a God-of-the-gaps view as a fall-back position versus treating it as an acceptable a priori assumption. The fall-back position becomes the automatic explanation if science doesn't quickly enough come up with an alternative answer and in that sense is a science stopper; it necessarily forces the theist and the atheist to opposite poles. The latter position, on the other hand, might be simply the a priori assumption that *"I believe God exists and that he could have used a materialistic mechanism that we haven't yet found and also that he could have stepped in and intervened supernaturally"*, and allows the theist and atheist to entertain different possibilities together.

As an analogy, consider a situation in which a mother agrees to pick up her two boys after hockey practice at 7:00, and that both boys find themselves still standing outside the ice rink at 8:30 with no indication that she's coming soon. The first boy begins with the a priori assumption that his mother loves him and wants the best for him and is reliable, while the second refuses to hold that assumption. Both entertain all kinds of possible explanations why she's late, and may even begin with some of the same obvious ones: she ran out of gas ... got lost ... had an accident ... car was stolen. But if they were somehow able to rule out those possible explanations, they would eventually find themselves going down diverging paths in their attempt to explain the problem, solely based on their a priori assumptions about their mother. The second boy could consider possibilities that were non-starters for the first: mother changed her mind and chose to watch her favorite TV show instead, or just didn't feel like getting up. The first boy, on the other hand, might come up with explanations that were non-starters or far-fetched from the viewpoint of the second: mother was indeed trying to reach them but had been abducted by an alien space ship.

In the same way, the theist and the atheist start with opposite a priori assumptions regarding the existence of God, and as such, when explanations for a scientific problem become hard to find, they are forced down different paths in their search for an answer. I've acknowledged the dangers to theists in taking the God-of-the-gaps approach, but there's also a danger in taking the anything-but-a-God approach, an absolute a priori rejection of the supernatural. A good scientist will remain open to all possibilities, and until someone finds proof – definitive, unassailable, hard evidence – that there is no such thing as a Being who operates in all ten dimensions that describe our universe, not just the four that we can perceive, then one needs to leave that possible explanation on the table. As Carl Sagan said: "the absence of evidence is not evidence of absence". This seems to be perfectly legitimate thing to do for those who endorse the SETI program (Search for ExtraTerrestrial Intelligence), launched by NASA in 1992. Using telescopes and sensors for a range of electromagnetic radiation wavelengths, SETI researchers have been scanning the heavens for regular pulses which could indicate intelligence (this research program is featured in the movie Contact). Even though they don't have any hard evidence that such extraterrestrial intelligence does exist, they're nonetheless quite comfortable accepting it as a valid possibility (as do I). Why the double standard? The answer to that will likely be an appeal to probability: astronomers have guestimated that there are likely trillions of planets in the

universe which could support life — half a billion in our own galaxy [59], let
alone all the other galaxies in the universe — and the chances are therefore
incredibly high that intelligent life must exist elsewhere. Well, if an appeal
to probability is a valid explanation, then an appeal to improbability should
be equally valid. And many trained scientists including myself find that, the
more we learn about the complexity of life (the genome and the genetic
code; the cell; living organisms; ecosystems), the more improbable it
appears that it all just happened, spontaneously and unaided. Again, why
the double standard?

(2) Anthropic principle, fine-tuning, and 'the Goldilocks effect' Much
has been said and written about the fact that a long list of physical properties
of the universe — one estimate [60] has this number at over 200 — are finely-
tuned to very precise values which are required for life on earth. These
physical properties range from: the strength of certain subatomic and atomic
forces; the gravitational constant; the mass of the proton; the mass of the
sun; the distance of the earth from the sun; our location within the galaxy;
the mass of the galaxy; et cetera. The point is made repeatedly that if any
single one of these parameters were out by a tiny fraction of a percent, then
life on earth would be impossible. And claims are then made about the
improbability for those values to be so closely aligned to the critical value,
and the immense improbability that all 200 of those values together would
be so closely aligned. This incredible improbability is then taken as proof of
God's existence and of creationism: it's one thing if a player in a card game
gets a royal flush (the most unlikely hand one can get) in a five-card deal,
but if the other three players are also dealt royal flushes in the remaining
three suits, then everyone is convinced beyond a shadow of a doubt that the
deck had to have been intentionally and carefully stacked by someone rather
than be randomly shuffled, and nothing will change their minds about that.
This whole argument is generally referred to as the Anthropic Principle. We
can also call it 'the Goldilocks effect': that a long list of physical properties
are not too big or too small, but 'just right'.

Clearly, if God were going to create life on earth, he would attend to
getting all those critical values precisely right. And let's be honest: if
someone wanted to create a universe that pointed to a Great Designer, could
you come up with anything more precise and delicately balanced than the
one we've got?

[59] Eric A. Petigura, Andrew W. Howard, Geoffrey W. Marcy. "Prevalence of Earth-size
planets orbiting Sun-like stars". *Proceedings of the National Academy of Sciences*.
doi:10.1073/pnas.1319909110 (October 31, 2013)
[60] Hugh Ross, *Journey Toward Creation*. directed by Robert Bontrager, 2005

But despite those two points, the improbability of those physical constants collectively taking the values that they have isn't proof of God's existence and intervention. Chance alone can indeed explain the same thing. While paddling a canoe past a very high rocky cliff, you notice a cedar tree growing out of one of the cracks in the rock half way up the cliff face. There are no other cedar trees, or even other trees or plants, growing anywhere within 50 feet up or down and hundreds of feet left or right. That cedar is completely all alone on that massive cliff face. How unlikely would it be for this cedar to find the very precise spot in the entire rock face where there was a tiny little crack that had accumulated just enough soil, and which happened to have a good exposure to the sun, and wasn't overly protected from the rain? Clearly it was a divine miracle: God must have planted it there. Or could it be just chance? Cedar seeds scatter randomly all over the place, and any that hit the cliff face would have just bounced off and dropped into the lake water below. Any that ended up in a crack with no soil, or underneath an overhang which blocked out any rain, or on a part of the rock wall which received very little sun light also would not have lasted long. But one out of billions of scattered seeds just happened to fall into that crack which had a little bit of soil and took root.   Divine intervention? Or purely chance? I recognize completely that it's highly less probable that all 200 of those cosmological constants would have such precisely defined values than for the cedar seed to fall into that one unique little crack, but that doesn't change my point ... 'highly improbable' does not constitute 'proof' of God's existence and involvement.

That is the rebuttal to the Anthropic Principle, and it's a valid one. It isn't so much that our universe is finely-tuned to support life, but that life is finely-tuned to survive in this universe. If those universal parameters didn't have a highly precise value, to within a fraction of a percent of that which is compatible with our form of life, then we just wouldn't be here to debate the matter. And if they were so, by chance, then we could be that lone cedar clinging to existence on a barren cliff face. And to increase the odds in their favor, the proponents of this 'all-by-chance' idea will appeal to multiverse theory, in which there are multiple (essentially infinite) other parallel universes in which all possibilities are tried out: most of those universes collapse into nothingness because the parameters are all wrong, but a small number of them continue on and support a diverse array of life forms, most of them probably completely different than anything we've seen on earth. Please understand me: I'm not arguing for or against the anthropic principle or multiverse theory. Instead, I'm saying to theists on the one hand that the immense improbability of all those parameters being 'just so' is not proof of God's existence. And I'm saying to atheists on the other hand that to claim this all happened by chance, and to strengthen that resolve by desperately appealing to multiverse theory, is nonetheless a belief system: two valid arguments that one has to believe in, just like theists might choose to believe that God was behind it all. For the record, I choose to believe that God was indeed behind it all.

(3) Intelligent Design   This chapter wouldn't be complete without a discussion of 'Intelligent Design' (ID) theory. First, a description of what this concept involves. Many people look at the universe around them and see all kinds of evidence that this world was carefully planned and crafted. The Anthropic Principle — that all the parameters of the universal laws are 'just right' to permit life to exist here on earth — is one such line of evidence. The incredible intricacy, detail and complexity of the genetic code and its associated machinery is another line of evidence: three books that I highly recommend are Stephen Meyer's *Signature in the Cell* [61] and *Darwin's Doubt* [62], as well as Michael Behe's *Darwin's Black Box* [63] (Behe is a bit more careful than Meyer to avoid terms like 'Intelligent Design'). For some people, the intricate web of animal species in a tropical rainforest or other ecosystem — with various plant and animal species interacting, co-operating and competing in balanced harmony and symbiosis — has all the appearances of having been planned and designed. These and other lines of evidence lead many people to the firm conviction of design and a designer.

   An earlier book in the ID curriculum is William Paley's *'Natural Theology'*, in which he describes someone finding an object on the ground — one filled with little gears inside, and on the outside a face inscribed with the numbers one to twelve and a pair of hands which rotate around the face in perfect synchrony with the time of day … in other words, a watch — and wondered where this object might come from. His answer: in contrast to a rock which he also found on the ground, this object's intricacy and detail clearly spoke of *"an artificer, who formed it for the purpose which we find it actually to answer …"* [64]. He used this analogy to explain the complexity of living organisms as obviously the design of a Divine Creator.

   But while William Paley may have popularized this idea that nature attests to a designer, it did not originate with him. Hundreds of years before

---

[61] Stephen C. Meyer, *Signature in the cell: DNA and the Evidence for Intelligent Design.* (HarperOne, 2009)
[62] Stephen C. Meyer, *Darwin's Doubt.* (HarperOne, 2013)
[63] Michael Behe, *Darwin's Black Box: The Biochemical Challenge to Evolution.* (New York, The Free Press, 1996)
[64] William Paley, *Natural Theology or, Evidences of the Existence and Attributes of the Deity, Collected from the Appearances of Nature.* (Oxford University Press, 2006)

him, Thomas Aquinas wrote in *Summa Theologiae*: "*We see that things which lack intelligence, such as natural bodies, act for an end, and this is evident from their acting always, or nearly always, in the same way, so as to obtain the same result.   Hence it is plain that not fortuitously, but designedly, do they achieve their end.   Now whatever lacks intelligence cannot move towards an end, unless it be directed by some being endowed with knowledge and intelligence; as the arrow is shot to its mark by the archer.   Therefore some intelligent being exists by whom all natural things are directed to their end; and this being we call God.*" [65]

Readers of the Bible would point out that even centuries before Aquinas, Paul the Apostle wrote: "*since what may be known about God is plain to them, because God has made it plain to them.   For since the creation of the world God's invisible qualities — his eternal power and divine nature — have been clearly seen, being understood from what has been made...*" (Romans 1:19-20).

It isn't only Christian writings. Three or four centuries before Paul, Plato wrote: "*In the first place, the earth and sun, and the stars and the universe, and the fair order of the seasons, and the division of them into years and months, furnish proofs of their existence*" [66]... 'their' referring to the Greek gods. His equally famous student Aristotle wrote: "*... so those who first looked up to heaven and saw the sun running its course from the rising to its setting, and the orderly dances of the stars, looked for the craftsman of this lovely design, and surmised that it came about not by chance but by the agency of some mighty and imperishable nature, which was God.*"

Going back yet a few more centuries, we have the Psalmist writing passages like: "*The heavens declare the glory of God; the skies proclaim the work of his hands. Day after day they pour forth speech; night after night they reveal knowledge. They have no speech, they use no words; no sound is heard from them. Yet their voice goes out into all the earth, their words to the ends of the world*" (Psalm 19:1-4). And around the same time, we find in the Wisdom of Solomon: "*For from the greatness and beauty of created things comes a corresponding perception of their Creator*" [67].

I haven't found out whether or not other earlier writings – including Babylonian and Egyptian texts – also contain the core idea that nature around us seems to speak of a Designer. But my point is not to show who first came up with the idea, but rather to show that this idea keeps

---

[65] Thomas Aquinas, *Summa Theologica*

[66] Plato, Book X of *Laws* (360 BC) (Project Gutenberg e-book; accessed Jan. 23, 2014)

[67] Wisdom 13:5, in *The Apocrypha* (or Deuterocanonicals)

reappearing continuously throughout history, whenever people take the time to stop and look around and think about the world they see.

Not surprisingly, many others oppose ID theory. One of the most vocal of these detractors in our era would be Richard Dawkins, who wrote *"The Blind Watchmaker"* [68] to directly challenge Paley's seminal book. More recently, Robert Pennock wrote *"Tower of Babel"* [69], in which he directly challenges ID theory. I've read many other such books, and listened to many speakers and podcasts coming from that viewpoint. Sometimes, I'm surprised at how emotional and vitriolic the opposition can be. They get conspicuously agitated and animated over this concept, although they could otherwise respond with a mere *"Oh isn't that idea just so silly"*. They certainly don't get nearly as worked up over other ideas that they might also find to be silly, like the 'Cosmic Turtle' which carries the world on its back. For those that get so inflamed over ID theory, I have to wonder if they're threatened because the idea is so compelling that they really don't have strong rebuttals against it, or the idea is so attractive to the lay audience that they worry about how many people will be 'duped' by it.

Some ID opponents might view ID as a side-step made by theists to get creationism back on the stage of public debate and into the school curricula. Certainly theists and creationists have embraced the idea. But ID is not equivalent to Christian creationism. Alternative versions of ID include the ancient Mesopotamian creation myths and the contemporary theory of panspermia (that we were planted here on earth by aliens from some far off galaxy). ID is also not the opposite of evolution per se, though it can be said to be distinct from any dogmatically underlying versions of Darwinian processes like completely random mutation and natural selection. ID theory is an alternative but valid explanation for a very complicated set of data which doesn't specifically point to any god, including the Judeo-Christian God. It's fundamentally not different from the rationale behind the SETI program: if the SETI scientists saw a regular or complicated pattern that couldn't be explained by non-living processes (for example, an X-ray-emitting star orbiting around another star such that the X-rays arrived at earth in regular pulses, somewhat like a lighthouse beacon), they would take it as evidence for extraterrestrial intelligence. In that context, it's ironic (or hypocritical) that other scientists using microscopes and molecular biological techniques can scan physiological processes and DNA sequences which are extremely highly ordered and complex, more so than a computer

[68] Richard Dawkins, *The Blind Watchmaker* . (Norton & Company, Inc., 1986)
[69] Robert T. Pennock, *Tower of Babel: The Evidence against the New Creationism.* (Cambridge, MIT Press, 2000)

code/program, but are obliged to view this as evidence for chance. Why not instead nod in assent that one valid explanation for the complexity of that genetic code and life itself is an intelligence of some kind? A number of years ago, evolutionary biologists pointed at the vast stretches of DNA which don't appear to code for any proteins, and were therefore initially referred to as 'junk DNA', and claimed that as the best evidence against ID (*"why would a Designer create those long segments of useless code?"*). But now we know that much of that 'junk' does serve critical roles in regulating the expression of our genes. Some of it codes for small bits of RNA (referred to as microRNA) that up- or down-regulate what the cell does with the other longer bits of RNA that do indeed code for proteins. It's all an incredibly complicated network of circuits and feedback loops that is often compared to the most sophisticated of computer programming. And experts in this area are hard-pressed to explain how this incredibly high degree of information could arise spontaneously through random processes. In other words, what had been one of the strongest arguments against ID has now become one of the strongest in favor of ID.

But now to address why I've put ID theory in the 'Problems for theists' section of this chapter. Theists like to talk about the intricacy, stupendous complexity, and perhaps even flawlessness of a living cell or the human body, and introduce God as the consciousness behind creation (or behind every iteration in evolution), producing these amazing machines that only a perfect intelligence could do. But science tells us in fact, that these machines are far from flawless. Each of us is born with a tailbone, something which seems to have lost all purpose. Some have said the same thing about the muscle which wraps around the airways and makes it hard to breathe during an asthma attack (referred to as airway smooth muscle, which has been the focus of much of my research career): we don't know why we have this muscle [70], and it seems we would be much better without it. 'Goosebumps' on your arm when you get cold? ... these are useful if you're completely covered with hair (fur) and need to trap a layer of warmed air around you as would have been the case for our primordial ancestors, but are absolutely useless if you've only got one or two dozen hairs per square inch of skin (like we currently do). Or the functionless eyes on subterranean animals, the remnants of hind limbs in whales and snakes, or the proviral sequences and pseudogenes I referred to above? Or behavioral equivalents of an appendix like the fact that many people are driven to sneeze when they look at a bright light: some attribute this to a

---

[70] Wayne Mitzner, "Airway Smooth Muscle: The Appendix of the Lung", *American Journal of Respiratory and Critical Care Medicine* 169 (2004), pp 787-790

'crossing of the circuits' in our brains, but the bottom line is that there's absolutely no obvious functional benefit. None of those speak for a very good designer to me.

However, some would say that we haven't yet learned their true purposes, and/or why we retain those useless features. For example, another question which has sometimes been used to challenge ID proponents was 'why do men have breasts? That previously made no sense at all from an ID perspective (nor did it make sense from an evolutionary perspective, by the way). Until we learned a little more about fetal development. All fetuses have at least one X-chromosome. Females have two, one of which needs to be inactivated shortly after fertilization or else both start coding for the same genes and that brings on all kinds of developmental problems. So both male and female fetuses have one active X chromosome busy contributing to the sequence of cellular divisions, organization of body tissues and organs, and gene expression which produce a human baby. For the first six weeks after fertilization, there's little difference between a male and female fetus with respect to that development. It's around the sixth week that the male Y chromosome starts to divert the sequence of developmental changes to begin producing a male. Nonetheless, those first six weeks have already seen the groundwork put in place for many female characteristics, including the initial stages of tissues which would otherwise produce fully female breasts given the right hormonal stimulation (even decades later).

But the eye is another organ whose function we do know quite well, one which has long been the focus (pun intended) of many creation/evolution debates, and one which calls into question the idea of an intelligent designer. In the retina, light has to first go through the eye's nerves before it hits the light-sensing cells (rods and cones) on the retina. This design impairs the resolution of the visual system, albeit very slightly. Engineers tell us that a more efficient design would simply place those nerves behind the rods and cones, thus improving the signal-to-noise ratio. Some ID proponents dismiss this criticism by acknowledging that, yes, the design could be improved, but that it nonetheless works perfectly well for what we need it to do: for those that have 20:20 vision, there's no need for them to be able to see any better. 'It's good enough'. But a good designer wouldn't aim for just 'good enough'. In order to frame a new wall in my basement, I have to hammer into place wooden studs that run from the floor to the ceiling: these provide solid supports onto which I'd nail sheets of dry wall that will later be painted or wall-papered. The best way to make those studs is to cut pieces of wood into lengths that reach all the way from the floor to the ceiling. But I could also haphazardly cut the wood into random lengths of roughly one or two feet long each, and then re-hammer those

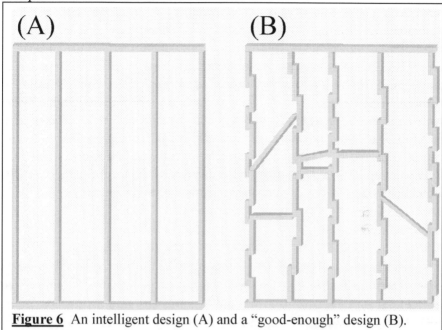

Figure 6 An intelligent design (A) and a "good-enough" design (B).

smaller pieces together, overlapping their ends by several inches in order to get a handful of nails into each overlapped joint, in order to make a fairly solid beam with the same ceiling-to-floor length (Figure 6). In theory, that patch-work beam could also bear the weight of the drywall. But you'd look at me funny if I did it that way. I could defend myself saying it's a 'good enough' design, but you'd be correct in saying it's still a poor design just the same. Getting back to our retina: yes, 20:20 vision is pretty good, but the design still isn't perfect. With all those nerves lying on the front of the retina, standing in the path of the light beams, resolution is decreased to some extent. One could argue that it isn't enough of a distortion to get too concerned about, but they definitely create a second bigger problem. The nerves all converge together to form the optic nerve bundle, which then has to first penetrate through the retinal layer before it can reach the brain, rather than simply projecting out the back of the retina: in the process, the nerve bundle crowds out the rods and cones and forms a blind-spot on the retina which wouldn't be there if all the individual nerves were behind the light-sensing layer. Not very efficient on the designer's part! Just like the recurrent laryngeal nerve travelling one or two meters too far down the neck of the giraffe before looping back and hitting the target that it missed by just a couple centimeters. There are so many other examples of poor or inefficient design. These examples are not what you'd expect from a perfect designer, but are exactly what you'd expect from an impersonal, iterative process that just builds in small increments, progressively adding more design changes on top of old designs. So be careful not to push ID theory too much, or you end up promoting a poor designer!

A greater concern though, is that ID theory doesn't insist that the intelligence behind it all has to be the God of the Bible; it could equally be Krishna, or Viracocca (from South America), or the extraterrestrials for which the SETI program is looking using public dollars (Raëlians take heart!). But that's an issue of faith, choice and interpretation, different matters altogether. Thinking ID thoughts may be good for one's personal faith – admiring God's creation – but it is not very good for evangelism: it's a tool that is too easily turned against the one who wields it.

CONCLUSION

Neither faith nor science need to be the point(s) on which theists and atheists divide themselves. My intent in this chapter is to promote more open dialogue, and less antagonism, between theists and atheists. The stereotype that the vast majority of scientists "*have no need of the God Hypothesis*" [71] is inaccurate, and the tension between science and faith is exaggerated. A recent survey of 1,700 scientists at major universities in the USA (with more in-depth follow-up interviews with 275 of them) did not find that an overwhelming majority were completely atheistic [72]. Instead, the survey found only 34% to be atheistic (and one fifth of these labelled themselves as 'spiritual atheists'), while nearly 50% of the scientists identify with some kind of religious label (27% had some belief in God, and 9% had no doubt about God's existence; nearly one in five is actively involved in a house of worship). Only 30% were agnostic, and only 6% were actively working against religion.

The public opinion polling agency Pew Research ran a survey in 2009 specifically targeting scientists about their religious beliefs [73]. They found 51% believed in some kind of deity or higher power, 41% did not believe in any supernatural power, and 7% remained agnostic. They are now running their own follow-up survey to how these views of scientists may have changed 5 years later (the results have not been published as of

[71] Pierre-Simon, Marquis de Laplace (1749-1827). French mathematician and astromer. A quote attributed to him in a conversation with Napoleon Bonaparte.
[72] Elaine H. Ecklund, *Science vs. Religion: What Scientists Really Think* (Oxford University Press, 2010)
[73] Pew Research Center. *Scientists and Belief.*
<http://www.pewforum.org/2009/11/05/scientists-and-belief/> accessed Sept. 20, 2014

the printing of this book), but they do comment in their report that these numbers haven't really changed over the course of the past century, citing another survey done in 1914 which found that 42% of approximately 1000 scientists believed in a personal God and the same number did not, as well as a 1996 poll of about 1000 scientists which came up with similar numbers (41% and 45%, respectively).

Likewise, science doesn't need to be the point on which theists divide themselves. I've already quoted a few of the findings from the Biologos survey which came to this conclusion (see pages 13 and 14). A more recent study [74] presented insights into what religious Americans (10,241 in total) think about science: nearly 50% of evangelicals believe that science and religion can work together and support one another ... 72% of evangelical scientists, and 48% of all evangelicals, see opportunities for collaboration between scientific and religious worldviews. This optimism was not fully shared by all Americans: 20% of the general population think most religious people are hostile to science, 22% think scientists are hostile to religion, and 27% of Americans feel that science and religion are in conflict. I was disheartened to read that, compared to the general population, *"Evangelical Protestants are more than twice as likely to take a 'conflict on the side of religion' stance"*.

One of the barriers that is often thrown up by atheists is the claim that they prefer to deal only with proven facts rather than beliefs. I hope they can now see that faith is being exercised on both sides of the discussion. This is particularly true when it comes to the questions of origins: of matter, of life and of species. On the other hand, I hope that the theists will be more careful about arguments that appeal to the God-of-the-gaps, to the Anthropic Principle, and to Intelligent Design: all three of these can so easily back-fire on the one trying to use those arguments.

---

[74] Elaine Ecklund and Christopher Scheitle. *Religious Communities, Science, Scientists, and Perceptions: A Comprehensive Survey.* Presented to the American Association for the Advancement of Science in February 2014.
<http://www.aaas.org/sites/default/files/content_files/RU_AAASPresentationNotes_2014_02 19%20%281%29.pdf>   accessed Sept. 20, 2014

5

The human family tree and our attempts to find God

What do I do with the Biblical story of Adam living 6,000 years ago, versus the scientific evidence for a much longer human history?

How do I reconcile the image of God I see in the OT with a very different image of God portrayed in the life of Jesus?

Was the human race founded by a single pair of humans: Adam and Eve?

Did they live 10,000 years ago? Were they special creations, or descendants of other hominid species?

If Adam is fictitious, then is Jesus also myth?

What about 'cavemen' and Neanderthals?

What about the other world religions?

Is one religion right, or more right than others?

Will God damn people forever to hell if they've never heard of Jesus or the gospel?

SCIENTIFIC EVIDENCE REGARDING THE ORIGINS OF HOMINIDS, INCLUDING HUMANS

The YE hypothesis holds that everything was created approximately 6,000 years ago. However, there are a lot of data available which suggest that hominids — human-like beings — have been around much, much longer than that. John Reader [75] gives a brilliant overview of the search for hominid fossils and tools, the various hoaxes and missing links, and the driving forces which led to our evolutionary success over other hominids. These forces include changes in our hands that led to stone tools, changes in our feet which led to bipedalism (standing upright) which may have freed up our hands to hold stone tools, and changes in our brains which may have facilitated the development of stone tools, but also made language possible. I highly recommend this book, especially to creationists who insist on the human/primate fossil record being largely contrived or incomplete.

Briefly, though, the data paint a picture of a series of waves of hominid species arising in Africa and migrating from there to other parts of the world. *Homo erectus* seems to have been the first, expanding into Eurasia from Africa just under two million years ago (a period referred to as the Early Pleistocene): as they migrated out of Africa, they were funnelled through a narrow strip of land bordered by the Mediterranean Sea to the northwest and deserts to the southeast. Another hominid species — *Homo antecessor* — arose in Africa and then left for Europe approximately 800,000 years ago. *Homo heidelbergensis* in turn arrived in Europe approximately 600,000 years ago, and some believe they then gave rise to Neanderthals, who interacted with, interbred with, and often competed for survival with our own species, *Homo sapiens.*

As for *H. sapiens* (Latin for 'us'), paleontologists, archaeologists and geneticists have amassed an incredible body of evidence which tell us that we first appeared in Africa, but then left that cradle approximately 200,000 years ago, spreading into South Asia (approximately 50,000 years ago) and Australia (approximately 40,000 years ago), and northward to Europe (approximately 30,000 years ago). From Asia, it is believed we crossed into North America via a land bridge between Siberia and Alaska before the end of the last Ice Age when sea levels were lower (presumably because so much water was tied up in the glaciers). It is generally agreed that we were in North America by about 15,000 years ago, and from there worked our way down to the southernmost tip of South America.

What is this 'incredible body of evidence' that backs up this story? Some of it will be quite familiar to the average person: fossils, bones, engravings and tools that can be radiologically dated that far back. But a number of really interesting and provocative genetic studies have given an entirely different set of data to trace our ancestry. Before I talk about those studies, I should give a brief backgrounder on some basic cell biology, particularly 'nuclear DNA' versus 'mitochondrial DNA'.

---

[75]   John Reader, *Missing links: In Search of Human Origins*. (Oxford University Press, 2011)

Mitochondria are small machines (also called organelles) within almost all cells, and are responsible for generating energy, mostly in the form of a chemical called ATP, although they also make other high energy molecules. The energy molecules are then used by the cells to accomplish all other cellular activities. Those mitochondria have little bits of their own unique DNA, on which are genes specific to their function as cellular power plants [76]. This fact, plus several others, suggest that mitochondria actually represent ancient bacteria which infected other cells and then took up residence within those cells and thereby became organelles [77].

The nucleus also contains DNA: in fact, it contains the vast majority of the genetic material that defines our hair color, our blood type, and almost all of the other traits and characteristics which make each of us unique individuals. The nuclear DNA that a baby inherits from its mother and father mixes and recombines during fertilization in a thousand different ways such that it becomes nearly impossible to determine which gene comes from which parent (which is in part why children from the same parents can look so dramatically different). The mitochondrial DNA of that baby, on the other hand, is inherited ONLY from the mother. That is, the egg cell contains not only the half copy of the mother's nuclear DNA, but also cellular machinery donated by the mother, including the mitochondria with its own unique and full copy of mitochondrial DNA. The sperm cell, on the other hand, has been stripped down to the barest minimum: essentially a half copy of nuclear DNA from the father plus a tail to move that package from A to B, but no mitochondria (and thus, no mitochondrial DNA). So without all that recombination of genetic information that is so important in the nuclear DNA, the mitochondrial DNA that the baby receives is identical to that of the mother, which in turn is identical to that of the grandmother, which in turn is identical to that of the great grandmother, et cetera, all the way back to a female ancestor many thousands of years ago.

Or rather, essentially identical, because all DNA can undergo spontaneous mutations for a variety of reasons. From time to time, there would have been a spontaneous mutation in the mitochondrial DNA, and when that happened, that new genetic sequence would then be passed down to all the daughters of that mother, giving rise to a new human family line slightly different from the family line carried by the sisters of that mother.

---

[76] SG Andersson, A Zomorodipour, JO Andersson , et al. "The genome sequence of Rickettsia prowazekii and the origin of mitochondria" *Nature* 396 (199): 133-140
[77] The idea is that they let the host cell take over many of the cellular functions needed for its survival, in exchange for those high energy molecules. This mutually beneficial parasitic relationship led to a much more evolutionarily successful kind of cell — the eukaryotic cells — that eventually led to modern multicellular organisms.

When one of the great-great-grand daughter cells developed a second mutation in its mitochondrial DNA, all the subsequent daughter cells in that line inherited both mutations, whereas their first-cousin cells only inherited the original/first mutation.

Based on this understanding of mitochondrial DNA, one genetic study took samples from women all around the world and from all kinds of racial backgrounds, and extracted their mitochondrial DNA. From those samples, it became possible to trace backwards the very gradual accumulations of those mutations in the mitochondrial DNA, eventually reaching a common ancestor who lacked all of those mutations. Their conclusion? ... the common ancestor ... the proverbial 'Eve' ... lived approximately 200,000 years ago [78]. Also, after taking into consideration all the different racial origins of the women who provided those samples, the convergence pointed to Africa as the birthplace of that 'Eve'.

A similar approach was used to look at the slow accumulation of mutations in certain pieces of the Y chromosome, which only males inherit (the Y chromosome is the one that has the genes that define a fetus as male) [79]. So, like the mitochondrial DNA being transmitted down an unbroken maternal genealogy, the Y chromosome DNA is transmitted down an unbroken male line of descent. In both cases, without any recombination between the genes from the two parents (which would blur the inheritance pattern). Just a slow and easily-followed accumulation of spontaneous mutations. In this way, samples taken from men indicated that the proverbial 'Adam' probably lived approximately 250,000 to 500,000 years ago, and also originated from Africa.

I fully expect that some creationists are jumping up and down right now saying: *"there's no way that this scientific evidence makes any sense if 'Adam' lived tens or even hundreds of thousands of years before 'Eve' and may not have even lived in the same part of Africa"*. However, there's absolutely no reason to expect that the earliest ancestor that we can trace down the maternal genealogy had to live at the same time, and in the same place, as the earliest ancestor that we can trace down the patrilineal one. Any more than saying it's necessary that the direction of the first thunder clap that we hear must line up with the direction of the first thunderbolt that we see, or the first cloud that appeared in the sky. There are several legitimate reasons why the 'Eve-data' and the 'Adam-data' don't converge

---

[78] RL Cann, M Stoneking, AC Wilson. "*Mitochondrial DNA and human evolution*" Nature 325 (1987): 31-36
[79] F.L. Mendez, T. Krahn, B. Schrack, et al. "An African American paternal lineage adds an extremely ancient root to the human Y chromosome phylogenetic tree". *The American Journal of Human Genetics* 92 (2013): 454-459

at the same place and time: part of the problem is that our tools and abilities to collect data are limited.

Another supporting body of evidence I'd like to summarize comes from decades of work done by Dr. Luigi Luca Cavalli-Sforza and his colleagues [80][81]. They looked at a number of genetic variations within one hundred and ten genes from samples taken from forty two different populations, and from those data generated an evolutionary tree summarizing how those different populations branched off from one another (that is, the approximate timing and sequence of the branchings). They then compared this evolutionary tree with the one that was generated by archaeologists who proposed the migration of *H. sapiens* out of Africa — first colonizing Asia and Australia, then Europe and eventually the Americas — and found a good match. But even more, they compared their genetic evolutionary tree to the evolutionary tree of the world's languages and also found it matched quite well.

THE GROWTH AND SPREAD OF HUMANITY

Unless you're going to say that God intentionally planted that human fossil and human genetic evidence to mislead scholars and curious lay people, an idea discussed above in chapter two, then "*a plain reading*" of the data given to us forces us to conclude that humans as a species goes back several hundred thousand years. Starting from a few small bands of individuals, which then had children, who then produced the grandchildren of the tribe, and then the great-grandchildren, et cetera, et cetera, producing an ever widening ancestral tree. The growth of the human population is thought to have been quite slow at first. This is because these were nomadic people who were hunter-gatherers. It would have been a very hard life: following and hunting herds of wild animals as big as mammoths, gathering fruits and nuts along the way, but never staying in one spot long enough to build permanent shelters. These bands of individuals would have to be relatively small: such a wandering existence couldn't support large groups, and could only nurture one or two infants at a time. So for thousands of years, the total number of *Homo sapiens* would increase only very slowly. But at some point, we learned how to live off the land — till the soil, plant

[80] LL Cavalli-Sforza, A Piazza, P Menozzi and J Mountain. "Reconstruction of human evolution: bringing together genetics, archeology and linguistics". *Proceedings of the National Academy of Sciences* 85 (1988): 6002-6006

[81] LL Cavalli-Sforza, E Minch and J Mountain. "Coevolution of genes and language revisited". *Proceedings of the National Academy of Sciences* 89 (1992): 5620-5622

crops, and keep pens of livestock — and build permanent shelters which protected ever larger families and helped us live longer, safer lives. All those changes had a dramatically positive effect on the growth rate of the human population. Jared Diamond does an excellent job describing the various factors that played into this change in our collective history in his book *Guns, Germs and Steel* [82], and I highly recommend that book too. The net effect was a dramatic, exponential rise in the number of humans living on the face of the earth. Currently, at the writing of this book, we number just over seven billion, according to the Population Reference Bureau [83].

But how many people have ever been born within the entirety of human history? The Population Reference Bureau have published an article addressing this very question [84]. They first explain why they went through the trouble to guestimate this number: "*somewhere, at some time, back in the 1970s, a writer made the statement that 75 percent of the people who had ever been born were alive at that moment*". They then lay down the assumptions made in estimating that number: for example, the average life span of individuals; infant mortality rates; life expectancy over the ages; major stresses on the human population, such as the Plague, or Black Death, or major wars; et cetera. It's a very interesting and yet quick read. The bottom line is that they guestimate that 108 billion humans have been born over the past 50,000 years (that estimate was made in mid-2011).

This is all background information for the next section, in which we consider the Genesis account of the unfolding of the salvation story.

THE IMPACT OF A MUCH LONGER HUMAN TIMELINE ON THE BIBLICAL STORY

From a YE perspective, the unfolding of God's redemption plan within human history was pretty straightforward. It begins with Adam in the Garden of Eden ('A' in Figure 7): with the Fall came the need for a redeemer. Just a few chapters later — albeit still within the opening acts of the story — God is making a covenant with Abraham ('*' in Figure 7), promising that "*all peoples on earth will be blessed through you*" (Genesis 12:3). According to Ussher, this happened around the year 1500 BC, or

---

[82] Jared Diamond, *Guns, Germs and Steel* (WW Norton, 1999)
[83] Population Reference Bureau. <http://www.prb.org> (accessed May 10, 2013)
[84] Population Reference Bureau *How Many People Have Ever Lived On Earth?* <http://www.prb.org/Articles/2002/HowManyPeopleHaveEverLivedonEarth.aspx> (accessed May 10, 2013)

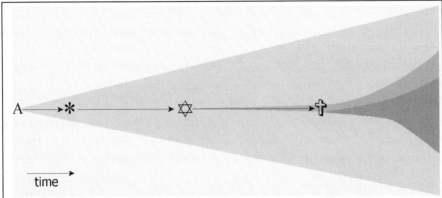

time

Figure 7 Young-Earth version of the ever-expanding human population. Adam ('A') gives rise to the whole human race, represented here by the lightest gray triangle, which gets wider over time as more people are born. His descendants include Abraham ('*'), David ('✡') and Jesus ('✝'). The Jewish and Christian faiths are represented by the darker gray shapes.

about a quarter of the way through a 6,000 year time-line. And as the OT unfolds, God continues to tell other individuals along the way more and more of the details of this rescue plan: Isaac; Jacob; David; Solomon; Isaiah; Daniel; Malachi; et cetera. A spotlight is put on the genetic line of David ('✡' in Figure 7), approximately at the year 1000 BC or half-way through the 6,000 year time-line, from whom we would eventually see the birth of Jesus and the whole salvation story unveiled completely ('✝' in Figure 7). Once Jesus arrived and his time here on earth was completed, it seemed that the story had come to an end. And yet, here we are 2,000 years later still waiting for the curtain to fall. I found it puzzling that things seemed to just continue going on. The explanation I was given was that God was waiting to give everybody the opportunity to make a choice: the gospel had to go out to all nations and to the whole ends of the earth. Only then would the final page be written and the book closed. It was like the story of salvation — revealed through the stories of Adam, Abraham, David and Jesus — ran like a red thread through the whole length of fabric representing human history. From start to finish. Except that it seemed that the finish never came, which always made me wonder what Peter meant when he wrote *"But when the end of time arrived, God sent His Son ..."* (Galatians 4:4; Aramaic version in Plain English).

But the OE point of view puts an entirely new perspective on that story within human history. Looking at the ever widening fan representing the human population over the past hundreds of thousands of years (Figure 8), look where Abraham fits in: he's the asterisk ('*') at the far, far, far, far

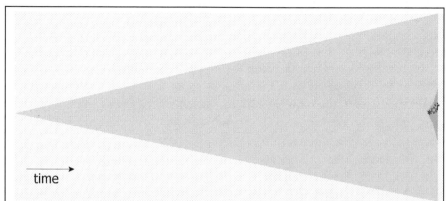

time

Figure 8   Old-Earth version of the ever-expanding human population. The Biblical genealogical record now fitted onto a longer time-scale more consistent with anthropological data in which the human race has been around for hundreds of thousands of years.

right. If you think I'm exaggerating where that asterisk should be placed, just consider that according to the genetic and archaeological records the human family tree began 200,000 years ago, and according to the Biblical record Abraham appears 4,000 years ago, or in the final 2% of that tree (some YE'ers will concede that the human family tree might be as long as 50,000 years, but even if one shortens up the human time-line that much Abraham still appears in the final 8% of that tree). And Jesus appears in the human family tree approximately where I've placed the cross ('✝'), almost at the very end of the page. So the whole Semitic line, including Abraham, Moses, David and Jesus, represents only a tiny little wedge in the whole of human history. And these individuals represent the entire salvation story. Rather than seeing the salvation story unfold throughout human history, it seems that the salvation story is told only after more than 90% of our collective history was behind us!?

Why would God do it this way: let humans go on for millennia ... living and dying by the billions ... before setting the story straight through Abraham - Moses - Jesus? Why would he place that asterisk ... Abraham, representing the beginning of the salvation story, God's grand solution for the redemption of people ... so far at the end of the entire history of the species he wanted to redeem? At least this new time-line for human history gave me a whole new perspective on Peter's comment: "*But when the end of time arrived, God sent His Son ...*" (Galatians 4:4; Aramaic version in Plain English; emphasis added); even if the human history went on for yet another thousand years from now, we'd still be looking at 'end times' theology.

But this in turn raised a whole new unsettling theological question in my mind, one that addresses the evolution of religious thinking as human history unfolded. The Bible is absolutely silent on whether God spoke to anyone other than the Abrahamic line in the Middle East (that is, Adam, Abraham, Moses, David, et cetera). Even though there were millions of other people spread all over Eurasia, let alone the rest of the globe, at the time. If he didn't, the only ones who would seem to benefit from the insider information revealed in the OT would be Abraham's household and the people who heard 'through the grapevine'. In other words, it would seem that almost all of those other people on earth at the time, and a vast majority of their descendants down through the ages, and all the people who preceded the Biblical patriarchs, had no idea that God was even speaking to people. Eventually, some other people would hear this good news: it might take only a few years for the people who were in Abraham's 'neighbourhood' (in the global sense), but certainly a few millennia for people who lived at the far reaches of the globe. In the meantime, countless billions would have lived and died without even knowing what God was doing, what he wanted from us, what he'd promised to do for us, et cetera. I don't know why God would choose to do it that way. But he must have known how billions would be clueless to any call to redemption or plan of salvation, and he would therefore make a way for those people to be included without ever having had a personal relationship with him.

That question is the focus of the next section.

HOMO SAPIENS AND RELIGIOUS THINKING

Paleontologists tell us that the distinctive characteristics of *Homo sapiens* include our proclivity to be problem-solvers, tool-makers and our ability to use language. In addition to those traits, though, another one of our clearly demonstrable intrinsic characteristics is an inner belief that *"there's something bigger out there"*: a Great Being of some kind. If you look across all societies today, all around the globe, the seven billion people that live on the face of our planet today, the vast majority of them believe in some kind of 'Great Being'. Some readers — especially Westerners — might want to think that atheists are in the majority today, but the evidence is just so contrary to that. And there's a mountain of paleontological and archaeological evidence going back thousands of years telling us that humans all through the past had this same intrinsic drive towards some kind of belief: human bones which can be radiologically-dated back to many tens of thousands of years are found buried with figures of religious artefacts and statues.

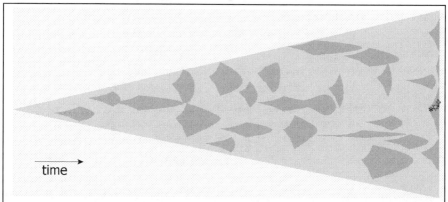

time

Figure 9 Evolution of humans and religion. Same human history shown in Figure 8, but now also including some of the other faiths and religions (darker gray forms) which appear and disappear over the course of time. Christianity as we know it is shown at the far right: the triangle containing Abraham ('*'), David ('✡'), Jesus ('✝'). All those other religions could not possibly benefit from the revelation given to the Semitic line.

Jared Diamond, a renowned scientist and Pulitzer Prize-winning novelist, wrote *"Virtually all known human societies have had 'religion', or something like it. That suggests that religion fulfills some universal human need, or at least springs from some part of human nature common to all of us. If so, what is that need, or that part of human nature?"* [85]. Blaise Pascal, French mathematician, physicist and Christian philosopher, said: *"There is a God-shaped vacuum in the heart of every man which cannot be filled by any created thing, but only by God, the Creator, made known through Jesus"*. Michelangelo captured our yearning for a God in his painting entitled 'Genesis': not only is God reaching out to man (Adam), but man is also reaching back out to God (Michelangelo heightens the tension of this encounter by painting a noticeable gap between the two).

As an aside, there's also evidence that the same was true of Neanderthals, a relative of *Homo sapiens*. In addition to their human-like qualities of having strong family and social units, and tool-making, and a genetic code which is nearly identical to our own, they also buried their dead with gifts and tools which indicates a belief in the after-life. It's not clear if other hominids — among them *H. erectus, H. antecessor, H. heidelbergensis*, et cetera — also shared this belief in an afterlife or a Great Being. So it would seem that all through human history — for hundreds of thousands of years — humans have sensed this Great Being, and some of

---

[85] Jared Diamond, *The World Until Yesterday*. (Penguin Group, 2012)

them have tried the best way they could to come to an understanding of who that Being is. By sitting on mountain tops and meditating. By pondering creation. Through discussions with other 'Great Being' believers and thinkers of their own time. And in a variety of other ways, humans have been busy developing different beliefs, theologies and faiths. For the humans that lived through the first 99% of our history — from 500,000 years BC until a few thousand years ago— this was all done without any input from what we would call the Bible. Not surprisingly, each one of them came up with a different story, though perhaps with some overlapping themes in common. In Figure 9, I've re-drawn Figure 8, which places Christianity in the context of an OE view of human history, but now added in representations for these various faiths and religions that came and died out over the course of time. We only know of some of those religions: the ones that still exist today or that have left enough archaeological artefacts for us to put their stories together. In Asia, there is evidence for prehistoric religion dating back to approximately 5,000 years ago — during the late Neolithic era in the early Harappan period — thousands of years before Abraham. Mesopotamian and Egyptian religions can be traced back to three or four thousand years BC, again long predating Abraham. In Siberia, researchers found frozen bodies and tools dating back to 24,000 years ago, and were able to clone out DNA from it which genetically linked Old World Europeans to New World North American Indians [86]: but more relevant to this section of my discussion, buried with the bodies they found many *"anthropomorphic Venus figurines, which are rare for Siberia but found at a number of Upper Palaeolithic sites across western Eurasia"*. In South America, thousands of miles and centuries removed from Biblical influences, humans came up with the Aztec and Mayan religions. Likewise, the Inuits in the North ... the aboriginals of North America and Australia ... the Polynesians ... the Druids ... the Norse Vikings ... the ancient (pre-Christian) Greeks and Romans ... and many others, all came up with their own unique ideas of who this Great Being is, and how that Being created all things, and gave special consideration to humans, all without any input from Biblical sources. During that part in our history where we see the development of literacy and the rise of urban society, just a few thousand years ago, we see a proliferation of holy books associated with particular belief systems: *"Judaism, Christianity, Islam, Zoroastrianism, Buddhism, Jainism, Hinduism, Confucianism, Taoism all developed sacred books to*

[86] M Raghavan, P Skoglund, KE Graf, et al., "Upper Palaeolithic Siberian genome reveals dual ancestry of Native Americans" *Nature* 505 (2014): 87-91

which was ascribed a high degree of authority and infallibility" [87].

    Christians might call all of these other religions misinformed beliefs, but let's be honest: they would have to be misinformed or uninformed if they were given no information (revelation) to begin with. It shouldn't be surprising if they developed sets of beliefs that would be inherently antagonistic to the Judeo-Christian beliefs that would eventually appear on the scene *"at the end of time"*. Because they and their society had grown up and developed for so long outside of the Judeo-Christian influence, they would be resistant and impervious to the new Biblical message. But does that make them guilty of doing anything wrong?

    Looking at it this way, I had to ask: *"How could God not expect that outcome?"* By creating a species with an inner yearning to understand him and find him but giving them no information whatsoever, letting them stumble around in the dark, groping at the walls of this maze we call 'life' and trying to figure it out on our own, he must have foreseen that most of them (us) might not get it right. In fact, a realistic expectation would be that none would get it right. Or by telling only one person among billions, and then waiting for the message to eventually filter down through the ages by word-of-mouth, billions of people would end up as outsiders, excluded from the truth, or growing up with uninformed half-truths, and therefore being 'lost for all eternity' as some Christians might say. That sounds unfair and unjust. Would he really damn those 99%'ers to hell because they did the best they could to understand him without any help from him, but got it wrong?

    But maybe he didn't leave them totally to their own devices. Maybe he did from time to time give them little glimpses of the truth. Little words of encouragement and prophecies to steer them in the right direction. Jews and Christians would make that claim for themselves. They point to scriptures that say he spoke to people like Adam, Cain, Noah, Abraham, Moses, Samuel, Elijah and many others to give each of them more and more pieces of the puzzle. What we now refer to as prophecies and covenants. Maybe he did the same for other people around the world and at other periods in human history? Could it be that those other faiths and religions were also given little pieces of the puzzle? Some Christians might find that idea hard to accept: that those other religions might have also been built on inspirations and revelations from God. And I also think that some of those Christians would dismiss it all away by saying: *"well, even if God did speak to them, they distorted the truth ... twisted God's words to them ... corrupted*

---

[87] Daniel Jeremy Silver, *The Story of Scripture: From Oral Tradition to the Written Word.* (Basic Books Inc. Publishers New York, 1990), p. 4

it with the ideas of man". Maybe that's true too. But on what basis can we not say the same thing about the religion handed down in the OT ... other than the basis that we don't want that to be true, or to have to admit it? The image of God that I see in the OT is just not the same as what we refer to as 'the full revelation of God in the person of Jesus Christ'. I just can't see Jesus saying that it's OK to slaughter the Canaanite children to make room for me and my people. Or blessed is the person who smashes the heads of children against the rocks because their parents have made life unbearable for me (Psalm 137:8,9). Or that I should stone to death my own son if he becomes disobedient or rebellious (Exodus 21:17; Leviticus 20:9; Deuteronomy 21:18-21). Or getting too worked up over whether or not I cook a goat in its mother's milk (Exodus 23:19; Exodus 34:26; Deuteronomy 14:21). And many other examples of very hard-to-swallow and hard-to-understand rules and regulations and events in the OT pages. What argument would I use against anyone who says that even if God did speak to the patriarchs of the OT, that their descendants added in their own ideas and distorted the true beautiful image of God into something much less appealing? (again, other than a fierce and blind unwillingness to have to admit that possibility)

So maybe the Inuit creation story or the Bhagavad gita or other wisdom literature from non-Jewish societies (for example, the Sumerians, the Mayans, the Druids) are cousins of the OT scriptures: literature inspired by the same divine author? When your first response is an immediate and visceral 'no', let me challenge you to answer how you can be so certain. We have no scriptural basis to say that God didn't also talk to people other than Abraham: to people living in China or India or South America, or the North Pole at the same time. Could it be that their diverse religions evolved from some message that God first gave them as well? And if so, what basis do we have for saying our religion is not simply another evolution of the same first message given to Abraham? How can I conclude that all of the Biblical beliefs that I was spoon-fed are more true than those other beliefs, or even that my beliefs are totally true and the other beliefs totally false? That maybe some of our 'biblical' ideas are a devolution of God's original message that he loves us and wants us to love each other? Which is why someone like Jesus had to come along and set it all straight, give us an example to follow, and show us 'The Way' ... the way to truly love God, and love our fellow humans.

There's a verse in the Bible that I had previously thought condemned all other religions: *"I am the Way, the Truth and the Life. No man comes to the Father except by Me"* (John 14:6). I realize now that it's contemporary Christians who may have added layers of meaning to those words, a meaning that perhaps Jesus wouldn't have intended. One thing many of them believe now is that the only way to be saved is by having a personal relationship with Jesus. But the vast majority of all people — 'the 99%' that I referred to above— can't have had a personal relationship with Jesus. Most of that 99% lived long before Jesus ever appeared on the face of the earth, and even some of that 99% who lived during or after the time of Jesus lived in parts of the world where his existence wasn't known. Another way to interpret that verse ("... *no man comes to the Father but by Me*") is that our access to the Father has nothing to do with 'our coming' and everything to do with 'his doing'. That is, he paid whatever price had to be paid for the shortcomings of all those 99% who would never know Him: just imagine them walking into God's presence absolutely dumb-founded asking themselves "*How on earth did I get here?*" And Jesus answers them: "*Don't worry about it ... it's my treat: I've taken care of all the arrangements*". This puts a whole new meaning on the word 'grace'. It also makes me see another passage of scripture in a whole new perspective, the parable of the workers who were hired at different times in the day, and therefore put in different amounts of work, and yet all of them got the same pay at the end of the day (Matthew 20:1-16).

ABRAHAM AND THE BIBLICAL STORY OF SALVATION

So there's no denying that there have been many different religions and faiths over the course of human history (Figure 9). Christians would say that Christianity is one of them that 'got it right'. I didn't say the only one that got it right ... there's no evidence, scriptural or otherwise, that Christianity as a religion is the only one to have gotten it right. Yes, John tells us that Christ himself claimed to be the sole and ultimate stairway to heaven: "*I am the way, the truth and the life. No one comes to the Father but by me*" (John 14:6). But he also said "*I have other sheep that are not of this sheep pen. I must bring them also. They too will listen to my voice, and there shall be one flock and one shepherd.*" (John 10:16). There are many ideas about who these 'other sheep' are, including the possibility that they might represent other non-human life forms on other planets in distant parts of the universe (not my idea), but there's no reason to say they couldn't represent other people from other religions here on earth over the course of human history.

The Bible also puts a bright spotlight on Abraham and his

descendants. Why might Abraham have been singled out? I've made the point above that many people(s) have come and gone over the last few hundred thousand years with widely different ideas about who God is. Most of them had certain ideas in common about the 'Great Being'. Just to name a few: that he created all things, is quite powerful (not all of them went as far as to say all-powerful) and transcends time. Why might Abraham and his descendants have had a unique understanding of God? Possibly, they were the first one to have caught a small glimmer of the true God. And as he and his descendants pursued that first soft ray of light, God revealed more and more of himself and of our relationship to him, ultimately being fully revealed in the person, ministry and teachings of Jesus Christ. Thomas Cahill gives an excellent description of this revelation, one that is well worth reading [88]. So what distinguished Abraham's understanding of God from that of other religions of the time?

That God is one god: monotheism versus polytheism. Many other religions, past and present, teach that there are many gods. Before Abraham, there were the polytheistic Babylonian and Egyptian religions. Other polytheistic religions which appeared after Abraham's time but have since died out include the Greek and Roman religions. Today, Hindus have many personal gods (murtis): in the Rgveda (an ancient sacred collection of Sanskrit hymns), there are thirty three devas, and one interpretation of the conspicuous word 'koti' (which can mean ten million) in the Vedas leads some to believe there are 330 million Hindu deities. Some religions, including contemporary ('New Age') religions, say we ourselves are all gods. Some of these polytheistic religions do teach that one of the gods is supreme among the rest (the Babylonian god Marduk; the Greek god Zeus; the Roman god Jupiter or Jove; the Viking god Odin), or that there is one ultimate reality (the Hindu Brahman; the Buddhist nirvana). But the OT teaches there is only one God: the fundamental confession of the Hebrew faith, referred to as the Shema, is *"Hear, O Israel: YHWH our God, YHWH is one"*. He does not have any rival gods.

That God is good and loving. The gods of many other religions are anything but good or loving. Anyone who has watched Mel Gibson's movie *Apocalypto* can get a graphic sense of how horrible was Kukulkan, the snake deity of the Mayans. The Aztecs had a similarly fearsome god: Quetzalcoatl. The Greeks, Romans and Norse had their gods of war (Ares, Mars and Odin, respectively). But the Bible teaches in many places that

---

[88] Thomas Cahill. *The Gifts of the Jews: How a Tribe of Desert Nomads Changed the Way Everyone Thinks and Feels.* (Bantam Doubleday Dell Publishing Group, 1998)

God is good [89]. I'm sure some readers are right now recalling stories from the OT which don't portray God as good or loving, but rather one of conquest. I'll come back to that later in Chapter 6, but suffice for now let me just ask a rhetorical question: have humans (and their authors and historians) ever been known to conscript the concept of God in a misguided attempt to justify horrible things that they do to other humans?

That creation and the physical world are good and to be enjoyed. The original form of Buddhism emphasizes the eradication of desire in order to achieve nirvana. Gnosticism in the 2nd century held that the physical world is evil and corrupt, and that salvation involves purging our souls from the physical body and gaining freedom from this world. In contrast, the book of Genesis emphasizes at each stage in the creation story that God declares it all good. And to be enjoyed: God's single command to creation and humans was *"Be fruitful and multiply"* ... go out and have sex! *"And the Lord God made all kinds of trees grow out of the ground — trees that were pleasing to the eye and good for food"* (Genesis 2:9). The Garden of Eden — whether a literal or metaphorical place — was a pretty cozy set-up!

That man needs redemption. We're familiar with contemporary ('New Age') teaching that, deep inside, we're all good. Some atheists believe that humanity in general is marching towards an ultimate Utopia, once we can cast off the corrupt ideas and ways that we inherited from our ancestors, including religion. Other religions, past and present, portray at least some segment of the human society — that is, those who are loyal to a particular deity — as good while the other segments of society loyal to other deities are evil and condemned. One of the central teachings from the Bible is that we are all fallen creatures, corrupted image-bearers of God. In fact, the idea is right there in the very beginning of the book: the 3rd chapter of Genesis (irrespective of whether you read this chapter as literal or allegorical). And it's developed throughout the OT as people — from individuals like David, 'a man after God's own heart', to whole nations such as the 'chosen people' of Israel — keep messing up. Often horribly. More importantly, the main theme of the Bible — in fact, the one that runs all through it, from start to finish — is that we have a way to be redeemed. This is the main idea behind the Levitical sacrificial system, and then the final sacrifice that Jesus made on the cross.

As Abraham and his descendants came to realize these truths, God revealed more and more of himself, and said that *"through your offspring all nations on earth will be blessed, because you have obeyed me."* (Genesis

---

[89] to cite just a very few of the many verses: Psalms 25:8; 34:8; 36:5-9; 100:5; 107:1; 135:3; 136:1; 145:9; Nahum 1:7

22:18). *"I, the LORD, have called you in righteousness; I will take hold of your hand. I will keep you and will make you to be a covenant for the people and a light for the Gentiles"* (Isaiah 42:6). And he gave them other hints and promises of a complete revelation. In the words of the Jews: the Messiah. One through whom *'all nations'*, including the Gentiles, would be blessed. Jesus claimed to be the fulfilment of the prophecies of the Messiah [90], and also said: *"No one comes to the Father but by me"* (John 14:6) and *"All things have been committed to me by my Father. No one knows the Son except the Father, and no one knows the Father except the Son and those to whom the Son chooses to reveal him"* (Matthew 11:27). Those claims need a whole chapter to explain (in fact, they're deserving of a whole other book), and I'll come back to it in chapters eight and nine. But in a few sentences, when everything is said and done, at the end of time, I could see Christ opening the doors and escorting into the very presence of God those who knew him and accepted his free gift, as well as many, many, many other people who didn't know him before having met him at the gates (see Matthew 25:31-46). But those who make a choice to reject that free gift – who, as Frank Sinatra and Elvis Presley put it, choose to *"do it my way"* – will have to hope that their way is at least as good as that of Jesus (could they ever hope to have found a better way than that?).

THE HISTORICITY OF ADAM

This chapter on 'The human family tree' would not be complete without an in-depth consideration of the person that Genesis names as the biological father of the entire human race. There are a number of questions that need to be addressed.

I've already explained in chapter three why I can't hold to a YE viewpoint any more, and I won't repeat that here. This necessarily means that I no longer find it possible to believe that Adam was a unique individual who, with Eve, lived approximately 6,000 years ago and fathered our race, nor do I find it necessary to do so.

But is it possible, or necessary, to just extend the timeline: to maintain that Adam and Eve go back 50,000 or even a few hundred thousand years ago, as some creationists are now doing? The answer to this question needs to be consistent with the genetic diversity seen within the human genome. Chapter three introduced the concept of 'alleles', and pointed out that a single human couple can account for only four alleles ---

---

[90] compare Luke 4:17-21 and 7:20-22 with Isaiah 29:18-21; 35:5-6; 61:1

two different ones on each of the woman's X-chromosomes, two more on the man's X- and Y-chromosomes --- unless you allow for the appearance of new alleles through mutation. Mutations can appear spontaneously, but it's a rare event and so therefore requires a lot of time. Six thousand years (or approximately 300-400 generations) is simply not enough. Even 50,000 years is rather short, especially when you consider a gene like the human leukocyte antigen complex with 59 different alleles: that period of time represents at best 3,000 generations (if you assume that the couples can reproduce at age fifteen). To better explain the large numbers of alleles that we see in the human genome today, you need a much longer period of time (that is, a much larger number of generations) and/or a larger number of starting couples (which collectively represent a wider number and variety of alleles). The alternative is massively higher rates of mutation in the past, but there's no evidence of that.

Is it necessary to maintain that they were a unique, 'specially-created' couple? I'd prefer to deal with that question in two parts.

First, 'specially-created'. Are humans just another branch on the evolutionary tree, or a whole different tree? Some theists can accept the idea that the plants and animals might have arisen through the processes of evolution, but draw the line at humans. For them, humans did not descend from some hominid ancestor, but were uniquely and specially-created. When I wondered about this, I ran into a road-block when I remembered the pseudogenes and proviral gene sequences that I describe in the opening pages of chapter two. We are definitely related genetically to the chimps and other great apes. If God was intentionally creating something completely new, something that was entirely distinct from the plants and animals, why would he use a genome that was virtually identical to that of the other hominid species, that had remnants of viral infections ('genetic scars') that chimps and apes fought off, and even genes with the same mistakes found in more distantly related animals like guinea-pigs (such as those in the gene for the enzyme L-gulono-γ-lactone oxidase, or those in the genes for growing a tail or making egg proteins)? Why would he create them with the same organ defects (I talked about the eye, the recurrent laryngeal nerve, the remnants of a tail). It's questions like those that make it hard for me to still hold to the idea of 'special creation'. Genesis distinguishes humans as being created 'in the image of God', but I doubt there are many theists who would insist on a biological interpretation of that phrase … that we have arms and legs and internal organs and gene sequences in order to reflect the same physical attributes in God. Instead, 'image of God' pertains more to the soul and/or spirit. But what exactly that means is a different matter altogether, one which is out of place in this chapter.

Second, 'unique'. Did the human race begin solely with these two individuals, or might there have been more? In chapter three, I already raised a theological reason for questioning the idea that there were only these two people to start the race off: this strategy requires a very uncomfortable amount of incest on the part of the first few generations of humans. Also, if Adam and Eve were not 'specially-created', and we instead derive our origins through some pathway more akin to the standard evolutionary model, then there is no such thing as a primal pair. Even though geneticists will talk about 'mitochondrial Eve' and 'Y-chromosomal Adam', they don't really mean that the human race began with just those two specific individuals. Neither, when scientists talk about a common ancestor shared by humans and chimps or another shared by mammals and reptiles, do they mean there was one individual animal who had some offspring that eventually gave rise to one species and other offspring in the same nest that became a separate species. Instead, these terms are always meant to be broad and corporate in nature: they represent whole populations of individuals over a very broad period of time. It's like saying that it was Germany after World War I that gave us Hitler, or Roman Catholicism that gave rise to Protestantism.

Some would counter my questioning of the historicity of Adam and Eve by saying that Paul clearly believed that Adam was a real person who brought sin and death into the world (Romans 5:12-21; 1 Corinthians 15:20-23). But Paul was a man of his time, and was educated in the ways of first century Greco-Roman and Jewish thinking. And a lot of things were changing at that period in time, not the least of which was Judeo-Christian thinking.

For example, there are many Biblical passages which suggested to the disciples at that time that the new message and kingdom which Jesus brought was meant only for the Jews, and they also had the words of Jesus himself: "*I was sent only to the lost sheep of Israel*" (Matthew 15:24-26). Which is why the early church leaders confronted Peter and demanded an explanation when he worshipped in the house-church of Cornelius, a Roman (that is, a Gentile). But that exclusive viewpoint was finally set aside by the discussion which followed Peter's vision of a blanket being lowered from heaven containing "*all kinds of four-footed animals, as well as reptiles and birds*" (Acts 10). The second chapter of Galatians provides another example of how they were struggling to reconcile their Jewish mind-set with the new Gospel message: the central issue was whether or not Gentile converts must become circumcised or not, but this gender-focused issue would also force them to rethink the nature of their new faith from the female perspective.

Another example: at one point, the early Christians were dead-set against eating meat offered to idols (Acts 15:20), but very soon afterwards reversed their thinking on that very point (1 Corinthians 8:4; 1 Corinthians 10:23-33).

At that time, they were quite accepting of slavery, even teaching *"Slaves, obey your earthly masters with respect and fear"* (Ephesians 6:5), and of the inequality of women (too many verses to list here), but many today would say that the ultimate message and truth of the gospel would take us beyond those ideas.

Even some things that we would now view as trivial seem to have been battle lines in the time of the apostles: *"Judge for yourselves: is it proper for a woman to pray to God with her head uncovered? Does not the very nature of things teach you that if a man has long hair, it is a disgrace to him, but that if a woman has long hair, it is her glory? For long hair is given to her as a covering. If anyone wants to be contentious about this, we have no other practice—nor do the churches of God."* (1 Corinthians 11:13-16). That last sentence underscores the passion with which Paul held that viewpoint — 'if any of you wants to think differently about this, then I've got nothing else to say to you'.

So let's be honest, there's certainly a lot of precedent even within the Bible itself for calling into question a hard-core teaching of the apostles. And Paul's every word need not be elevated to the status of bed-rock unshakeable dogma; I'm not saying he's wrong, but rather that it's OK to probe and question his teaching. In some of his writings, he's aware or suspects that a particular point he's making is his own thinking and not necessarily revelation from God. *"To the rest I say this (I, not the Lord) ..."* (1 Corinthians 7:12). *"Now about virgins: I have no command from the Lord, but I give a judgment as one who by the Lord's mercy is trustworthy"* (1 Corinthians 7:25). *"In this self-confident boasting I am not talking as the Lord would, but as a fool."* (2 Corinthians 11:17).

In other places, he said things that he and his contemporaries genuinely believed but that we moderns might question. For example, he thought that human souls could be found *"under the earth"*, existing in some kind of subterranean caverns (Philippians 2:10; Psalm 55:15). Does that mean that mining companies today need to take appropriate safety precautions when they start digging? He also referred to the 'heavens' (2 Corinthians 5:1; Ephesians 4:10) and the third heaven (2 Corinthians 12:2), and was therefore probably thinking, as many in his day did, that there was one level in which earth-bound bodies moved (birds, arrows and baseballs), another level in which the celestial bodies moved (sun, moon and stars), and yet another level beyond those in which heavenly bodies moved (God, angels, human souls), and that the third heaven would have been situated somewhere directly above the Middle East (that is, they weren't thinking about the fact that earth is a sphere and that 'up' in Palestine is not the same direction as 'up' in China or Argentina or Australia). So if he firmly believed those ideas, does it mean that it might be possible some day for us to ricochet a satellite or space probe off the streets of gold in the New Jerusalem, or reach Heaven (as in Paradise) by rockets? Paul claimed to be the very worst of all sinners (1st Timothy 1:15-16) ... does that mean he was?

Or Paul might say something that he wasn't claiming to be factually accurate, but did so to make a point. For example, the writer of Psalm 14 asks if there are any who seek after God, but Paul turns this into a statement by quoting a modified version of this: *"... there is no one who seeks God ..."* (Romans 3:11). I and many others would adamantly claim differently on this point: even before they embrace Christianity, there are many people who are indeed trying to find God in all kinds of blind and misdirected ways (as per Figure 9).

So if Paul depicts Adam as an actual person, does that make Adam's existence an irrefutable fact? Is the claim of this 1st century Roman-Jewish theologian sufficient evidence for us to have to re-interpret or discard all kinds of modern scientific evidence to the contrary? Alternatively, is it possible that Paul just had a worldview that reflected the thinking of that part of the world at that time, and/or that he was just simply using the concept of Adam, Eve and the Fall in the garden as a teaching tool — an illustration — of sin in our lives and our need for redemption? He may also be trying to emphasize the universal nature of his message: he saw himself as the Apostle to the Gentiles, yet he's trying to present to that non-Jewish world a message which had previously been very much a tribal (Jewish) story. He might therefore be using the concept of Adam to bring us all, both Jews and Gentiles, under one umbrella.

Jesus himself never mentioned Adam, even though his sole purpose on earth was to answer the theological problem we inherited from Adam and Eve in the garden. I find that astounding: if humanity's fundamental flaw could be traced to that one couple who actually lived and transgressed in the Garden, and Jesus was the sole solution to that problem, specifically sent for that purpose, why would he never even mention Adam and Eve by name. He could have easily done so when he was debating with the Pharisees: *"Haven't you read, he replied, that at the beginning the Creator 'made them male and female,' and said, 'For this reason a man will leave his father and mother and be united to his wife, and the two will become one flesh"* (Matthew 19:4-6; also in Mark 10:6-9). He's quoting here from Genesis, which uses the noun "adam" in two very different ways.

In some places, "adam" is used as a personal name: it's the Hebrew word for "man", and the first human created is given that name. It's a little bit of an eye-roller that the first man takes on the very unimaginative name "Man" (and the first woman is given the name "Eve", which means "source of life"). This name is also a play on words because "adam" also means ground or earth or dirt, from which he was made: so "adam" is made from "adam".

But in other places, Genesis refers to *"ha adam"*, which means *"the adam"*. Hebrew doesn't put the definite article – the word 'the' – in front of personal names: it never refers to *"the Abraham"* or *"the David"*. So 'ha adam' is not a personal name. Instead, 'ha adam' refers to a representative man: it means humankind, not *"the guy named Man"*.

So getting back to the main point of this section, the quote in Matthew and Mark given above is the only time that Jesus comes even close to mentioning *"Adam"*, and he uses these two passages from Genesis which refer to *"ha adam"*. But more importantly, it needs to be recognized that when Jesus quoted these texts, which themselves focus on the institution of marriage, he was talking about humanity not a couple, and was addressing a sociological matter – divorce and marriage – not teaching science or genealogy or ancient human history.

For all these reasons, I don't think one has to believe in Adam or Eve as literal, historical figures.

But for some people, this then raises a much more fundamental question which has absolutely huge consequence for Christians: if we now agree that Adam and Eve are fictitious, then do we have to concede that Jesus is also myth? The gospels of Matthew and of Luke both recount the genealogy of Jesus Christ. Interestingly, the two are different in several places [91], but both trace the lineage of Jesus back to Abraham, the father of the Jews, and then Luke continues on from there to connect Jesus with the biological and spiritual fathers of the entire human race, concluding with "... *the son of Adam, the son of God.*" (Luke 3:38).

I certainly don't question the idea that Jesus is a real historical figure. Despite the claims of some Bible-debunkers, the historicity of Jesus is unassailable: there are too many written records of his existence. And not

---

[91] People frequently jump on those discrepancies as proof that there are errors in the Bible and thereby question the credibility of the Bible, and even of Jesus. The notes in my NIV Study Bible state: "*A more likely explanation, however, is that Matthew follows the line of Joseph (Jesus' legal father), while Luke emphasizes that of Mary (Jesus' blood relative).*" I've also heard that one traces the royal line of Jesus while the other traces the priestly line of Jesus, since the Messiah would fulfill both roles.

just Christian writings (the books within the New Testament, plus many other books which were not included in the Bible), but also writings from non-Christian authors living at the same time (such as the Jewish/Roman historian Josephus) and those living shortly after the death of Christ who would have been able to validate the claims. Also, it's hard to explain the foundation of the Christian church — within the crucible of intense persecution from the occupying Roman military government and antagonistic Jewish leaders — upon the name and teachings of a mythic person who they conspired to have been born and died less than a generation prior, but who they actually knew never existed.

How, then, do I explain the genealogy of the real person Jesus being traced back to a mythic Adam? Where does the genealogy transition between the mythical and the historical?

Many believe that Moses was involved with the authorship of Genesis (I'll write in greater detail on this question in chapter eight of this book). That writing would have occurred around the year 1500 BC, which is 400 or 500 years after Abraham, and a couple thousand years after Adam. The best cutting-edge technology for data storage during the period spanning Adam to Abraham was found in the Mesopotamian empire: its priests and intellectuals carved all their writings on clay tablets. This may have been a workable solution for a stationary civilization with massive stone libraries (like the Mesopotamians), but would have been impossibly impractical for a desert-wandering group of Bedouins such as the Semites were. The tablets would be heavy, clumsy, and easily broken during the countless donkey and camel rides through the desert over thousands of years. As such, the writings of the author(s) of Genesis would likely have been based on a very long oral tradition. Anyone who has played the game 'telephone tag' — in which a message is whispered from one player to the next repeatedly and comes out quite differently at the other end of a long line of players — can understand how an oral tradition is not the most reliable, especially over a couple thousand years. I've heard many people speak emphatically and dogmatically about how ancient societies were able to keep an error-free oral tradition, to an extent that is absolutely unparalleled in modern society. But on what evidence do they base that claim? In the majority of the cases, their only evidence is that they heard this to be true from someone else, and/or they want it to be true. But there's no way anyone can go back and determine nor prove how accurate was the oral tradition of the Biblical patriarchs. The best we can do now is conjecture; one of the worst things we can do is be indefensibly dogmatic about what we hope is true without any hard evidence. Sociologists and anthropologists who have actually studied the phenomenon of oral tradition in contemporary illiterate societies have evidence that seriously challenges its reliability. Daniel Jeremy Silver – a now deceased Hebrew scholar, Jewish rabbi, and Adjunct Professor of Religion at Case Western Reserve University – wrote: *"So impressed have some students been by what they believe to be the fidelity of the oral transmission of narratives and legal formulas that they have come to overdramatic conclusions about the reliability of the Bible's reports of events occurring centuries before they became a part of Israel's written record"* [92]. Some societies were indeed able to pass down poems and songs for centuries, but that is made more reliable by the rhyme and rhythm that those forms of communication possess: even a minor change in wording can suddenly make a given line in a poem *'sound wrong'*. This isn't the case for the kind of text that we find in the first few books of the OT, which describe events that presumably occurred before the Hebrew language was developed or even the development of the Mesopotamian language/alphabet which gave that to us (more on that point in chapter eight). It's true that more recent societies which can cloister large numbers of their people into secluded temples and charge them with endless memorization and recitation are able to produce individuals who retain in memory huge tracts of text such as the Torah, the Rig Vedas, or the Quran. But that kind of scenario doesn't apply to the small groups of Semitic families herding sheep and wandering deserts and speaking an Akkadian tongue for one or two thousand years before any oral (and Akkadian) tradition was committed to a Hebrew text (the origin of Hebrew language and written text around the time of David is described in more detail in chapter eight).

So what reason do we have to discount the idea that the writer(s) of Genesis built up — as in, concocted or synthesized — a pre-Abrahamic genealogy many years after the event? They might have been able to remember fairly clearly back to some long-deceased predecessor, but then would have to struggle a little bit harder to remember details about that predecessor's father or grandfather and therefore would have to suppress a little bit of uncertainty and add just a sprinkle of fabrication to keep the story going. And as they tried to go back yet another generation or two, they would have to be yet a little more liberal with those sprinkles. In that way, more and more layers of fabricated story could be added to a factual history until history fades into myth as the mists of time close in.

In this context, it's interesting to note that Matthew's genealogy of Jesus is specifically broken up into three groups of fourteen: *"Thus there*

[92] Daniel Jeremy Silver, *The Story of Scripture: From Oral Tradition to the Written Word.* (Basic Books Inc. Publishers New York, 1990), p.52

were fourteen generations in all from Abraham to David, fourteen from David to the exile to Babylon, and fourteen from the exile to the Messiah" (Matthew 1:17). Like many ancient societies, the Jews often attached numerical meanings to letters, and would add up the numbers represented by the letters in a name: fourteen was the number for David [93]. So to the Jews, three groups of fourteen screamed out "house of David", in the same way that "number-ninety-nine" brings Wayne Gretzky to mind for many hockey lovers, and the phrase "double-oh-seven" immediately brings to mind a different persona for most of the rest of us. It's like an author writing a novel about a character who *"lives in apartment #007 in the Double-Oh-Seven Condominium on Zero-zero-seventh Avenue"*; without being told anything more about this person, you already know a lot about who this character is and what he does and how important he'll be in the developing storyline. This provocative time-line — three groups of fourteen —appears to be a human construct, an artistic flourish on a story being told, rather than an actual fore-ordained outcome of God's detailed plan, because if you compare the genealogy in Matthew 1 with the stories given in 2nd Chronicles, you see that Matthew skips several generations to maintain this symmetry [94].

There's one more rebuttal which might be made against my claim that the Adam and Eve described in the first three chapters of Genesis were probably mythical characters. As I already acknowledged above, Paul describes Adam as a real person who brought sin and death into the world, and Jesus as the *"last Adam"* who brought life and reconciliation (Romans 5:12-21; 1 Corinthians 15:20-23). As such, some might accuse me of overturning the entire redemption story. If there was no Adam, there was no Fall in the garden, and therefore no need for Christ's work on the cross: Christ therefore died in vain. I disagree completely. The Bible is certainly clear that we all have sin in us. And if we're honest, we can see that inside ourselves. We're too often plagued by selfish motives and self-destructive desires. Too often, our dealings with our fellow human are less than honourable. We don't love enough, respect enough, care enough. That's in all of us. And in some of us, that leads to other things: cheating, lying, hatred, theft, rape, torture, murder, war, et cetera. I'm not a murderer simply because my great-great-grandfather was. True justice would not hold me accountable for some sin or crime that one of my ancestors committed. But I do have a sinful streak simply because I'm human. And

---

[93] The Hebrew word for 'David' is 'DVD', with 'D' and 'V' being the 4th and 6th letters of the Hebrew alphabet: therefore, 'David' = 4+6+4 = 14
[94] see 2 Chronicles 21:4 to 26:23, and compare with Matthew 1:8

that sinful streak has blossomed into a unique set of sins to which I will have to admit. And that's what I see was the reason for Christ's work on the cross. I'll come back to these points in the next chapter.

I fully realize and expect that some conservative Christians will react strongly against the contention that Adam may not be an actual historical person. I don't feel it has to undermine any belief in God, in our sinfulness, in the gospel message of Jesus Christ, nor the Bible itself as an inspired text ('inspired' does not have to mean 'inerrant and infallible'). I'll write later in this book (chapter eight) in more detail about how I've come to reconcile my faith with questions like this.

CONCLUSION

So, approximately one hundred billion people have spent millennia trying to figure out who this 'Great Being' is, most without any of the resources that we take for granted (particularly books like the Bible, the Torah, the Quran, the Upanishads or Bagavad Gita, et cetera) and have come up with dozens ... hundreds? ... thousands? ... of different theological paradigms (Figure 9). Is one religion 'right', or more right than others? They can't all be precisely right: some are in stark contrast to others. Perhaps none of them is precisely right. Personally, I think many religions have something good to say: there are some kernels of truth in many of them, and some have incredibly valuable things to teach us. But I also think they all have some misconceptions and even some truly hideous warts, not least among them being Christianity (here I'm referring to the selling of indulgences for salvation, the Crusades and Inquisition, the suppression of women, religiously-based arrogance and condemnation of other people, et cetera). Where do I stand? ... chapter nine.

6

The Fall and Original Sin

Were Adam and Eve really the first people?

Was there a Garden of Eden?

Was there a specific tree?

Was it an apple? And a snake?

Are all people cursed because of something Adam and Eve did?

What is 'Original Sin'?

Does Genesis three provide a literal description of actual history?

Will God really send so many basically good people to an eternal hell?

Would God send people to hell just because they didn't know Jesus?

This chapter is quite a departure from the ones before, which dealt with the tensions between science and the Bible. But nonetheless this is also one of the big questions that threatened to undo my faith.

One of the tenets of Christianity which trips up so many people is the concept of 'original sin'. I recently learned that this isn't just a Christian idea: ancient Mesopotamian texts which predate the Jewish Biblical texts also refer to it. Thomas Cahill summarized the Sumerian viewpoint on this: "... *human beings were full of evil. 'Man behaves badly,' pronounces Ut-napishtim sagely. 'Never has a sinless child been born,"* warns a favorite

Sumerian proverb." [95]

    I grew up with a Calvinist viewpoint which is particularly harsh on this point. Basically, all humankind is spiritually dead, damned to hell, because of this Original Sin. Even babies who are newly born, and are years away from being able to speak or even form thoughts, are said to be tainted with Original Sin. People who have never been taught about the Christian concept of God are saturated with Original Sin. Even though they are generous, helpful, positive, pleasant, compassionate, and courteous people — they're doomed to hell because of Original Sin.

    Very sobering thoughts. Very hard to swallow.

    So what is Original Sin? Even though the word pair 'Original Sin' is never found even once in any of the widely-accepted translations and transliterations of the Bible — it was a term coined by Augustine in 396 AD, long after the Bible was canonized — many Christians would trace it all back to Adam and Eve. To the Garden of Eden. To that very familiar story of the first two people who ever existed. Walking together in a paradise, eating from any plant or tree they saw (except for that nasty tree of knowledge), playing with the animals, including the snakes and lions, and even walking and talking to God Himself. And God told them they could do whatever they wanted, but just don't touch that one tree over there, the one called *"the tree of the knowledge of good and evil"* (Genesis 2:17). But along came some serpent-like being (contrary to popular thinking, this would not have been a snake, because this being seemed to have legs which were later 'revoked'). And at the urging of this serpent, one of them is convinced to try some of the fruit — 'after all, it's only going to make you more like God', a praiseworthy motive in its own right. Don't we all want to be more like God? And then the other was co-opted into this act of treason by taking a bite. Because of that one single act — well, two acts actually — the proverbial theft of cookies from the cookie jar, all hell broke loose. The animals are condemned to turn on each other in savage carnivorous competition, the ground to produce thorns and thistles, women to have pain in childbirth, men to sweat and toil for the rest of their lives trying to make a living (what does this say for women taking epidurals before birthing their baby, or men who have easy air-conditioned office jobs?) and all generations of humans from then on to be tainted with 'Original Sin' and condemned to hell.

    But not everyone is a 'Hitler'. How can such a loving, compassionate God condemn so many apparently fundamentally loving,

---

[95] Thomas Cahill, *The Gifts of the Jews: How a Tribe of Desert Nomads Changed the Way Everyone Thinks and Feels.* (Bantam Doubleday Dell Publishing Group, 1998), page 61

compassionate, good, generous people to hell just because they're descendants of two people who we're told lived several thousand years ago. How could he destine so many babies — we would call them *innocent* babies — to the fires of Hell, simply because of that one act of Adam and Eve? What a seemingly over-the-top response to what seems to us to be such a small, insignificant act. I mean, it's not like Adam and Eve went on a psychopathic, murderous spree and horribly tortured and mutilated some other innocent human (if there were anyone around to assault) ... or uttered the most blasphemous, blood-curdling, jaw-dropping, defiant curse against God Himself ... or committed a range of other possible egregious acts that would make anyone conclude that: yes, they had it coming and brought it on themselves. No, they just picked an apple from the tree, despite God's command that they not touch it, with the simple naive intent of 'becoming more like God'. What could be so wrong about that? And why attribute the penalty of that heinous sin to every living human being ever since? And why make it so that even the very best attempts at being good and doing good would not be enough to get us into Heaven? It just seems to be so lop-sided. It's no wonder that so many non-believers, when told about the Good News, just recoil in confusion and disgust, saying *"that stuff's all fine for some people, but it's not for me"*.

Some would respond with: it's not that they simply took a bite from the apple, but that they deliberately disobeyed a direct command from God. He explicitly directed them not to take of that fruit, and they just went ahead anyway and did exactly that. *"In your face God!"* Literally, since they must have known that God sees everything and knows everything. Okay. That ratchets the offense up a few notches: Adam and Eve defied God directly. They told God in no uncertain terms that his rule meant nothing to them (there was only one rule at that point: "don't eat from **that** tree"). Maybe I could understand the two of them getting kicked out of Eden for that kind of rebellious insult. But why condemn all the animals and plants, and even the ground? And why all of humankind for the rest of eternity? What would our response be if some Dutch couple named Mens and Vrouw saw a sign on the Whitehouse lawn reading 'Do not step on the grass', went ahead and did just that, leading the government of the United States to immediately expel all people of Dutch descent. In fact, they then extended this penalty to all people in general, from all US territory for the rest of perpetuity, and imposed an onerous tax on all dogs and cats? Wouldn't we label that a bit of a misdirected over-reaction? (Note: this does not mean that I think the USA is the Garden of Eden).

And why would God set the stage for that anyway? Why not give them something more like the ten commandments ... do not kill, do not steal, et cetera ... or something closer to Jesus' more positive commandment: love God with everything that is in you, and your neighbour as yourself (Matthew 22:37-40)? Why such a strange commandment like: Eat from any and every tree in the Garden except that one over there — you can't miss it: it's right there *"in the middle of the garden"* (Genesis 3:3) — with the neon signs around it flashing *"Not this one"*, and *"DO NOT EAT"*, and even a few well-directed arrows pointing right at it, strobe lights blinking, a couple spot-lights beaconing out into the sky to even catch their attention and help them find their way back to it if they happened to stroll beyond sight of the tree. It's almost like a dare. Why draw that line in the sand which will determine the fate of all creation and all history over such a seemingly insignificant act?

Although I'd tossed questions like that back and forth for many years, I never really engaged myself in trying to find an answer. On the one hand, I didn't have the courage to really question God on that. But on the other hand, and more to the truth, I was content to put those questions on the shelf for another day. It wasn't really central to my day-to-day existence, and therefore not really that important to me. Ignorance is bliss!

Then I read *The Kite Runner*, by Khaled Hosseini [96], and it completely challenged my theology. My brief summary of this book is this (don't worry, I don't think this will spoil it for anyone who hasn't read the book yet). A boy makes a decision and commits an act of betrayal that he regrets for the rest of his life. It haunts him and tortures him. And because of that, he seeks with all his heart and mind to pay for that sin. To be reconciled with not only the friend whom he betrayed, but also with Allah. In our Christian terminology, he just desperately wants forgiveness and to be right with God ... the only God he ever knew or heard about. For years he agonizes how to find this redemption. Unfortunately, because of his context — living in Muslim Afghanistan — he has no Bible, no missionary, no TV evangelist, or any other source of Christian teaching to help him find the way. My understanding of Christian theology told me that meant he was destined to hell. Though he just wants to get right with Allah (the same God as that of Abraham), he had no hope at all for eternity. And that tore my heart. It really shook my religious conviction. It made me ask God how that could be? At that same time, I had begun to interact more closely with people who were of a Muslim background. I worked with them, went on business trips with them, socialized and talked with them, and they invited my wife and me to their home for dinner. In talking with them, even about religious things, and seeing how they lived, I came to see that they were

---

[96] Khaled Hosseini, *The Kite Runner* . (Riverhead Books, 2003)

fundamentally good people who also wanted to be right in the eyes of their God. Unfortunately, their God was not the same as my God. (Or is He? More on that later).

More recently, I read *The God Delusion* by Richard Dawkins [97]. I'd read other books of his, and seen him many times on TV and in documentaries, and was therefore quite familiar with his fervent anti-God stance. But I had to admit that he raised a number of very good questions, very challenging questions, including some of the ones I've mentioned above. One of his points was that he is very much a scientist, someone who bases his conclusions on evidence. In all other areas of his life, if the evidence pointed to this conclusion, that's what he would believe. If the evidence pointed against a conclusion, he discarded that belief. If there was no evidence, he withheld judgement on the matter. So when it came to God, he just had no evidence to believe. He had never spoken with God; had never seen God, touched God, nor heard God. There was just no evidence. So why believe, especially with such passion and conviction? That got me thinking. I had to admit the same myself: that I'd never actually talked with God (sure I talked <u>to</u> him, but couldn't claim to have talked <u>with</u> him in any way comparable to how I talk with people) or touched him or seen him. So why did I believe? I realized that it does just come down to faith. Not evidence leading to an irrefutable conclusion. But faith. Fortunately for me, I had that faith because of the teaching I received from my parents, the numerous pastors whose teachings I'd heard, the many Christian mentors and friends who impacted my life, the fact that I'd read the Bible through many times, as well as the many Christian books I'd read. All of that combined with personal experiences to spark an indescribable confirmation that one feels but can't pin down. Which was all great for me. But what about the people who never had access to that, like the kid in *The Kite Runner*? Or people like Richard Dawkins who had heard these things but was designed by God to have a very analytical mind, and who needed hard evidence to understand. Just like the disciple Thomas, who said he needed to put his finger into the holes in Jesus' hands, and to put his hand into Jesus's pierced side, before he could believe. At least Thomas had Jesus standing right in front of him. Could speak with Him. Could hear from Him. What about Richard Dawkins? Why did God make it so hard for someone like Richard to believe?

But let's return now to the main question of this particular chapter: the nature of Original Sin. While listening to a pod-cast about the historicity of Adam, a point was made that completely floored me. Excluding the first

---

[97] Richard Dawkins *The God Delusion*. (Bantam Books, 2006)

five chapters of Genesis, Adam is only mentioned twice in the entire remainder of the Old Testament: in a genealogy of Abraham given in 1 Chronicles 1:1, and in Hosea 6:7 (which is strange in its own right because Adam is there said to have *"broken the covenant"*, although there's no mention in Genesis of any covenant made to/with/by Adam). And yet I had been taught throughout my entire life that this was the very central message of the Bible: that we were all cursed because of Adam (and Eve) and that God had a plan of salvation that would remove that curse. If that was the very core theme of the entire Bible, if the sin of Adam and Eve in the garden was so fundamental to the whole salvation story, why were their names not scattered everywhere throughout the OT, especially in those parts that dealt with sin, guilt, sacrifice and redemption? The OT covers at least 4,000 years of history, describing in great detail the interactions between God and humans, including all the rituals and sacrifices needed to address sin, and never once mentions that we've inherited the guilt of Adam which prevents people from having fellowship with God (please note carefully, I wasn't referring to whether the OT said anything about 'sin'... it does indeed do that in scores of places ... but whether it talks specifically about 'the sin of Adam'). Even Jesus doesn't mention the names of Adam and Eve, or make even a vague reference to them as the original source of our sin, nor to the Fall in the garden, let alone make those ideas the core of his teaching (he does allude to the first created beings in Matthew 19:4-6 and Mark 10:6-9, but that's in the context of the nature of the marriage relationship, and has nothing to do with the nature of sin).

In case the reader doesn't understand why this omission of mentioning 'Adam' is such a huge issue, imagine reading a collection of books which are deemed by historians to be the ultimate treatise on World War Two – the reasons why it started, how 'our side' could win, the weapons and strategies that were developed, and historical accounts of the many individual battles – but Hitler is mentioned only a few times in the first few pages of the first book in the series, and all the other books of that series fail to even mention him at all. Wouldn't that be strange? He was the entire reason we had that war, and his name should feature prominently throughout the entire collection of books.

It's true that the theme of our inherently sinful nature is picked up much later in the NT, especially by Paul. But one reason he might be doing that is to extend the reach of the gospel message. He makes it very clear many times that he sees himself as the Apostle to the Gentiles: he's trying to present to the non-Jewish (Greek and Roman) world a message which had previously been very much a tribal (Jewish) story. He therefore appeals to and emphasizes the idea that we (Jews and Gentiles) are all one and the same through our common ancestry, which he (Paul) traced back to Adam.

Altogether, this whole concept of Original Sin receives very little attention in Jesus' teaching, but begins to gain traction during the 1st century AD in the teachings of the disciples and apostles, and then blossoms in the hands of Augustine of Hippo in 396 AD.

These experiences and thoughts and questions helped me to begin to see faith, and Original Sin, in a whole new light. Once again, I think we need to return to the story of Adam and Eve in the Garden of Eden, and more importantly, to the concept of Original Sin, and look at it from a new angle. One not colored by centuries of human (mis)interpretation. Yes, I know this sounds pretty pretentious and audacious. Please understand: I don't presume to be smarter or more educated or more insightful than many religious scholars before me. I do claim, however, to have wrestled with this question of Original Sin, to have been repulsed privately by the apparent lack of love and justice in that traditional interpretation of the event, and to have been muzzled to silence and embarrassment when trying to witness to colleagues and friends who raised questions like the ones I pose above — but to eventually have come to a new interpretation that I find quite satisfactory and defensible.

Original Sin, in my mind, is not Adam and Eve taking a bite out of the apple. Instead, it's the fiercely independent and self-centred spirit we all have within us. Whenever we're told explicitly what we can't do or can't have, we all have to fight a deep-seated urge to defy exactly that: it's a fundamentally human characteristic. As Mark Twain put it *"There is a charm about the forbidden that makes it unspeakably desirable"*. Two millennia before that, the Roman poet Ovid wrote: *"We are ever striving after what is forbidden, and coveting what is denied us"*. Original Sin is that strong-willed selfish tendency to say *"I don't need you, get out of my way, I can take care of myself, thank-you"*. Pride. Mine. Me, me, me. Even though God provides for everything we need — right from a whole garden full of fruit trees and perfect weather, to the very stairway to heaven — all we can say is: *"I can do it myself"*. *"Of course I'm going to heaven: I've been a good person"*. *"I don't need religion ... I'll make my own way"*. Or some of us say the converse of this: *"I'll never get to heaven: I'm not good enough"*. In all these sentences, we betray the viewpoint that we are the masters of our own destiny. God holds out the way for us, and we turn our back and follow our own course. And God, in such an immense display of love and respect, honours our free-will choice. He says: *"You want to do it your own way? So be it"*. It breaks his heart, but he'd rather have you freely and willingly choose his way than force a merely robotic obedience from you. That's the Original Sin that we inherit from the proverbial Adam and Eve. I think sin is our intrinsic nature of wanting to do it by ourselves, and for ourselves. God honours our desire to go it alone: the problem is, the Bible teaches that we just can't make it on our own (I'll elaborate on that below).

But how does that interpretation change things for the poor Muslim boy in Afghanistan who will never hear the gospel, or the baby who will never grow old enough to make a conscious decision, or Richard Dawkins who will go his own way until he's forced to the conclusion by irrefutable evidence? Or the people who lived before the time of Jesus and therefore could never come to put their faith in him for salvation. Or those who lived far away from Abraham back in the day when God was talking to him but apparently not to anyone else in the little hamlet of Haran, or even the booming empire of Babylon?

I think the Bible teaches that we'll be judged according to the information we were given ... that to those who have been given more, more will be expected of them, and conversely, to those who had less opportunity or information, there'll be less stringency and more grace. Those people will be judged according to what is written on their hearts and their conscience (Romans 2:12-16).

Some will have been confronted with the teaching that there is a God, and that he sent Jesus to make a way for us to be right with him: if those people reject that outstretched hand of God and say *"I don't need it"* or *"I'll do it myself"*, that's the free choice they make. And they'll have only themselves to blame (Hebrews 6:4-6).

Others will never hear about God, or Jesus or the Bible. But they'll have an awareness that there is something or someone much bigger than themselves out there: the 'Great Being' or 'God'. That there is an ultimate right and wrong. That lying and stealing are wrong, let alone killing. Those ideas don't come only from the Bible: they're built right into all of us (Romans 1:18-20). And some will respond to that positively. They'll marvel at creation around them, and in their own way, praise some version of 'the God' for it. They'll go on living their lives, but when they see someone in need, they'll help. When they themselves are in need, they'll turn to the 'Great Being' that they sense. They'll turn to him just like kids turn to their parents: children are completely dependent upon their parents ... run to their parent at the first sign of trouble ... want to share their personal achievements and triumphs with their parents. Don't forget, Jesus said: *"Unless you change and become like little children, you will never enter the kingdom of heaven"* (Matthew 18:3). At other times, when these people see an injustice, something that they feel would displease 'the God', they will seek to end it or make it right, sometimes in ways that would offend us 21st century Westerners. I believe that God will honour their limited understanding of him, and love them for their heart attitude (1 Corinthians 4:5).

On the other hand, some of their peers who have also never heard about our version of God, Jesus or the Bible, but who nonetheless are aware of a 'God-being' and right and wrong, will consciously choose to follow their own path. They will lie, steal, horde, kill and destroy for their own gain. They will glory in their own ability, and see themselves as entirely self-sufficient. The masters of their own destiny. They'll conclude that they don't need any help from the 'Great Being'. That it's all about them. The fruit of the garden is theirs for the taking. Pride. Selfishness. Fierce independence. Original, and unpardonable, sin. God weeps, but nonetheless honours the free-will choice that they've made.

And then there are those who are unable to make that conscious decision. Their brains never matured sufficiently, either because they were too young or through some kind of debilitating disease. They won't be able to form the thoughts leading to an 'other'-minded, compassionate, love versus a self-sufficient, self-indulgent, selfish independence. They haven't crossed that line, and God won't hold them accountable for that.

This new view not only helps me explain the question of our final judgement, but also to explain Christ's death on the cross. I find it hard to believe that God merely required someone's death and spilt blood before he could overlook our many and sometimes petty acts of transgression. *"Sure I can forgive you, but first let me vent my anger on something, anything. I just need to get it out of my system."* This makes it hard to take Paul's injunction to *"let not the sun go down upon your wrath"* (KJV; Ephesians 4:26). The savageness of Christ's death wasn't necessarily God's idea: that's just the way the Romans did executions back in those days. Instead, I think God was using Christ's death --- gory as it was --- as an object lesson to show us how to be saved. Here is God's solution to this Original Sin of selfish independence: God himself comes down, giving up a pain-free, guiltless life, to show love, compassion and mercy, even accepting the guilt of everyone else and taking on an excruciating death, so that all who follow him and his example will have eternal life. I think God is showing us that the way to eternal life is giving up a self-centred life. Living for others: first and foremost for God, but then equally for our fellow human being. Remember Jesus' answer to the question *"which is the greatest commandment?"* ... it was *"love the Lord your God with all your heart ... and soul ... and mind ... and love your neighbour as yourself"* (Matthew 22:35-39). Christ's death is the template for us: he modelled 'The Way' for us. We need to do the same as he did. To take up our own cross, daily

(Luke 9:23). To give up ourselves, and our selfish ambitions. To care for the poor, the widows and orphans, the sick and imprisoned (Matthew 25:31-46, the sheep and the goats metaphor). That's God's answer to Original Sin, and our path to eternal life: give ... love ... build ... bring healing ... think about others before yourself. The Bible is just packed full of verses talking about how we need to care for each other, both the saved and unsaved. *"I have set an example that you should do as I have done for you"* (John 13:15).

Some might still insist that people will not find redemption unless they 'accept Jesus Christ into their heart', even though there's no scriptural reference for this wording *"accept into their heart"* (so where did it come from?). They'll hold this exclusionary viewpoint based on Jesus' saying: *"No one comes to the Father except through me"* (John 14:6). But let's put that isolated excerpt into context: Jesus tells them *"I go to prepare a place for you ... and I'll come back to get you so that you may be where I am ... you know the way to where I am going"* ... Thomas says: *"Lord, how can we know the way to where you're going?"* ... Jesus answers: *"I am the way ... no one comes to the Father except through me"*. Jesus shows us the way to God the Father, the pathway to be saved, the stairway to heaven. 'The way' is the life-example that Jesus modelled for us through the pathway of complete sacrifice, love, service, giving. That's why he called himself 'The Way' (John 14:6), and his teaching was called 'The Way' in Acts 9:2. It's the opposite of the many paths of self-sufficiency, selfishness, defiance and independence, which is our natural default setting. This is also why the Bible also teaches that we need to be born again: we need to put to death that old nature of selfishness and have a new nature of selflessness begin to grow in us.

So what do I do with the story of Adam and Eve? Is it a literal description of actual history? Were they the first two people who ever existed? Was there a Garden of Eden? Was there a specific tree? Was it an apple? That last question is easy. There's no place in the Bible that says it was an apple. Somehow, history has inserted that into the picture. Someday I'll have to research when and how that happened, and who did it.

But the other questions I just raised are a bit harder and more controversial. I feel that I don't have to believe there was actually a first man named Adam and a first woman named Eve. If I had more reason to do so, I could still acknowledge that it's possible that God interrupted the course of natural history by suddenly introducing these two individuals. But I'm not forced to believe that: I can equally see them as metaphorical, and can therefore more easily explain the fossil record of human evolution, let alone answer the moral questions I've raised above. Instead, I think Adam and Eve and the story of their fall could be representative of an awakening of the human species. More specifically, they would represent the groups of humans existing at that time in our evolutionary history that came to an understanding of self, and an awareness of others and God. God breathing the breath of life into man in Genesis 2:7 could represent him nurturing that awareness of self and selflessness. The Garden of Eden could represent a carefree existence in which people lived like the animals: just going out and eating, living and existing, blissfully unaware of their mortality and finiteness. They would have no concerns about provisioning for the future. They would be naked: vulnerable to the elements ... completely open and honest with each other... not fettered with taboos about sexuality, gender, superiority, wealth, skin color, et cetera But at some point their thinking crested a metaphorical plateau, they got a taste of the knowledge of good and evil, and they suddenly saw everything around them from a new perspective. They suddenly had fears about the future, their mortality and finiteness (they became scared of God, and hid), about their relationship with others (the concern about being naked and vulnerable). But at the same time they now had that spark of divinity — the breath of God — which compelled them to find the 'Great Being'.

7

Other stories in Genesis

Was the Flood story adapted from other religious writings?

Did God fail?

Who were the Nephilim?

Angels having sex with humans?

What is the Tower of Babel story all about?

Why did God destroy Sodom and Gomorrah?

Do I take these stories as historical, or the OT equivalent of parables?

In the previous chapter, we considered God's response to Adam and Eve eating from the Tree: the condemnation not only of all humans throughout history, but also the animals, plants and even earth's soil itself. All because of the actions of two individuals. But Genesis also recalls other responses of someone portrayed as God which, if I am allowed to be honest, might be blown out of proportion. In the Flood story, we have the global destruction not only of all humanity, but also *"all life under the heavens, every creature that has the breath of life in it. Everything on earth will perish"* (Genesis 6:17) because people have displeased him. In the Tower of Babel story, the disruption of human collaboration because they sought to build a city and a tower. In the Sodom and Gomorrah story, the utter destruction of *"those cities and the entire plain including all those living in the cities—and also the vegetation in the land"* (Genesis 19:25) because of their wickedness, and the turning of Lot's wife into a pillar of salt simply because she looked back (Genesis 19:26). These stories, and others, really challenge the Good News message, and make it really hard to say "*Smile: God loves you*". They reinforce the image of God being stern and judgmental. And it's for that reason alone that I really want to challenge whether we need to take those stories literally, or if possibly they represent stories that have been shaped by human minds from an ancient, patriarchal, Near Eastern viewpoint.

THE FLOOD

There are many accounts from ancient civilizations all around the world of a flood which caused global destruction, or at least destruction over an exceedingly wide regional area [98]. From ancient Hindu Vedic texts, to Babylonian and Greek mythology, the Mayans in South America, Aboriginals in North America and those in Australia. Of course, most readers know that the book of Genesis describes a Flood which caused nearly complete global destruction of all human society and even life in general, with the exception of one family and an ark full of representative animal species. Those that hold to a literal reading of Genesis say that this was the definitive flood event, and that all other flood accounts from other civilizations have borrowed from that narrative, or at least are separate accounts of the same event. But let's look at this question of precedence.

According to the timelines and genealogies given in the OT and collation of that biblical history with world history (see Chapter 2), the Flood story described in Genesis chapters six to nine would have occurred approximately around the year 2350 BC. But many of those other flood stories from other civilizations long pre-date the story of Noah's flood. I'm sure the response of many readers to this statement will be simple denial: "*it's their word against ours*". However, a better approach to being properly informed, to really knowing the truth, is to investigate it rather than assuming or being unjustifiably dogmatic. I know some will choose not to do this because they simply don't want to be convinced otherwise. But I feel we need to be able to look at the facts and follow where the data lead.

One authoritative and eye-opening source I found on this subject is a recent book written by David Montgomery, entitled '*The Rocks Don't Lie: A Geologist Investigates Noah's Flood*'. As the title suggests, the bulk of the book looks at geological evidence interpreted by an expert in the field.

---

[98] R. Norman Whybray, *Introduction to the Pentateuch*. (Grand Rapids, MI; Wm. B. Eerdmans Publishing Co., 1995), ch. 3

But he also has an excellent chapter which looks at ancient literature and flood accounts. In particular, he writes about George Smith of the British Museum deciphering ancient Sumerian / Mesopotamian texts that he had just unearthed: *"The blocky symbols of ancient cuneiform told of a divine warning about an impending flood conveyed to a righteous man, the building of a great boat, the riding out of days and nights of rain, and the eventual stranding of the boat on a mountain when the floodwaters receded. Smith's excitement echoed throughout the museum. How could the biblical flood story be inscribed on a broken clay tablet excavated from a Sumerian library older than the Bible itself?"* Montgomery goes on to describe how more clay fragments and sleuthing revealed details such as: caulking the boat with bitumen; loading it with the builder's family and beasts of the field; the flood killing all living things; the sending out of a dove, a swallow and finally a raven to search for dry ground; the boat resting on the mountains of Nizir when the flood receded; the righteous boat builder named Utnapishtim, upon exiting the boat, offering up a burnt sacrifice to the deities, and the latter being 'well pleased' with this offering. As those who are familiar with the Biblical story of the Flood already know, all of these details are also present in the Genesis account, albeit sometimes with slight modifications.

A common response from Christians to this is that it was the Sumerians and others who borrowed the ideas from Biblical scriptural writings and their authors. But how do we know which way the borrowing went? On both sides of the argument, we don't have the original texts, but rather copies of those originals. The Sumerian clay tablets referred to above date to approximately 1600-1700 BC [99] [100] [101] [102] [103], while the Dead Sea scrolls (which are foundational for OT writings) only date as far back as 400 BC [104]. At this time, there's no way to know for certain which original writings preceded which: Mesopotamian or Hebrew. But what sounds more likely? That a sophisticated, established and world-dominating empire

[99] Alfred Rehwinkel, *The Flood: In the Light of the Bible, Geology, and Archaeology.* (Concordia Publishing House, 1957)

[100] David R. Montgomery, *The Rocks Don't Lie: A Geologist Investigates Noah's Flood* . (WW Norton & Company, 2013)

[101] *The epic of Gilgamesh: The Babylonian epic poem and other texts in Akkadian and Sumerian.* Translated and with Introduction by Andrew George. (Penguin Books, 2000)

[102] David Damrosch, *The Buried Book: the loss and rediscovery of the great epic of Gilgamesh* (New York; Henry Holt and Company, 2006)

[103] Alexander Heidel, *The Gilgamesh Epic and Old Testament Parallels.* (University of Chicago Press. 1946)

[104] Henry H. Halley, *Halley's Bible Handbook.* 24th edition. (Zondervan Publishing House, 1965), pp 843-846

(Babylon) ... with centuries or millennia of cultural history and tradition ... would hear about the origins story of some uncultured and unimportant (from their point of view) nation (Israel) which was soon enslaved by a rival empire (Egypt), and would then decide to adopt the origin story of that pathetic nation as their own? Or is it more likely that a small but growing nation (Israel), which sees itself taking the spotlight on the world stage, would assimilate and re-interpret the origins myths of the 'mighty but soon-to-be-defeated and ungodly' nations around it?

Also, it's worth considering this question in the context of the recorded enslavement of Israel in Egypt. There's no way yet to know whether or not the Hebrews had sacred scriptural writings before settling in Egypt (the OT doesn't say they did), but if they did, those texts would not have been in Hebrew, since that latter language didn't develop for another millennium later (more on this in chapter eight). Whatever texts that might have existed would have been written in some derivative of Sumerian script, since that's the culture from which Abraham originated and all the cultures in that ancient Near Eastern neighborhood were heavily influenced by that superpower. And if the Israelites did have any kind of religious writings before Egypt, it's a matter of opinion as to whether they would have been allowed to keep them during the peak of this 400-year-long brutal enslavement. The book of Exodus describes this as a brutal and complete enslavement for 400 years: *"The Egyptians came to dread the Israelites and worked them ruthlessly. They made their lives bitter with hard labor in brick and mortar and with all kinds of work in the fields; in all their hard labor the Egyptians used them ruthlessly"* (Exodus 1:12-14). The book of Exodus then describes how Israel was led out of Egypt by Moses, who is then held to be the author of Genesis. Here's the important point: according to the Exodus account, Moses, although born a Jew, had been adopted by the daughter of Pharaoh, the ruler of the Egyptian empire (Exodus 2:8-10), and therefore was likely schooled in the Pharaoh's courts (see Acts 7:21-22). The Egyptian empire is noted for many things (everyone has heard of their pyramids), not the least of which were tremendous libraries which housed the world's knowledge at that time, including copies of the Sumerian texts referred to above: how can we not wonder whether Moses was taught or even read for himself any of those Sumerian texts as he grew up? The date of the Exodus is debated, with claims ranging between approximately 1500 to 1000 BC, but the point is that all those dates occur long after the dating of those Mesopotamian/Sumerian fragments. In the next chapter, I'm going to return to this question of who wrote Genesis and what source material they might have used to write stories like this one about the Flood. But unless one takes the view that God dictated the very words of those five books to the authors of Genesis, then it would be hard to refute the possibility that the Genesis texts were influenced by those earlier Mesopotamian texts. Did the authors of the Pentateuch, whoever they were, adapt and re-tell those Sumerian accounts from a Jewish perspective, in the same way that Paul on Mars Hill took the Greek altar dedicated to an unknown God as a starting point for his sermon: 'Let me tell you about this God whom you don't know ...' (Acts 17:22-31)? When the Sumerian texts describe 'Ea' as the god who instructed Utnapishtim to build a huge vessel to escape the impending flood, did they recognize Ea to be 'Yahweh'? Were they providing a Hebrew light and interpretation on Egyptian, Mesopotamian, Sumerian and Babylonian knowledge and tradition? How can we know differently?

Setting aside the question of whether the biblical flood story preceded accounts from other ancient civilizations (who borrowed from whom?), many have tried to reconcile a literal reading of Noah's flood with the scientific findings of modern archaeologists, geologists and biologists. How that flood could explain the stratification of rock layers. Whether the torrents of receding water could be so powerful as to carve out colossal geological features like the Grand Canyon while at the same time be gentle enough to leave the bodies of insects as delicate as dragonflies intact to later fossilize, or animals with the food they were eating still in their teeth, and embryos still developing within eggs and/or within the mothers' bodies. Whether the ark could be big enough to hold all the representative species of the planet (one estimate was that it would be the size of an aircraft carrier, but how could that be built by just a few people)? Could Noah gather enough food and supplies for that many animals? Would eight people be enough to take care of the necessary animal husbandry for a whole year (I've shovelled out a horse's stall as a teenager, and would have shuddered at having to do that for a pair of elephants, a pair of giraffes, a pair of wildebeests, ...)? How, after the doors of the ark re-opened, certain animals which live in only one part of the world arrived at their unique destinations: the koala bear to Australia; the Emperor penguin to Antarctica; the polar bear to the Arctic; the llama to Chile. How we humans could have more than sixteen alleles for any given gene if there were only eight humans on the planet 3,000 years ago (less than 200 generations ago). Many books have already been written which raise questions like these or try to answer them [105], and I don't intend to simply recapitulate here much of what they say. But there are three other questions that I do want to address here.

---

[105] John C. Whitcomb and Henry M. Morris, *The Genesis Flood: The Biblical Record and Its Scientific Implications.* (P & R Publishing, 1960)

The first of these is: why God would do it this way. Not: why would God do it period? Genesis already gives that answer clearly: *"The Lord saw how great man's wickedness on the earth had become, and that every inclination of the thoughts of his heart was only evil all the time. The Lord grieved that he had made man on the earth, and his heart was filled with pain. So the Lord said, 'I will wipe mankind, whom I have created, from the face of the earth — men and animals, and creatures that move along the ground, and birds of the air — for I am grieved that I have made them."* (Genesis 6: 5-8). As an aside, the Genesis account says several times that this judgement was sent because of the violence that was in the land, so it's a little bit ironic that the problem of violence is dealt with by destroying every living thing — human, animal and plant —and the complete demolition of the face of the earth. But setting aside the morality of destroying the whole human race (except for Noah and his immediate family), my first question is instead *"Why would God do it this way?"*: with a global flood, which would also destroy every living thing and completely fracture and scar the face of the planet? Why not simply use some other naturalistic phenomenon which was only lethal to humans. For example, a virus or bacterial disease, such as the Plague or Black Death. Or something supernatural which was equally selective for humans (for example, simply blinking them out of existence)? In the words of the current debate raging across the United States, the Middle East, Central Asia, and many other countries around the world: why not use drones and smart bombs, rather than carpet bomb the area or send in whole armies to completely level the country?

The second question is: what was accomplished by this global destruction? We're told that it was done because of the wickedness of mankind: that *"every inclination of the thoughts of his heart was only evil all the time"* (Genesis 6:5). Then, after squashing flat the whole earth, and after the Flood waters had receded and the animals are brought out to replenish the earth, God says that he won't repeat this destruction *"even though every inclination of his [mankind's] heart is evil from childhood."* (Genesis 8:21). So it seems we're starting all over again, metaphorically 'with a clean slate', but the problem was never fixed. God declares that humanity is still wicked through and through. It's only inevitable that within a few generations the situation will be exactly what it was before the Flood. So what was the point of this horrible act? What did it achieve? Did God fail?

The third question has to do with why there are so many versions of a Flood account from so many diverse civilizations. Again, some take this as hard evidence that there was indeed a global flood: one that literally engulfed the entire known world and wiped out all human civilization as well as all other land- and air-dwelling life. Okay, that's one conclusion one could draw from the plethora of flood accounts (in the next paragraph, I discuss another, very different, one). And if it were indeed such a global phenomenon — involving such a volume of water that all the world's mountain ranges were covered, and then that volume of water receding to some other place — then I guess it would indeed have had to be a divine intervention. But it still leaves the question of why God would choose to do it that way.

However, some think it might just have been a localized, regional flood that would have left intact many animal populations (and possibly other human civilizations) in disparate parts of the globe. It's worth pointing out that, according to the dating scheme proposed by Ussher, the Flood would have occurred in the year 2349 BC, yet historical records from China and Egypt skip through that date without any mention of a massive world-wide flood that would have wiped out their civilizations. Likewise, there are tree ring data from bristle cone pines going back tens of thousands of years, including 5,000 year-old trees still alive today in the Western United States, old enough to have survived the Flood, that show no evidence of such a cataclysmic event. And the ice-sheets in Greenland with individual annual layers going back 100,000 years don't show evidence of layers which appear to have melted and re-frozen nor been mixed with silt (as would happen if they were covered with dirty floodwater), even though they do show layers with the dust from the Krakatoa and Vesuvius eruptions.

I'll admit that the wording of Genesis chapters seven and eight do claim that this was a global flood --- *"The waters rose and increased greatly on the earth, and the ark floated on the surface of the water. They rose greatly on the earth, and all the high mountains under the entire heavens were covered."* (Genesis 7:18-19) --- but this could equally refer to only that part of the earth that the Hebrew writers knew about at that time (that is, the Mesopotamian region only). For example, hundreds of years later, when Joseph is said to be the acting ruler over the Egyptian empire, Genesis says *"all the world came to Egypt to buy grain from Joseph, because the famine was severe everywhere."* (Genesis 41:57). I highly doubt that people were arriving in Egypt from China or South America to buy grain. When the Israelites are about to enter Canaan, God himself says to them: *"This very day I will begin to put the terror and fear of you on all the nations under heaven. They will hear reports of you and will tremble and be in anguish because of you."* (Deuteronomy 2:25). Do you think the North American Indians were concerned about the Israelites in Canaan? When the Bible says that *"... Jews from every nation under heaven ..."* (Acts 2:5) were gathered in Jerusalem to witness the Holy Spirit coming down at Pentecost, is it referring also to Inuit Jews, Chinese Jews, and Jews from Peru or Australia? (I'm not saying there were Jews in those countries at that time, but the wording does imply that there were because they were each 'one of the nations under heaven'). For these reasons, I don't think we need to interpret Genesis's use of the concept "global" in the same way that we would today. Perhaps the Genesis account is instead a story built up by the ancient patriarchs, possibly by borrowing extensively from other cultures (again, I'll deal with this in much greater detail in the eighth chapter).

There's another valid explanation — one from sociology — as to why there might be so many accounts of a tremendous flood which wipes out civilization. A very large fraction of human civilizations are found near water. Whenever you see a satellite picture of the earth's surface at night, take notice of all the bright lights – cities – which are localized to the coasts (Figure 10). If those satellite images could also display the inland bodies of water, you'd see that most of the other (non-coastal) pin-points of light are situated at the edges of lakes and rivers. Large human populations are more likely than not to be found at the edge of some large body of water (ocean, sea, lake, river). This is partly because life needs water to survive, and cities of people require huge amounts of water. It's also because many agricultural and industrial activities need water, and because it's very easy to transport goods and people by water. Things are different now: with our technology, we can build cities in the middle of the desert. But down through the ages, especially in ancient times before the extensive development of roads and motorized vehicles and cross-country travel, people have tended to congregate by the water's edge. And for this reason, flooding has been a relatively common event in the human experience. It's very common for any given generation at any time in history to remember a particularly terrifying and devastating flood event. Floods of cities situated by a sea or ocean are often the result of tsunamis, hurricanes and cyclones. Right now, many people are worried about the flooding that might be caused by global warming and the melting of earth's glaciers: The New York Times provide an interesting interactive web-page which shows several major cities around the US and the loss of land that would result if sea level changed by amounts ranging from five to twenty five feet [106]. Floods of cities situated near rivers and lakes are more likely due to massive rainfalls (for example, during hurricanes, cyclones, or monsoons) or the breaching of

---

[106]   The New York Times, Sunday Review "What Could Disappear" <http://www.nytimes.com/interactive/2012/11/24/opinion/sunday/what-could-disappear.html?_r=0> (accessed May 10, 2013)

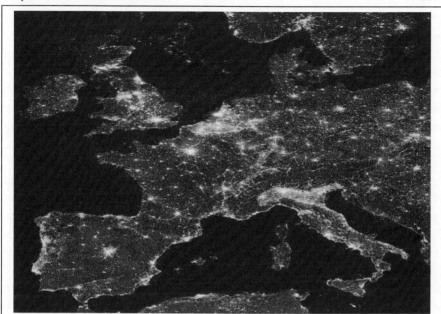

Figure 10 Satellite view of Europe at night-time. Used by permission obtained from NASA Earth Observatory.

some form of dam (for example, one made of mud, rock or ice) suddenly giving way and draining an entire lake or river onto an unsuspecting populace. Floods are everywhere, and reported in the news many times every year (I would even hazard to say every month of the year).

The bottom line is this: as humans tried to understand their relationship with the gods, a few archetypal stories would materialize. One recurring theme in the world's religions is humans displeasing the gods. And if a god was going to destroy a whole civilization in judgement of their sins, a flood was something that people could easily relate to from personal experience or first-hand eye-witness accounts from the village elders at fireside gatherings of the community. It certainly was a very frequently recurring problem in ancient Mesopotamia (that name means "land between rivers"), Egypt (situated at the mouth of the Nile River) and other parts of the Middle East. Massive destruction of a whole human population by flooding is much more common than an equivalent level of destruction caused by earthquake, volcanic eruption, fire, wind, lightning or any other means including bacterial or viral plague.

Finally, much is made about the fact that so many different accounts from various civilizations around the world talk about some kind of boat on which the survivors brought animals. But if you accept that floods have been an incredibly common experience in human history, and almost certainly the tool of destruction that the ancients believed a god would use against whole societies of humans, then answer me this: how does one escape a flood? A boat! And if you come from a pre-modern society that always had to stockpile food for the next half year or so until the next harvest ... **before** the time of rescue operations and relief efforts mounted by neighboring countries using airplanes, boats and other machines ... what would you do as you were scrambling onto that boat? You would grab some sacks of grain and some livestock, and maybe scoop a few other animals out of the raging waters to make some stew with. And if you, as an ancient flood survivor, believed that you were spared because of the good grace of your particularly divine protector, or otherwise wanted to appease the still simmering anger of the destroying divinity, what would be the first thing you do when you step out onto dry land? You would thank the one divinity and/or submit to the other divinity. And how did everyone communicate with divinities in those times? They offered animal sacrifices. So are these parallels with the Genesis story of Noah really all that surprising?

I'm now totally inclined to believe that this explains the origin of the Babylonian/Sumerian flood story in the Epic of Gilgamesh, and that the writers of the Pentateuch borrowed from those much earlier texts in trying to understand YHWH (God).

THE NEPHILIM

A very bizarre little vignette appears in the sixth chapter of Genesis, immediately before the account of the Flood, but I've chosen to deal with it after my discussion of the Flood, where I introduced the ancient Mesopotamian texts. You'll understand why in a moment.

First, the vignette: *"When men began to increase in number on the earth and daughters were born to them, the sons of God saw that the daughters of men were beautiful, and they married any of them they chose. Then the LORD said, 'My Spirit will not contend with man forever, for he is mortal; his days will be a hundred and twenty years.' The Nephilim were on the earth in those days — and also afterward — when the sons of God went to the daughters of men and had children by them. They were the heroes of old, men of renown."* (Genesis 6:1-4).

Where do I begin? What might a traditional or literal interpretation mean by 'sons of God' in contradistinction with 'daughters of men'? The context suggests to me that they're spiritual beings, since they're apparently different from humans. Would that make them angels? (Somehow I don't think they'd be called 'sons of God' if they were demons.) I didn't know that angels could have sex with humans. Do they have sperm? And even if they did, does their sperm have all the right complementary chromosomes to produce a viable fetus (given what we now know about reproduction between species, unless you're claiming that angels and humans are the same species)? In Mark 12:25, we read that angels don't marry, but this says nothing about whether they have gender or engage in sex. On the other hand, maybe these 'sons of God' were aliens, which would also distinguish them from 'daughters of men'; but I wouldn't know what to do with that conjecture. And irrespective of who these beings are that are having sex, what does any of that have to do with God not wanting to "*contend with man forever*"? Could it mean that the progeny of this apparently unholy communion inherited eternal life from their sons-of-God-fathers, which would explain why God fixed the problem by limiting lifespans to 120 years? Did they somehow represent a threat to God, given that he felt he had to step in to impose this limitation? How else can one 'contend' with God such that the problem is fixed by limiting a lifespan? I have to admit that my questions are starting to get stranger than the story itself.

On the other hand, it makes a great deal more sense if we suggest that this was yet another story borrowed from the ancient Mesopotamian texts. But to explain why I say this, let me first give you some quick facts: a Mesopotamian Mythology 101. The Babylonians wrote about a supreme triad: Anu (the Sky God), Enlil (the Earth god), and Ea (a deep ocean God). Then there was a pantheon of lesser gods: the kindly Mother Goddess, Lady of the Gods; the violent Adad, god of the storm; Sin, the Moon God; Shamash, the Sun God; Ishtar, the goddess of sexual love and war; the list goes on and on. One of those lesser goddesses, Ninsun, created/birthed a human named Gilgamesh, who is therefore one of the sons of the gods and yet human. Enlil sent a massive flood to destroy humans because they were reproducing like flies yet not dying, and their increasing numbers were keeping him awake at night with all their noise. (Seriously: I'm not making this up.) But the plan fails due to the intervention of Ea and Utnapishtim (as described in the section above), and so the gods decide to better control the humans by limiting their lifespans.

So, it makes more sense to me that the authors of Genesis, when they developed their own account of the Flood sent by YHWH to destroy humanity, they not only used the Mesopotamian texts to develop the flood story itself, but at the same time tried to integrate these other details in the Mesopotamian myth texts. Details like the phrase in the Bible: "*When human beings began to increase in number on the earth*" ... and God 'contending' with humans ... and solving the problem by limiting their lifespans ... and the *"sons of God"* reproducing with *"the daughters of men"* producing *"the heroes of old, men of renown."*.

THE TOWER OF BABEL

Shortly after the Genesis account of God destroying humanity because he *"saw how great man's wickedness on the earth had become, and that every inclination of the thoughts of his heart was only evil all the time"* (Genesis 6:5) and was grieved by their violence (Genesis 6:11,13), we have yet another story of him intervening in the activities of people. But from our 21st century and Western point of view, many of the recorded details of this story are simply inconsistent with a God of love and power. Briefly for those who aren't familiar with the story recorded in Genesis 11:1-9, 'The Lord' hears that people are up to something big in the plains of Shinar, goes to check it out, feels a need to disrupt their activities, so decides to put an obstacle in the way to keep them in their place.

In at least two ways, this story greatly diminishes the power and grandeur of God.

First, in contrast to the idea that God exists everywhere and knows all things, here he *"came down to see the city and the tower that the men were building"*. Not very omnipresent or omniscient. But second, and more strangely to me, is his response to the sight that he now sees, having come down to look: *"If as one people speaking the same language they have begun to do this, then nothing they plan to do will be impossible for them. Come, let us go down and confuse their language so they will not understand each other."* (Genesis 11:6-7). I don't know who the 'us' is that he refers to. If it's the angels, why does he seem to be explaining or justifying his actions to them? If it's the other members of the trinity, why did he have to return to heaven to confer with them about how to handle this situation (since he had already 'come down' to check things out, and was now inviting them to 'go down' again to respond to what he or they saw)? It just challenges my notions of omnipresence and omniscience.

Second, there's the capriciousness of God's response to this one city, or this one activity of people. It isn't a response to wicked acts, like the story of Sodom and Gomorrah which we'll come to in the next section. All we're told about their motives for building the city and the tower is that they: (1) wanted to reach to the heavens; (2) wanted to make a name for themselves; and (3) didn't want to be scattered.

Regarding motive #1, isn't this simply humans wanting to explore? All through our history we've walked/marched to every corner of the land masses we stand on, sailed across every sea/ocean, and now we're trying to move out into the cosmos using satellites, probes, space stations and rockets. I think God put within us that inclination to explore: perhaps it's related to his command to 'subdue the earth'? Or maybe it's just that urge in us to find God himself? In that sense, this could represent a literal attempt to reach heaven. The ancients believed that the sky was a solid dome — an upside-down bowl — that rested on the mountains and which contained the celestial bodies: I'll come back to this idea in great detail in chapter eight. So perhaps they thought they could build a tower that literally (in their world-view) brought them to the front door of heaven. But I don't believe God would be threatened by that. I mean, how high can you make buildings out of sun-baked brick and mortar anyway? Ten stories high? Maybe twenty? Does God face a greater threat today from the towers and buildings that we can now build, which far, far exceed the heights and scales of anything that could have been built in the year 2000 BC? Is heaven a physical place that can 'be reached'? Others will say that this tower which reaches to the heavens was a 'ziggurat', a religious structure dedicated to a foreign god. Okay, but *Homo sapiens* has been setting up other religions for millennia? Why was this one so deserving of destruction?

As for motive #3 — not wanting to be scattered — why is that so bad? People have often recognized the efficiencies of urban living, and/or wanted to gather together in close-knit groups with common interests: churches, denominations, ethnic families, rotary clubs, Star Trek conventions, rock star fan clubs.

I've heard more than one person say that this represented a direct act of disobedience of God, since we were commanded to *"fill the earth"* (Genesis 1:28), not gather together into cities. Although the text does quote God as saying "*Be fruitful and increase in number. Fill the earth and subdue it*", I wouldn't call this a command to disperse, and there's no indication of a penalty if humans don't disperse (such as the command to "not bite into the apple" and the penalty indicated if they chose to defy that command). Besides, if that were the case, then God would have said something to Cain as well. The first thing Cain is said to have done after killing his brother (over jealousy of God's acceptance of their offerings) and being banished from his family is to build a city (Genesis 4:17). (as an aside, 'building a city' seems to me to be a very strange thing to do if the only people around at the time are you, your two parents, your dead brother, and your wife, who appears out of nowhere in this very confusing story).

Motive #2 seems to me to be the main reason that 'the Lord' (whoever that was in this story) would condemn this action of humans. This desire to make a name for oneself has been the ambition of countless billions of people all through history. But perhaps this was more an act of arrogance, something that would lead to pride. I don't see anything wrong in simply having an honest but contained pride in a great achievement. Otherwise we should stop giving out first prizes for things and stop having races, sports competitions, graduation ceremonies, et cetera. But when that pride eclipses our perception of dependency on God, and we essentially see ourselves as our own gods or at least masters of our own destiny, that's where the trouble starts. Perhaps that's what 'the Lord' meant when he said *"nothing they plan to do will be impossible for them"* ... successful completion of this tower might lull humans into the false sense of self-sufficiency: that we are our own gods. So it wasn't so much that we represented a threat to 'the Lord' or might storm the gates of heaven, but that we were a threat to ourselves. But again, that level of pride and arrogance has been repeated all through history: why was this one singled out for judgement?

Finally, there's the oddity of God's solution to the problem: let's confuse their languages and then they won't be able to work together. Haven't people with different languages been co-operating on various levels (commerce; war; building projects) since the dawn of time? Did he not anticipate British and French teams digging 'the Chunnel' underneath the English channel a few thousand years later? Or the building of the International Space Station by dozens of different countries speaking different languages? Or the accomplishments of linguists who recovered long-lost languages using computers, mathematics, and artefacts like the Rosetta stone? Anyone who has immersed themselves into an entirely different culture and picked up enough of the local language within six months to converse comfortably can attest to what a short-term solution this confusion of languages would have been. Even people who have lost the ability to speak or hear at all can still function quite well in society: in fact, think about the story of Helen Keller, the woman who was born without the ability to speak, hear or see, and who still learned how to communicate! Clearly, diversity of language is not a big obstacle for humans.

I'm also puzzled that the story begins with the line *"Now the whole world had one language and a common speech"* (Genesis 11:1), when the previous chapter describes a world full of different languages. Chapter ten provides a long list of the various Canaanite people groups existing at that time (and historians confirm that these groups had different languages [107]), and the concluding verse of each of the three sections of these clan groups

---

[107] William G. Dever, *Who Were The Early Israelites and Where Did They Come From?* (Eerdman's Publishing Co., Grand Rapids / Cambridge, 2006)

refers to their distinct languages: ... the Japhethites: *"From these the maritime peoples spread out into their territories by their clans within their nations, each with its own language"* (v. 5) ... the Hamites: *"These are the descendants of Ham by their clans and languages, in their territories and nations"* (v.20) ... the Semites: *"These are the sons of Shem by their clans and languages, in their territories and nations"* (v. 31; emphases added).

In the end, I can only chalk this story up to the authors ... an ancient people ... trying to explain the diversity of languages, and possibly explore the tension between the human and the divine: the former always trying to reach beyond their place in the cosmos, and the latter putting them back in their place.

THE DESTRUCTION OF SODOM AND GOMORRAH

After recounting three stories of God's displeasure with people and his acts of judgment against us, we have yet another genocidal destruction story: in Genesis chapters 18 and 19, the destruction of Sodom and Gomorrah. Again, I think most readers are familiar with the story, but for those who aren't: briefly, God hears about the wickedness of a particular pair of cities, goes to check out whether the rumours are true and/or how bad things are, concludes they are in fact very bad, and destroys the cities by fire and brimstone, but not before warning a righteous family to flee (but killing one of their members for not following instructions). Much of what I'll write about this story is similar to what I wrote about the story of the Tower of Babel above.

On the one hand, this story diminishes the power and grandeur of God. Although God is otherwise said to be omniscient and omnipresent, he here confides with Abraham that he's visiting the city because: *"The outcry against Sodom and Gomorrah is so great and their sin so grievous that I will go down and see if what they have done is as bad as the outcry that has reached me. If not, I will know."* (Genesis 18:20-21). Why did he need to *"go down and see"*? Why did he say: *"If not, I will know"*? Most Christians would say that he would already have known, because he is everywhere and knows everything.

On the other hand, God comes across as extremely capricious on three counts: in how he deals with humanity in general (the two cities as a whole) and with two individuals (Lot, and Lot's wife).

First, these two cities are destroyed because there aren't even ten righteous people living in them (Genesis 18:23-33). The justice of this judgement would be more evident if there was any indication that all the other city's inhabitants had been taught what was right versus wrong but chose to break God's commands: but this all takes place long before God delivers his laws to Moses ... long before there were synagogues or churches ... long before prophets and religious teachers. They hadn't yet rejected any instruction because they'd never received any (at least, we're never told otherwise). In the absence of that religious instruction, is it surprising that the outcome was any different than what is written about the Israelites in the book of Judges: *"every man did what was right in his own eyes"* (Judges 17:6 [NASB]). By the way, on this point of the nature of the wickedness of Sodom and Gomorrah which was so deserving of utter destruction, many Christians might say it was sexual in nature, primarily with respect to homosexuality, because of the strange anecdote in the first half of chapter 19. But a very different reason [108] is given in the book of Ezekiel, in a prophecy against the city of Jerusalem: *"Now this was the sin of your sister Sodom: she and her daughters were arrogant, overfed and unconcerned; they did not help the poor and needy. They were haughty and did detestable things before me. Therefore I did away with them, as you have seen."* (Ezekiel 16:49-50). Evidently, God was equally concerned with their self-indulgence, with their indifference to the poverty all around them, and with their arrogance, as he was about their morality. I find it hard to believe that those two cities were distinct in these respects among all other cities of that particular time, let alone innumerable other cities since then: all through history, and even into today, we have shown the same lack of concern for our hungry and poor, the same arrogance, and the same moral laxity as is described for Sodom and Gomorrah. So what does this say about God's justice in singling out only these two cities to be destroyed?

Second, the capriciousness of God also comes out in the way he deals with Lot (Abraham's nephew) and Lot's wife. Although God destroys two entire cities because they lack even ten righteous people, he first warns Lot to flee with his family, which suggests (at least to me) that those were the few remaining righteous people in that city. Yet, in a very curious scene which preceded this story, when the men of the city call out to Lot: *"Where are the men who came to you tonight? Bring them out to us so that we can have sex with them"* (Genesis 19:5), consider the response from Lot: *"No, my friends. Don't do this wicked thing. Look, I have two daughters who have never slept with a man. Let me bring them out to you, and you can do what you like with them. But don't do anything to these men, for they have come under the protection of my roof"* (Genesis 19:7-8). This doesn't sound

---

[108] Walter Brueggemann, *Interpretation: A Bible Commentary for Teaching and Preaching.* (John Knox Press, 1982)

to me like the words of a righteous man (2nd Peter 2:7 refers to Lot as *".... a righteous man, who was distressed by the depraved conduct of the lawless ...."*). This story, together with another one a couple chapters later in which Lot's daughters conspire to get Lot drunk in order to become impregnated by him, justifiably leads Richard Dawkins to exclaim *"If this dysfunctional family was the best that Sodom had to offer by way of morals, some might begin to feel a certain sympathy with God and his judicial brimstone"* [109]. When I weigh the relative merits of demanding the right to rape visiting guests versus encouraging, or at least condoning, the rape of one's own daughters, I don't see why Lot deserved protection while his friends deserved destruction. On the other hand, this strange response is entirely consistent with an ancient, patriarchal viewpoint in which hospitality and respect of house guests were highly valued, and women were treated like mere property.

On top of this, when Lot and his family are then warned to flee the city, their instructions given by the two emissaries (that is, not by God himself) are simply *"Flee for your lives! Don't look back, and don't stop anywhere in the plain! Flee to the mountains or you will be swept away!"* There's no indication from the text that looking back had moral or lethal consequences, and yet Lot's wife is said to have been turned to a pillar of salt simply because she looked back (Genesis 19:26). It must have been pretty hard not to be curious when one can hear an entire city being destroyed by fire and brimstone. And not just any city, but in fact the very one that you lived in, which contained all your earthly possessions, your neighbours, your friends, possibly also your relatives. But in this case, 'curiosity killed the cat'. It just comes across as an extreme punishment for not following instructions. Note that I didn't write *"... punishment for not following God's command ..."*. One could argue such a direct disobedience of God's command would be a sin in the same category as Adam and Eve's direct disobedience by biting into the forbidden fruit and therefore equally worthy of harsh judgment. But there was no indication that this was a strict command that carried a death penalty, and it wasn't given by God but by his messengers (who admittedly represented God).

CONCLUSION

Why do I feel the need to focus a critical light on all these other stories of Genesis, as well as the story of creation in my 2nd chapter? Two

---

[109] Richard Dawkins, *The God Delusion* (Boston/NY; Houghton Mifflin Co, 2006)

reasons.

First, rather than being precisely literal, historical, unbiased accounts which stand up to the measuring stick that we apply to today's historical and scientific documents, I see these as being the best attempts of a writer, or a people, from several millennia ago to understand the origins of things and of a nation, and to explain humanity's relationship with God. To some extent, I agree with Jared Diamond, acclaimed scientist and author, about why humans down through the ages have shown a propensity for religion: religious teachings and writings serve a valuable function in explaining things, and thereby *"defuse our anxiety over problems and dangers beyond our control"* [110]. While he was in Egypt, Moses almost certainly saw the Sumerian tablets: in addition to the flood account, George Smith found that those Mesopotamian texts contained stories *"describing the creation of the world in six days as well as man's temptation and fall"* ... *In their account of the world's creation, the cuneiform tablets told of the initial chaos from which the universe was made and how, after each step along the way, the gods pronounced their creation good. Smith even found a tablet telling of the fall of a celestial being corresponding to Satan"* [111]. They tell of the great Aruru, the universal mother, creating a man from clay: *"... she pinches 'off a piece of clay, casts it out in open country,' where it becomes Enkidu, the warrior ...."* [112], and of *"... the jealous goddess Ishtar, who had a sacred 'tree of life', guarded by a serpent, ..."* [113] Those tablets also describe the life-times of the Sumerian kings as unbelievably long (thousands of years) before the Babylonian Flood but dropping suddenly to contemporary lengths after the Flood: this is exactly what Genesis does with the life-spans of the patriarchs before and after the Genesis Flood. Those Egyptian libraries would have had texts from other civilizations with comparable creation stories, as well as stories of gods destroying humans with floods, or fire and brimstone, or various plagues ... of gods having sex with humans and thereby producing giants or monstrous people (much like the Nephilim) [114] ... stories of people trying to rise above the limits imposed by the gods, and the gods then putting the humans back into their place (much like the Tower of Babel). Is it so unreasonable to suggest that Moses

---

[110] Jared Diamond, *The World Until Yesterday*. (Penguin Group, 2012)
[111] David Montgomery, *The Rocks Don't Lie: A Geologist Investigates Noah's Flood*. (WW Norton & Company, 2013), ch. 8
[112] Thomas Cahill, *"The Gifts of the Jews: How a Tribe of Desert Nomads Changed the Way Everyone Thinks and Feels."* (Bantam Doubleday Dell Publishing Group, 1998). page 23
[113] Thomas Cahill, *"The Gifts of the Jews: How a Tribe of Desert Nomads Changed the Way Everyone Thinks and Feels."* (Bantam Doubleday Dell Publishing Group, 1998). page 62
[114] Robert N. Bellah, *Religion in human evolution: from the Paleolithic to the axial age*. (Harvard University Press, 2011), ch. 7

might have adapted stories and explanations which had already been widely circulating for many centuries by the previous Akkadian, Sumerian and Egyptian civilizations?   Used them to explain the origins of things? Material things like the universe, life, humanity, pain in childbirth, why snakes don't have legs and elicit a deep-seated fear in humans, rainbows in a desert environment, the nation of Israel?   And immaterial things like language (Genesis 11:1-8), agriculture, the arts and metallurgy (Genesis 4:17-22), human sexuality (Genesis 2:18, 23-24), sin (Genesis 3), guilt, shame and the distinctly human need to be clothed (Genesis 3:7-12, 21) (in distinction to all the other animals)?   Acts 7:21-22 says: *"... Moses was educated in all the wisdom of the Egyptians ..."*.   And wouldn't it be even more reasonable if it were the post-exilic scribes who wrote the Pentateuch, who also had the Persian literature, knowledge and wisdom to supplement the Babylonian and Egyptian writings?

But second, and more importantly, I take exception to these stories as literally true because they portray God as harsh, impulsive, capricious and punitive.   They distort an image of God as being loving, kind and just. Completely different from the image of God that I see in Jesus Christ.   And I find it hard to accept them as is, without attributing them more to the folklore of an ancient Near Eastern people … Iron Age tribesmen.   I simply can't endorse these stories while telling my friends and colleagues that God loves them.

So why then do we have those stories in Genesis? Can they serve some other purpose than providing an accurate historical account of the beginning of all humankind in general?

To start with, they have importance to the Jewish people.   The OT was written by Jews for Jews, and these stories helped them root themselves in world history, to define who they are and declare the God that they worshipped [115] [116].   So many other civilizations — the Egyptian, Babylonian, Persian, Greek and Roman empires; the Chinese; the Inuit; the Mayans — likewise have stories and myths which describe where they came from, with the help of their unique patron gods.

But the OT writings also have some broader theological value for gentiles like ourselves in the 21st century.   They portray God as in control, and humans always failing God.   Inasmuch as they show God often casting judgement and destroying things, they equally show God stooping down to

---

[115] William G. Dever, *Who Were The Early Israelites and Where Did They Come From?* (Eerdman's Publishing Co., Grand Rapids / Cambridge, 2006)

[116] Peter Enns, *"When was Genesis Written and Why Does it Matter? A Brief Historical Study"* The Biologos Foundation. <www.biologos.org/projects/scholar-essays > (accessed Jan.-11-14)

help and redeem humanity: by clothing Adam and Eve ... putting a mark on Cain to protect him from vengeful siblings ... saving Noah and his family ... saving Lot and his family ... several times promising a saviour who will redeem them ... safeguarding the Jewish nation which would eventually bring us that promised Messiah ... et cetera. So I won't throw it all out. But neither will I hold the Genesis texts up to a higher level of authority than they ask for themselves.

8

Putting Genesis into context

How did we get the Bible?

Are 'the Bible' and 'God's word' the same thing?

Isn't all scripture inspired and given to us by God himself?

Who wrote Genesis? The Pentateuch? The Bible?

Infallibility and inerrancy of scripture?

Can we call into question the wording of scripture?

What's the danger in reading Genesis in a less literal light?

What's the danger in reading Genesis too literally?

HOW DID WE GET THE BIBLE?

So my honest and sincere searching for how to reconcile scripture with science (chapters two, three, four and five), as well as with my senses of morality and theology (chapters six and seven), led me to take a good close look at the Bible. Why is it so hard to reconcile with so many plain and simple concrete facts all around me, as well as with so many more abstract beliefs, moralities and philosophies? What exactly is the nature of the Bible's authority? These and many other similar questions motivated me to take a much closer look at its origins, inspiration, authority, inerrancy, and infallibility. But before we talk specifically about those ideas, it's important to understand how we received this book we call the Bible. Unfortunately, many people including contemporary Christians know very little about this.

The Bible is not a book that was hand-written by one human author. I'm sure most readers knew that already on a surface level, but it's useful to take a really close look at this fact and keep it front and centre as we talk about Biblical authorship and inspiration. Almost every other book that the average person will read today will have had one author, and every one of those books will have been written with an explicit intent that each chapter has a specific place in the developing storyline or message of the book. Some of those chapters might have numbered sections to help the reader place the various thoughts in context or within a framework. All of those books will also have been authored with the punctuation in place, and will have been submitted to the publisher with all the pages fully intact and in order.

None of these points apply to the Bible. None.

Many dozens of different human authors delivered to us the various books of the Bible. In most cases, those authors never met nor communicated with each other. The books they wrote did not have numbered chapters or numbered verses (those were added thousands of years later by Archbishop of Canterbury Stephen Langton in 1227 AD): every sentence just ran right into the next, without any of those kinds of linguistic clues that the reader is now moving into a new idea or section. In many cases, the books didn't even have punctuation. In case the importance of that last point is missed by the reader, consider the different meanings of these two sentences when you simply change the punctuation:

"The man passed the orange dog, panting quickly."
"The man passed the orange? Dog panting quickly!"

This may not be the most elegant example, but it does make the point that punctuation can make a big difference, and it's up to the interpreter of the original Hebrew texts to decide which meaning makes the most sense.

Further complicating matters is the fact that ancient Hebrew had consonants but did not employ vowels, leaving it to the reader to insert the ones that made sense [117]. For example, the sequence of letters *"MKSNDRBLDRMT"* can have different sets of vowels inserted and be translated in English either as *"My key is under blue door mat"* or as *"Mike is an adorable dear, mate"*. The context of the surrounding sentences helps in deciding how to translate. Nonetheless, ambiguities remain and cause problems for translators. It is for this reason that some suggest the story of

---

[117] Daniel Jeremy Silver, *The Story of Scripture: From Oral Tradition to the Written Word.* (Basic Books Inc. Publishers New York), 1990

Elijah being fed by ravens while hiding from King Ahab (1 Kings 17:1-6) could equally be translated that he was fed by wandering Arabs.

Each of the writers of scripture authored one or a few books which in their mind was a stand-alone manuscript: they didn't know that their writings would be stitched together with other writings from authors who lived hundreds of years before or after them (Figure 11), and which lived in a village or city that was far beyond the distance that an average person would travel in a lifetime. Those other authors might as well have been on another planet.   When the authors of Isaiah finished writing that book (there's considerable debate as to whether Isaiah wrote the entire book himself, or whether others also contributed), neither God nor the human writers then said: *"Great, that's #23 out of 66. Now let's get Jeremiah to start #24"*. In many cases, these authors didn't know the other authors, nor had ever heard of them (again, given their separation in place and time). As

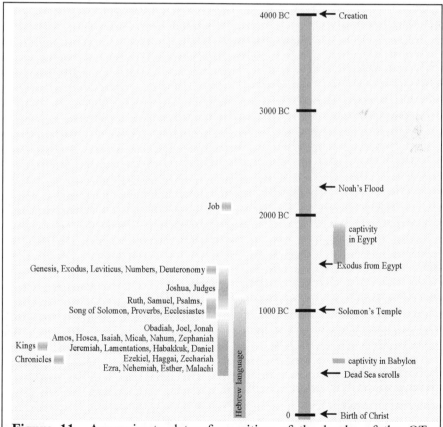

<u>Figure 11</u>   Approximate dates for writing of the books of the OT. Landmark biblical events are also shown. Notice the Biblical events which occur before the appearance of the Hebrew language itself.

Daniel Jeremy Silver noted, the gospel writer Luke did not know that his scroll would later become a part of scripture – holy writings – when he wrote his document: Luke simply *"indicated in his opening chapter that he knew of several inadequate biographies of Jesus and intended his book to be a useful and accurate correction of their failings; in his explanation of his purpose, there is not a word that he had prepared his scroll under the guidance of the Holy Spirit. Many of Paul's letters were clearly written as private letters to a particular church"* [118] (or individual in the cases of Titus, Philemon, Timothy, et cetera). Most of these texts were written as scrolls, and had no punctuation, and very little in the way of formatting (for example, indented paragraphs; headings; et cetera). Also, those 39 books of the OT were not the only Hebrew religious writings around at the time: hundreds of authors would have penned thousands of manuscripts describing other stories, other people, other genealogies, other songs and hymns. Those different manuscripts were then copied and re-copied, sometimes into other languages. (At this point, one could get into the issue of errors made and propagated in those reproductions. I won't discuss that here: it's a huge and highly contentious matter, about which much has been written. Suffice to say that many errors and 'apparent contradictions' exist. I'll leave it to the readers to pursue this themselves if they wish). Copies were then collected by libraries, synagogues, and individuals who were interested in them on an intellectual or spiritual level and/or saw them as art pieces. Only the copies of copies now exist anymore: we've long ago lost all the originals. In fact, most of the oldest copies exist only as fragments. The collections of writings varied from one place to another, depending on availability of the copies, the level of interest that each collection holder had in a given author or subject or historical/religious period, et cetera. As time went on, different scrolls came to be recognized as more authoritative than the rest and were kept and read regularly at the synagogues (particularly in the case of Judaism) and/or in home churches (particularly in the case of the nascent Christian church). In the year 325 AD — long after the life and ministry of Jesus, and also long after the birth of the Christian church — the Roman emperor Constantine called together Christian leaders to meet in the city of Nicea (present day Turkey) and come to a careful consensus on several theological and administrative matters. One of those matters was to identify which of the many manuscripts should be officially recognized as holy and inspired by God: 'canonized'. It was this Council of Nicea that gave us an initial version of the present day Bible (Figure 12). Not that

---

[118] Daniel Jeremy Silver. *The Story of Scripture: From Oral Tradition to the Written Word.* (Basic Books Inc. Publishers New York, 1990), p. 30

there's always been agreement on this canon: even as recently as 1522 AD, Martin Luther – the father of the Protestant Reformation – was advocating the removal of the books Hebrews, James, Jude and Revelation from the canon because they didn't line up with his theology.

Also around this time, the Greeks had all these books, written in Hebrew, translated into the common Greek language (which most of the civilized world spoke at that time): the Bible so produced is now called the Septuagint, which means "seventy" (referring to the seventy Greek-speaking Hebrew scholars involved in producing it). A little later, Pope Damasus I in Rome commissioned Jerome to translate all the Christian texts into Latin, producing the Vulgate (which is rooted in the Latin word for "common", as in "commonly used"). In 1604, King James VI of Scotland and I of England gathered together scholars and translators to translate those Hebrew, Greek

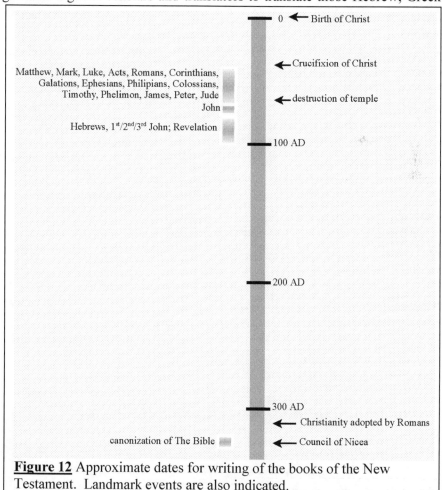

Figure 12 Approximate dates for writing of the books of the New Testament. Landmark events are also indicated.

and Latin texts in order to produce an English version of the Bible which would be officially approved by the Church of England (they took seven years to do this).

So why was that lesson in history necessary? To emphasize the point that the Bible represents only a few handfuls of scrolls, out of many thousands of different writings existing at the time. In Luke 24:45-47, Jesus refers to writings which don't match up easily with any text in the various Bibles I've looked into, which might suggest there was at that time another OT book that we've since lost, or that he was summarizing and paraphrasing several different writings. We've also lost books which are cited by OT writers: the Annals of Samuel the Seer (1 Chronicles 29:29); the Records of Nathan the prophet (1 Chronicles 29:29; 2 Chronicles 9:29); the Records of Gad the Seer (1 Chronicles 29:29); the Visions of Iddo the Seer (2 Chronicles 9:29 and 12:15); the Records of Shemaiah the prophet (2 Chronicles 12:15); the Book of the Wars of the Lord (Numbers 21:14); the Book of Jashar (Joshua 10:13); the Annals of the Acts of Solomon (1 Kings 11:41); Annals of the Kings of Judah (1 Kings 14:29). Other texts from Judeo-Christian writers and which are not included in my Protestant Bible include: the book of Enoch; Ecclesiasticus; the Wisdom of Solomon; the Acts of Thomas; the Revelation of Paul; the Apocalypse of Peter; the Gospel of Peter; the Gospel of Philip; the Gospel of Judas; the Gospel of the Nazarenes; the Gospel of Truth; Gospel of the Ebionites; the Epistle of Barnabas; Paul's letter to the Laodiceans; 3rd Corinthians; as well as many other texts which have been retained within the Roman Catholic Apocrypha. Depending on your Christian roots, some texts have been added or discarded, such that the Protestant Bible has 66 books, the Catholic Bible has 73, the Greek Orthodox Bible has 76, and the Ethiopian Orthodox canon has 81 books.

In summary, out of the hundreds or thousands of ancient writings which existed at that time, the books which have been kept in whatever version of the Bible you hold sacred today had been written over the course of nearly a couple thousand years by a few dozen different authors, then copied and re-copied, and translated and re-translated many times.

AUTHORSHIP AND INSPIRATION OF SCRIPTURE

An often quoted verse in the Bible reads *"all Scripture is God-breathed and is useful for teaching, rebuking, correcting and training in righteousness"* (2 Timothy 3:16). The King James Bible uses the wording

"All scripture is given by inspiration of God ...".

Most people, when they read or hear that verse, unconsciously substitute the words 'all scripture' with 'the Bible'. This verse (and this substitution) is an anchor point for people who hold emphatically to *"the infallibility and inerrancy of scripture"*, words and claims that are not made within or by the Bible itself. These two terms are a human invention ... derived doctrine... and they draw an unnecessary and dangerous line in the sand for unbelievers: just find one mistake, and we'll be forced to chuck the whole thing.

It's worth pointing out, though, that Paul wrote that particular verse almost 300 years before the Bible actually came into existence at the meeting of the Council of Nicea (Figure 12), which collated for us the present day Bible out of the many manuscripts which were available at that time, and there were indeed a great many other manuscripts circulating within Christian circles at that time. Daniel Jeremy Silver – of whom I already mentioned had impeccable credentials regarding Hebrew scriptural scholarship (see page 122) – put it this way: *"in Hellenistic times, the Temple in Jerusalem had a sizeable library which included, among many other works, scrolls that ultimately would be chosen as part of the Hebrew scripture. Many of these rolls, those that would be chosen and those that would not, were studied and believed in biblical times. Few besides the Five Books of Moses were treated as sacrosanct. No one was disturbed to find different versions of various classical narratives in circulation, nor to find scribes who copied them adding and emending"* [119]. So Paul clearly wasn't referring to 'the Bible' as we know it when he spoke about 'all scripture': the Bible itself didn't yet exist as an entity. Also, some of the books which were eventually included within the Bible hadn't yet been written when Paul wrote that verse, including Hebrews and all five of the books which are generally attributed to the apostle John (John's gospel; the three epistles of John, and Revelation) and possibly also 1st and 2nd Peter, and Jude. Although there may not be total agreement over the exact dating of their writing, the general consensus is that those ten books appeared many years or even decades after Paul's writing to Timothy (Figure 12).

So, when Paul wrote *"all Scripture is God-breathed ... "* to Timothy, what exactly did he mean by *"all Scripture"*? He likely was referring primarily to the books of the OT which were recognized by the Jewish leaders to be holy, and which were kept in the synagogues and read frequently (for example, see Luke 4:16-20 where Jesus himself is asked to

[119] Daniel Jeremy Silver, *The Story of Scripture: From Oral Tradition to the Written Word.* (Basic Books Inc. Publishers New York, 1990), p.5

read).

Next, what does it mean to say scripture is *"God-breathed"* or *"by inspiration of God"*? The apostle Peter gives us a passage that is often quoted in this context: *"... no prophecy of Scripture came about by the prophet's own interpretation of things. For prophecy never had its origin in the human will, but prophets, though human, spoke from God as they were carried along by the Holy Spirit"* (2nd Peter 1:20-21). But Peter is talking about a particular sub-genre of scripture ... prophecy ... and more specifically about prophecies pertaining to Jesus Christ as the Jewish Messiah. Other sub-genres which are quite distinct from prophecy include historical and anecdotal writings (for example, much of the first half of the OT), worship writings (for example, Psalms), wisdom literature (for example, Proverbs and Ecclesiastes) and Law texts (for example, Leviticus and Deuteronomy). Whatever it is that 2nd Peter is saying about the divine authorship of prophetic literature, there's no reason to automatically apply that to these other forms of literature. If you think differently, then I'm curious what you do with passages like Ecclesiastes 10:19 *"A feast is made for laughter, wine makes life merry, and money is the answer for everything."* or Ecclesiastes 8:15 *"So I commend the enjoyment of life, because there is nothing better for a person under the sun than to eat and drink and be glad. Then joy will accompany them in their toil all the days of the life God has given them under the sun."* And what you do with passages that conflict with respect to genealogical or other historical details.

Let's explore more closely the question of inspiration of the Pentateuch, since this contains the more problematic passages I wrote about in the previous seven chapters of this book. The study notes in my NIV Study Bible say: *"Historically, Jews and Christians alike have held that Moses was the author/compiler of the first five books of the OT"* [120]. That word 'compiler' is important: there's a lot of evidence that these five books were pieced together from many different sources and different authors. These different sources are characterized in part by very different writing styles (which, to linguists and scholars, can be like signatures or fingerprints), repetitions of certain stories with a few divergent details, striking similarities between the Pentateuch text and texts from other cultures, et cetera.

Moses may have been a prominent compiler in the putting together of the Pentateuch, although it's obvious that he had some additional human help, since Deuteronomy ends with Moses climbing Mount Nebo, talking briefly with God, then dying and being buried by God himself in a spot that

---

[120] NIV Study Bible. Notes regarding the book of Genesis.

nobody knows about (Deuteronomy 34:6)... who wrote that addendum? Numbers 12:3 gives us another indication that someone other than Moses contributed to the Pentateuch: it reads: *"Now Moses was a very humble man, more humble than anyone else on the face of the earth"*, which would otherwise be a very boastful comment for such a humble man to make. On the other hand, many biblical scholars make a strong case for the idea that the final version of the Pentateuch was written and compiled by Jewish scribes roughly a millennium after Moses, during and/or after the Babylonian exile (approximately 500 BC) [121] [122]. As Brueggemann puts it: *"there is no doubt that the text uses older materials ... is almost certainly sixth century and addressed to Babylonian exiles ... serves as a refutation against Babylonian claims"* [123]. Either way — whether the Pentateuch was largely compiled by Moses or by religious leaders in the Babylonian exile — it becomes important to consider the origins of the sources of their inspiration. How did they come up with the ideas that were written down in the text of Genesis (and the rest of the Pentateuch, for that matter) when they wrote about the Creation event, the Fall, the Flood, et cetera? There are only four options:

One, the author(s) saw the events first hand and wrote down exactly what they saw. However, the Creation story is supposed to have happened around the year 4000 BC (according to the timelines provided in Genesis itself), whereas Moses lived around 1500 BC, and the post-exilic scribes lived around 500 BC. I'm not aware that anyone would stand their ground on this first option.

Two, God dictated the stories to them, word-for-word, a view that some have described as 'divine ventriloquism'. Muslims believe this is how they received the Quran (although through the messenger angel Gabriel, not God himself). However, there are many discrepancies in the Biblical text, even though many Christians are adamant that scripture is inerrant and infallible. This view of divine ventriloquism would make God directly responsible for those errors, as well as the criticisms I've raised throughout chapters two to seven, and even calls into question his reliability. Those that hold this view have to come up with some explanation for the discrepancies between different books, as if God somehow 'had a senior's moment' and got his facts a little confused. I'm not going to list these discrepancies here

---

[121] R. Norman Whybray. *Introduction to the Pentateuch.* (Grand Rapids, MI; Wm. B. Eerdmans Publishing Co., 1995)

[122] Daniel Jeremy Silver, *The Story of Scripture: From Oral Tradition to the Written Word.* (Basic Books Inc. Publishers New York, 1990)

[123] Walter Brueggemann, *Interpretation: A Bible Commentary for Teaching and Preaching.* (John Knox Press, 1982), p.24

or get into specific examples of errors. Many others have written about this topic: it's a favourite subject for debate among those that want to do away with the Bible completely.   Any interested readers can research this themselves. David Montgomery devotes one chapter to the various debates about the inerrancy of Scripture and the many contradictions and errors found in the various ancient versions of the Bible (Hebrew versus Greek versus Latin) [124]. Daniel Jeremy Silver raises another interesting point pertaining to the idea that God is the direct author of the Biblical texts: *"The Deuteronomic histories (Samuel-Kings) actually cite earlier annals. Those who claim the whole Bible to be revelation are, therefore, forced to affirm the absurdity that God, like any professional historian, needed to provide footnotes to validate his observations"* [125].

Three, the author(s) of Genesis received their inspiration from God through impressions, visions, insights, et cetera. God guided their thought processes as they meditated and developed their theology, and pondered what to write down for future generations. A problem with this idea is that sometimes the thoughts and words that came out might still be tainted to some degree by the author's own thinking, experiences, prejudices, history, culture, social norms, et cetera. In fact, this is what I do see in certain places in the Bible. For me, Psalm 137 is the perfect example of this. Some readers may recognize the beginning of this psalm, since it was popularized on the radio in 1978 by a disco group who called themselves Boney M: *"By the rivers of Babylon we sat and wept when we remembered Zion ..."*. It's a lament from Jewish captives suffering horribly under Babylonian rule. But not many people remember how the psalm ends, and many of those that do know how it ends aren't sure what to make of it: "O *Daughter of Babylon, doomed to destruction, happy is he who repays you for what you have done to us — he who seizes your infants and dashes them against the rocks*" (KJV). I certainly don't believe God dictated those words to the writers of that psalm, nor do I think he moved them to that kind of hate and revenge. I have to believe that that's an example of the writers of that Psalm inserting their own sentiments and values into the Scriptural text: the fingerprints of people marring God's intended message. Likewise I can see the value system of Ancient Near Eastern authors legitimizing OT stories which are deplorable and unacceptable by today's standards ... Lot offering his virgin daughters to be raped rather than violating his houseguests (Genesis 19) ... a priest taking a prostitute for his wife and giving her to a gang of men to be

[124] David Montgomery, *The Rocks Don't Lie: A Geologist Investigates Noah's Flood*, ch. 8. (WW Norton & Company, 2013)
[125] Daniel Jeremy Silver, *The Story of Scripture: From Oral Tradition to the Written Word*. (Basic Books Inc. Publishers New York, 1990), p. 30

raped, then cutting up her body into pieces when he finds her dead the next morning (Judges 19) … the prophet Elisha calling down a curse on a group of boys because they were taunting his baldness, resulting in two bears coming out of the woods and mauling forty-two of the boys to death (2 Kings 2:24). In the same way that human values may have crept into these stories, the writers of Genesis (and the rest of the Pentateuch) would almost certainly have been influenced by their exposure to other creation narratives which were circulating throughout the world of that time, or even that they read for themselves in the courts of the Babylonians and Egyptians (possibly also the Persians and Greeks, if you accept that Genesis was finalized much later).

Four, the writers of Genesis intentionally and overtly adapted those other narratives from the cultures surrounding them, but now making YHWH the central player. Providing a Hebrew light and interpretation on Babylonian, Sumerian and Egyptian knowledge and tradition of that time; again, much like Paul did on Mars hill when he re-interpreted the Greek statue to the unknown God. There's a subtle difference between this fourth option and the third one. To clarify: in this fourth option the author literally gathers one or more of those non-Hebrew manuscripts, lays them open on the desk in front of himself and adapts or incorporates those other texts as he begins writing. In the third option, those other non-Hebrew manuscripts are only hovering as memories and subconscious influences in the back of his mind, but competing with God for input just the same and it's up to the author to sift through the two inputs.

For me, the first and second options are untenable, for the reasons already given. So that only leaves options three or four. Readers today can get a sense of what that inspiration looks/feels like, since the Bible extends that kind of inspiration to believers in general in Matthew 10:19-20 (the same instruction is given in Mark 13:11, Luke 12:11-12 and Luke 21:14-15), John 16:13, Acts 1:8, and 1 Corinthians 2:12-13. But that inspiration doesn't guarantee a flawless delivery: whether you accept the third or the fourth option I list above, either way the Biblical stories come to us through humans who left some of their own fingerprints on God's message. God's desire to involve people in the revelation and unfolding of his plan for man carries with it the potential for mistakes being made. In the story of the Israelites clamouring for water at Kadesh during their march through the desert, God could have just as easily spoken the water into existence himself, or to the rock to produce the water, but he chose to use Moses to do this. Moses let his emotions (frustration? anger? arrogance?) get in the way and he 'got it wrong' and God reprimanded him severely (Numbers 20:8-12). When the Greeks who had gathered in Cornelius' home-church also *"received the word of God"* (Acts 11:1) with the same manifestations described for the Jewish recipients in Acts 2, the leaders of the Christian church brought their Jewish mind-set into play and immediately criticized what was going on. They thought the whole new Christian movement was only meant for the Jews, but they too 'got it wrong' and had to be corrected by God (Acts chapters 10 and 11). There are just so many examples of God using humans to accomplish something rather than doing it himself, and those humans inevitably 'get it wrong'. Why can't we also accept that maybe the ancient writers brought their mindsets into play and they got parts of it wrong?

With respect to the writing of Genesis in particular, we do need to take into account how the message that God wanted to give us was filtered by the human minds and hands that received it and wrote it down. Would its authors or its intended recipients have understood something like the Big Bang ... matter/anti-matter ... gravitational forces producing cosmic bodies ... genetic mutations and natural selection ... et cetera? How could they ever comprehend the concept of billions of years? When God started interacting with humanity thousands of years ago, would he tell the story in a way that made sense to ancient people who were pre-scientific and Mesopotamian in their thinking, or would he tell it in a way that would be incomprehensible until a modern, Westernized society would appear 6,000 years later? Clearly the story had to be finessed and modified (colloquially, we say 'dumbed down') in order for its original hearers to understand and relate to it. Moreover, the writers of Genesis must have been influenced by the narratives of other cultures all around them. The nation of Israel was immersed within the Mesopotamian, Egyptian, Babylonian and Persian empires, at the very least as captives and slaves (the Biblical stories of Moses, Joseph and Daniel, even portray them as centre-stage players within those empires).

It shouldn't be surprising that the OT stories look so much like ancient Mesopotamian stories: linguists tell us that the Hebrew language in which the Bible was written didn't even exist until after those Mesopotamian societies were well developed, including their stories of the deities [126]. The Semitic alphabet (from which the Hebrew, Aramaic, Ammonite, Edomite, and Moabite languages arose) wasn't devised until around the year 1700 BC and the earliest evidence of the Hebrew language

---

[126] Thomas Cahill, *The Gifts of the Jews: How a Tribe of Desert Nomads Changed the Way Everyone Thinks and Feels.* (Bantam Doubleday Dell Publishing Group, 1998)

itself dates to around 1000 BC [127] [128] [129] [130] [131]. So those stories which tell of events which occurred as far back as 4000 BC (Creation; the Fall; Tower of Babel; the Flood; et cetera) or even 2000 BC (the stories of Abraham, Isaac and Jacob) must have been passed down in a Mesopotamian form: oral stories spoken in a Sumerian or Akkadian tongue for centuries or millennia until they evolved or matured into fully Hebrew stories. Also, remember that the Bible tells us that Abraham originated from the city of *"Ur of the Chaldees"* (Genesis 15:7), which was of Sumerian origin and even older than the Assyrian and Babylonian cultures. Joshua reminds the Israelites that *"Long ago your forefathers, including Terah the father of Abraham and Nahor, lived beyond the river and worshipped other gods"* (Joshua 24:2). It was those wandering nomads --- Abraham's family --- who were thoroughly Mesopotamian in their language and culture, who gave us the earliest stories in the Bible (unless one subscribes to the idea that the stories were developed or invented much later, during the Babylonian exile). A wandering society such as the Abrahamic/Israelite one would not have carried immense collections of clay tablets (which was the way people in Mesopotamia at that time recorded stories), so their stories must have been passed on in oral form. It's conceivable that, once they integrated into Egyptian society, the Hebrews committed those stories to papyrus scrolls. But that would have required some collusion on the part of the Egyptians and it would be hard to believe that those Egyptians would allow the Israelites to keep libraries of scrolls during the peak of their enslavement when the Egyptians decided to brutally oppress them. So it's quite likely that the Hebrews carried those stories still in oral form as they left Egypt (again, the dating of that event is disputed, but many would say that it occurred somewhere around 1500 to 1000 BC; others deny its occurrence altogether [132]). It was only sometime later – some scholars say it was during the Babylonian exile in the year 600 BC --- that these stories are actually written in a Hebrew tongue. And the earliest fragments of Hebrew writings

---

[127] Peter Enns, ""The Old Testament and ancient Near Eastern literature", in *Inspiration and Incarnation: Evangelicals and the Problem of the Old Testament.* (Grand Rapids, MI; Baker Academic, 3rd printing, 2007), ch. 2.

[128] William G. Dever, *Who Were The Early Israelites and Where Did They Come From?* (Eerdman's Publishing Co., Grand Rapids / Cambridge, 2006)

[129] Seth L Sanders, *The Invention of Hebrew.* (University of Illinois Press, Chicago, 2009)

[130] Israel Finkelstein and Neil Asher Silberman: *The Bible Unearthed: Archaeology's New Vision of Ancient Israel and the Origin of Its Sacred Texts.* Simon and Schuster, New York, 2002.

[131] Daniel Jeremy Silver, *The Story of Scripture: From Oral Tradition to the Written Word.* (Basic Books Inc. Publishers New York, 1990)

[132] William G. Dever, *Who Were The Early Israelites and Where Did They Come From?* (Eerdman's Publishing Co., Grand Rapids / Cambridge, 2006)

date back to only a few hundred BC [133]. As Peter Enns wrote: *"... regardless of when Genesis was written and in what language, it still reflects an ancient Near Eastern worldview that clearly is significantly older"* [134].

This idea that the OT writings are tainted by human involvement helps to explain other cringe-inducing stories in the Bible. Foremost among these are the descriptions of the conquest of Canaan, in which we're told that God directs the Israelites to go into various cities and territories to slaughter all the inhabitants in order to clear space for the incoming Israelites. Sometimes the commands specifically include the women, children and animals of those cities. In 1994, the whole world reacted in horror as the Hutus slaughtered the Tutsis in Rwanda. I've already written about the world's response to another similar genocide in Syria (page 10), and many other such horrible events have happened before and since. In each case, the perpetrators of those atrocities were condemned and deplored by the average person, as well as by the contemporary church. And yet when similar stories are given in the OT books of Numbers, Deuteronomy and Joshua, they are embraced as perfectly acceptable: these stories are sanitized by the justification that *"God ordered it"*. Personally, I find it oh so very hard to see a God of love and mercy issuing that kind of command, but find it much easier to see a people coming up with the idea themselves and justifying their acts of violence in the name of a god.

Some people remark on the fact that, despite there being so many different Biblical authors spread out over hundreds of years, isn't it amazing how much the different books concur. But two things need to be said. First, all those books were written within a very closed Jewish society with similar perspectives. Some would claim that there were in fact huge divisions within Jewish society, but any divisions between two groups of Jews would pale in comparison to the differences between a Jewish group and a Chinese group, for example. Second, the books of the Bible concur because they were specifically selected at the Council of Nicea: other contemporary books written by other Jewish/Christian authors that deviated from the main line (for example, the Gnostic Gospels) were rejected by that Council. So the concurrence among the different books is, at least in part, an artefact of the selective authorship and the selectivity of that Council.

One final comment on this matter of inspiration: we need to think not only about whether/how the original authors were inspired, but also

---

[133] Henry H. Halley, *Halley's Bible Handbook.* 24th edition, pp 843-846 (Zondervan Publishing House, 1965)

[134] Peter Enns, "The Old Testament and ancient Near Eastern literature". in *Inspiration and Incarnation: Evangelicals and the Problem of the Old Testament.* (Grand Rapids, Michigan; Baker Academic, 3rd printing, 2007), ch. 2, page 52.

about three other groups of people who were involved in the process of handing down the Bible to us. First, the Masoretic scribes who inserted the vowels and accents into the ancient texts hundreds of years after the latter were first written. These insertions had the potential to change the meaning of a word or even the sentence. Were those scribes equally inspired? Second, the Council of Nicea, which selected the books and manuscripts that would be incorporated into our scripture. There's no record of them having been inspired or divinely chosen: they were convened by the Roman emperor Constantine, a recently converted Roman general whose career aspirations included unifying and fortifying a crumbling Roman empire and then ruling it. You can read into that whatever vested interests you think he might have had. Finally, the various translators of the texts from one language to another: this too would require inspiration, since meaning is often lost and/or created during that transition. For example, two different sets of translators can take the same cryptic message from some long-lost civilization, and the one comes up with the phrase "out of sight, out of mind" while the other translates it as "invisible lunatic". Many comedies are based on the confusion that results when two different people interpret the same words differently: one that most readers might recognize today is Abbott and Costello's *"Who's on first?"*

The 'inerrancy and infallibility' of scripture

For some people, this is a bed-rock issue. But does the Bible itself ever claim to be infallible or inerrant? The short answer is: no.

Paul described it as *"useful for teaching, rebuking, correcting and training in righteousness"* (2 Timothy 3:16). This word 'useful' isn't exactly the strongest that he could have possibly used if he was aiming at 'inerrant and infallible'. Imagine there was some kind of threat that could destroy all of humanity and civilization, and world leaders declare *"we need the brightest mind available to solve the problem"*, and your best friend names you saying *"he would be useful in this situation"*. Not exactly a ringing endorsement, would you say? Other versions, including the King James, translate this word as 'profitable'. Both renderings are indeed positive, but certainly don't say 'infallible' or 'inerrant' to me.

In several other places, the Bible says that its writings give direction, encouragement, enlightenment. *"For everything that was written in the past was written to teach us, so that through the endurance taught in the Scriptures and the encouragement they provide we might have hope"* (Romans 15:4). *"Your word is a lamp for my feet, a light on my path"*

(Psalm 119:105). But neither of these convey the unbending dogmatism of 'inerrant and infallible'. Psalm 119 is an incredible love song aimed squarely and solely at the value and attributes of God's instruction – nearly every one of its 176 verses refer to the latter using the singular and plural forms of law, word, statute, commandment, judgement, precept, ordinance, testimony – and one could claim that they hint at inerrancy and infallibility (I myself don't make that claim). But those 176 verses aren't referring to the historical parts of the OT such as the creation accounts, the Flood and other destruction stories of Genesis, or the conquest of Canaan (these were completely separate scrolls/books when Psalm 119 was written), and certainly not to any of the books written after 1000 BC (that is, after the approximate dating of the writing of the Psalms) which make up the bulk of what we now call the Bible. Although Psalm 19 reads *"The law of the Lord is perfect ..."* (v. 7), it too doesn't seem to be referring to anecdotes like the Flood story or the Nephilim (otherwise, why would it refer to these as *"the Law"*?), nor to the Bible as an entirety (since most of the Bible was written centuries or millennia later). Besides, the word 'perfect' that it uses can also be translated blameless or complete rather than flawless, which is why the same word is used to describe the writer of this Psalm (v. 13) and another Psalm writer (119:1). No matter where I find passages of scripture that talk about scripture itself, I don't find wording that says 'inerrant and infallible' to me. What else can I conclude but that this doctrine of inerrancy and infallibility is also a product of the human mind?

That made me wonder where this doctrine came from. Augustine wrote to Jerome in 405 AD about the inerrancy of scripture [135]: *"I have learned to yield this respect and honor only to the canonical books of Scripture: of these alone do I most firmly believe that the authors were completely free from error. And if in these writings I am perplexed by anything which appears to me opposed to truth, I do not hesitate to suppose that either the manuscript is faulty, or the translator has not caught the meaning of what was said, or I myself have failed to understand it."* Notice that he specified 'the authors' as being completely free from error, not necessarily the books themselves, and also that he felt free to raise questions about the manuscripts if they didn't quite make sense to him. For example, he also held emphatically that Creation was a single instantaneous event, rather than being spread out over six separate days [136]. And church fathers (sorry ladies) ever since have shown varying dogmatism on this point. The invention of the printing press began to focus attention on the exact wording

---

[135] Augustine. Letter 82.3
[136] Augustine, *The Literal Interpretation of Genesis*

of the biblical texts. It was in the mid-1800s that Protestant scholars put out the idea of 'plenary verbal inspiration': that every word of the biblical text was the very word that God intended. But it's only been in the past century that the heat has been turned up to boil on this issue. I can't help thinking now that this fundamentalist movement is a defensive (over)reaction to the steady encroachment of science and societal norms into territories long held by Judeo-Christian thinking. It represents a palisade, an entrenching, a last-ditch effort against what it sees as 'attacks'. Unfortunately, that starts to sound like paranoia on the part of the church.

I've heard people comment on how amazingly well God preserved his word for us down through the centuries. One needs to be careful about how dogmatically to make a claim like this, because the fact is it doesn't look like the preservation went too well. There's been a complete loss of all the original texts, and far too much fragmentation of the copies of copies, and too many errors, variants and translational problems in the texts that we now have. If God intended for the very wording to be precise and reach us in an inerrant state, he could have preserved it much better. Some try to step over this problem first by referring to the errors as 'apparent errors' or 'apparent contradictions', as if that adjective somehow softens or removes the problem. It doesn't. The contradictions are still there, whether we qualify them with words like 'apparent' or 'perceived' or any other adjective.   Others will fully acknowledge that there are errors and contradictions in the copies we have today, but will insist that the originals were inerrant. The problem is that we haven't had the originals for at least one or two millennia. We only have copies of copies of copies. So there's no way to justify the insistence that the originals were inerrant. We might choose to believe that, but we can't know that for certain. One scenario that's consistent with the data at hand is that the originals had errors which were gradually cleaned up as copies were made and the errors noticed, but we just haven't finished 'fixing all the typos'. I'm not claiming this to be the case, just saying that it's a possibility that explains the data at hand, and that we simply can't know for sure that the originals were inerrant and infallible.

So I didn't find anything in the Bible that supports the claims of inerrancy or infallibility. Nor did I find any passages that distinctly said the Bible was written by God, nor dictated by God, although certainly inspired by God. In fact, the passages I found did not rule out the possibility that the Bible is a diary of the human experience with God. That it was written by humans who were searching after the God of Abraham, trying to understand him, learning things about him, taking 'one step forward and two steps back'. Making mistakes along the way. Peter Enns pointed out that in the same way that Jesus is referred to as 'The Word' (John 1:1-18) and is believed to be both human and divine, so the Bible is also God's word and is both human and divine [137].

So if the Bible doesn't plainly reject that idea – but leaves the door open on the idea that it is just as much a human document as a divine one – then I don't any longer feel wrong in using that view to help make sense of those otherwise very-hard-to-understand passages of scripture. It becomes much easier to solve many (all?) the problems I've referred to in this book if you take a much more lenient stance. It's very hard to explain the conflicts that Genesis has with science, or the Biblical stories of ethnic cleansing and the treatment of women, if you try to hang on to words like 'literal', 'inerrant' and 'infallible'. But it's much easier and more reasonable if you see the Bible as written by men from an ancient Near Eastern patriarchal viewpoint, with some truth revealed by God wrapped up within human ideas. And I would extend this beyond just the book of Genesis: the OT books as a whole were written to Jews, its religious commands written to a Jewish theocracy, its scientific explanations written to a pre-modern audience, its historical accounts written to a budding Jewish nation who didn't have the journalistic standards that we do. We have to work to find out how much of it pertains to us non-Jews in the 21st century. Just because the suggestion to treat some passages of Scripture as allegory raises some difficult, even scary, questions about other passages doesn't mean we should therefore turn a blind eye and not do that hard work of understanding what the message is, who it's from and what it means.

A friend who is also a pastor challenged me on this, asking essentially what right do I have to pick and choose how I read Biblical passages, and what I accept or believe or reject? My answer is that everyone does it to some extent, including the most fundamental, conservative, Bible-thumping individuals among us. When they read about the smoke coming from God's nostrils (2nd Samuel 22:9), and the many references to God's arms and feet. About the rivers and trees clapping their hands (Psalm 98:8; Isaiah 55:12). About the storerooms within the sky for snow and ice and rain and lightning (Job chapters 37 and 38). When the dietary laws teach that it is a sin to eat lobster or shrimp (Leviticus 11:10 and 12) or to cook meat with milk (Exodus 23:19; Exodus 34:26; Deuteronomy 14:21). In these passages and many, many others, we sift out the core truth hidden in the literary devices (metaphor, allegory, hyperbole, rhetoric, parable, poetry) and limitations of the human authors (world-view,

---

[137] Peter Enns, *Inspiration and Incarnation: evangelicals and the problem of the Old Testament.* (Grand Rapids, MI; Baker Academic Press, 3rd printing, 2005), p. 17

cultural and scientific sophistication). We read those passages through the lens of our own times, our own understanding and accumulated knowledge not just about the world and science, but also about God himself.

Some will declare that this is the beginning of a slippery slope. I think that response is just a popular slogan or learned reflex to avoid critiquing what one believes and why. Those more conservative individuals among us who talk about a 'slippery slope' need to see that they themselves are also on that same slope (albeit perhaps a part of the slope that isn't quite as steep). And furthermore, that the slope is man-made, an artefact of our elevating the Bible to an unnaturally high level, because I don't believe God would create such a precarious situation that requires a complete jettisoning of all faith if one finds even a single mistake or error in the text.

WHAT'S THE DANGER IN READING GENESIS IN A LESS LITERAL LIGHT?

I recently asked one fellow believer that question, and his answer was: "*In my mind, it all stands or falls together*". That worries me. That puts far too much on the line ... raises the stakes far too high. We needlessly hand a nuclear bomb to our detractors and dare them to "*just find one little thing wrong with the text and I'll be forced to reject the whole thing*". If you put all your eggs in one basket, what happens when the handle breaks? I've seen people, including family members, cast off their entire faith simply because they couldn't believe all of it, and therefore they felt they had to throw out all of it.

If you approach dating and marriage with the idea that there is one, and only one, person who you're destined to spend the rest of your life with, then dating becomes an incredibly risky endeavour fraught with the danger of missing the right choice, and in so doing utterly messing up your entire life. The decision doesn't have to be so razor-edged. In the same way, if your view is that the whole Bible has to be literally God's very words — every passage being complete, inerrant, and infallible — then to start considering certain parts of it as allegory or metaphor suddenly becomes the beginning of a slippery slope, at the end of which you're forced to the conclusion that you have to "*chuck the whole thing*". Does it have to be all or nothing?

I asked another friend: "*Why should I accept the book of Genesis as literally true?*" His answer: "*Well, to begin with, Jesus endorsed it*", to which I asked: "*but was that for the sake of his audience?*" Jesus himself said he was sent to the Jews, the lost sheep of Israel (Matthew 15:24). So to best get their attention, he used the scriptural writings which they valued above everything else except God himself; something they could relate to; something that was woven into their very lives. At one point, Jesus referred to the story of Noah: *"As it was in the days of Noah, so it will be at the coming of the Son of Man. For in the days before the flood, people were eating and drinking, marrying and giving in marriage, up to the day Noah entered the ark; and they knew nothing about what would happen until the flood came and took them all away. That is how it will be at the coming of the Son of Man"* (Matthew 24:36-41). Okay, on the one hand this reference could be seen as a bona fide 'endorsement' of the actual Flood story. But on the other hand, Jesus could be using an image that his Jewish listeners would have visualized many times as children and as adults: an image of a depraved humanity focusing on the temporal, oblivious to the eternal, until it was too late. He could have been simply using an allegory that this Jewish audience could relate to. Today, when talking to a younger audience, one might refer to a movie clip to emphasize a point: *"... just like when Skywalker was battling Darth Vader, and the imperial storm-troopers were closing ranks around them, and then Yoda ..."*. Doing so doesn't imply that you believe George Lucas's *Star Wars* is actual history. It's just a useful communication tool to convey imagery and make a point. I'd make the same argument for Jesus's reference to Jonah and the whale (Matthew 12:40): a picture paints a thousand words. I didn't find Jesus making any references to the six days of creation, and most importantly, I thankfully did not find anything which could be remotely construed as his support for stories like the conquest of Canaan. There were other instances where he appeared to be using the imagery of certain OT characters or stories as an anchor for the theology he was teaching: morality (Matthew 5:21, 27, 31, 33, 38; 15:3,4), the Beatitudes (Matthew 5:1-10), and stories of David (Matthew 12:3-8), and Solomon (Matthew 6:29; 12:42). There were other instances where it's clear he wanted a literal reading/interpretation from the OT: when he was being tempted in the desert (Matthew 4:6), and when he claimed to be the fulfilment of the law (Matthew 5:17) and of many prophecies of the coming Messiah (Matthew 11:1-5; 13:11-17).

WHAT'S THE DANGER IN READING GENESIS TOO LITERALLY?

I alluded to the answer to this question in the introductory chapter of this book. My own experience was that Genesis almost robbed me of my faith!   On the one hand, because of the increasing tension between a dogmatic interpretation of a YE theology and scientific discoveries of a very old earth arising through naturalistic processes, I thought I had to choose between faith versus fact; between scripture versus science. On the other hand, when I read many of the stories in Genesis and other parts of the OT, I saw a God who was too often displeased, angry, vengeful and wanting to punish and destroy; rather than a God of love. For both reasons, I found it harder and harder to share my 'good news' with people around me. I could have followed the example of many other Christians around me, including members of my own family: at least keep silent about my faith, or at worst abandon the whole thing.

That's my own personal experience. But let's now look at the experience of Christians in general down through the ages. In order to maintain a certain interpretation of scripture, the church has frequently had to go to great lengths and through amazing contortions. As an illustration of this point, consider the geocentric theory: the idea that the sun — and the whole universe for that matter — revolves around the earth (chapter two). It was so mind-numbingly easy for astronomers and physicists to draw a diagram of a tiny sun and its circular orbit around a centrally placed and much larger earth, and to represent that with an actual model of a little shiny ball on a stick spinning around another stationary ball. But then they added in the moon, also orbiting around the earth, but had to scratch their heads to figure out how to explain the various phases of the moon as it waxed and waned between what we call a new moon and a full moon. And it got even more complicated when they tried to add in the various planets as they raced across the sky, some faster than others, and some even seeming to slow down and then speed up.   They kept making ever more complicated diagrams, and models with all kinds of added gears to reproduce the changes in orbital speeds and rotations of those cosmic bodies. All because an interpretation of Genesis seemed to demand it. Until they accepted the simplest explanation: the heliocentric theory. Then it became possible to draw very simple diagrams, and make elegant physical models. And move on from there to ever greater discoveries about our solar system and the rest of the universe.

In the same way, creationists who insist on a certain interpretation of Genesis, have to devise ever more complicated models, scenarios and explanations in order to explain the origins of everything. Proposing the concept of 'apparent age' to explain some discrepancies. Attributing the abundance of evidence of a gradual evolution to God wanting to test our faith. Suggesting the existence of an earlier earth ruled by Lucifer — long before Adam, Eve and the Garden of Eden — which was destroyed by God, in order to explain the very long age of earth's rocks and the fossil record. God temporarily relaxing the rules around incest until Adam and Eve's children and grand-children could get the human race started and then later adding a harsh penalty against it, or creating husbands and wives for those children but not including that detail in the 'historical' account. Tremendous torrents of water from a receding flood explaining major geological features (for example, the Grand Canyon), while at the same time declaring that those waters were gentle enough to leave animals intact and sometimes with the food still in their mouths, to be eventually fossilized. And further, that those dead animals settled out in various layers, from less complicated to more complicated to give us the layers in the fossil record; except that it would be the larger, heavier animals (that is, those that were more complicated or evolved) that would sink faster than the smaller, lighter (less evolved) animals. Explaining how Tubal-Cain could be born shortly before the Bronze Age and a couple thousand years before the Iron Age but still have "*forged all kinds of tools out of bronze and iron*" (Genesis 4:22) by invoking cryptic generations and unusually long life-spans.

I could go on with other examples of how certain interpretations of Genesis require ever more hand-waving and tenuous explanations and cognitive dissonance to explain simple scientific discoveries. But the same thing is also done to explain discrepancies at a moral or theological level: for me, this is so much more hideous and dangerous.

For example: in order to justify the conquest of Canaan — which includes the slaughter of women and babies — we invoke concepts like 'holy war' and 'just war' and 'divine justice'. We try to convince ourselves that it was better for those babies to be killed because they went straight to a blissful existence in heaven but would otherwise have been raised by godless, immoral, idol-worshipping heathen parents. Wouldn't it be better for the Israelites to simply adopt those children (and even the animals, and assimilate those adults who were open to exchanging their understanding of God), and thereby rescue them from such a godless life. Some might answer back that those children would lead the Israelites astray, into a worship of the very same idols which their biological parents worshipped. My rebuttal to that: not if they were adopted young enough, when they're just so malleable, or even when they're older and could be taught about the much greater God of love. If one were to come back yet again that those children would rebel anyway because they were destined (by God?) to do so, this argues against free choice.

Another explanation that I've heard several times to justify the extermination of these heathen nations was that they were so incredibly evil, which demands the question why God made exceptions for the Aztec religion, or the church in the Dark Ages, or 1940s Germany under Hitler, or many other evil civilizations and societies. In fact, it is often said that they were so evil that they sacrificed their children. Is there not something ironic in a command which goes something like: *"I want you to go in there and slaughter their children because they're so wicked that they slaughter their own children"*?

I've also heard the argument that the nation of Israel had to keep itself genetically and racially pure in order to ensure that the Messiah would truly be from Abraham's seed and of David's line. But irrespective of whether they were racially pure or not, any and all descendants of Abraham and David would still be of Abraham's seed and David's line. Why not allow the gentiles to have an equal role in the unfolding of the plan of salvation? Ruth was a Moabite (which was a group of people that God had long previously commanded should all be slaughtered!?) and was part of the lineage of Jesus (Matthew 1:5). Likewise, Rahab, was from Jericho (and a prostitute), a city in Canaan which was also designated for complete destruction, but she was granted asylum by two Israelite army spies (Joshua 2; although this was clearly acceptable to Joshua, there's no mention that this was at God's command), and later became the wife of one of Jesus's descendants (Matthew 1:5; Hebrews 11:31). On the other hand, if there was in fact some kind of spiritual necessity for a pure (that is, inbred) blood-line, then couldn't an omnipotent and omniscient God keep that line pure without resorting to genocide, or shorten up the time-line so that it didn't stretch out for thousands of years and run the danger of getting 'contaminated'?

Another example: in order to justify the way women are portrayed in scripture, it becomes necessary to develop theologies around the fact that it was Eve who sinned first; that women are the weaker sex; that God gave authority to men over women; that the man is the head of the household; that women should not teach men. (At least not Westernized men: it otherwise seems perfectly all right for those same women to become missionaries overseas and teach men in third world countries.) My rebuttal: why not simply attribute those ideas to an ancient, patriarchal, Semitic way of thinking about women. It was, after all, only that kind of men who were involved in the writing of those scriptures.

And a third one: in order to satisfy a desire to accumulate wealth at all costs, we emphasize how God commanded us to *"fill the earth and subdue it. Rule over the fish of the sea and the birds of the air and over every living creature that moves on the ground."* (Genesis 1:28). And so we pillage the earth, plunder its resources, especially in third world countries who have to bear the cost of the despoiling and pollution which is needed to produce cheap goods for us. Somewhat related to this third point, some people are growing concerned with how easy it becomes for 'Christianized' nations to justify war against certain countries, to become comfortable with the nuclear option, and to nudge world events ever closer to an apocalyptic end, simply because *"this was all foretold in the scriptures. It doesn't matter if it all gets destroyed: it just brings us that much closer to glory"*. My rebuttal: God wants to bring heaven to earth, not people to heaven.

Or we could talk about how easily the church can condemn people and lifestyles (for example, the venomous rhetoric about homosexuality) and other religions. Or condone the burning of witches. Or justify slavery.

HAVE WE GONE TOO FAR?

The point is that by attributing too much literal meaning to the words of books like Genesis, and forbidding any questioning of those texts, we end up with a theology that distorts the image of a loving God, and gives that theology a degree of authority that we take away from God. We start to worship the book itself, rather than God. We put that book on such a high pedestal that it becomes a god to us. A friend of mine who is a pastor told me that this well-recognized problem in the church today is sometimes referred to by him and his colleagues as 'Bibliolatry' (in case it isn't immediately obvious to the reader, this is a play on the word 'idolatry'). Or we Christians get caught up in fruitless internal battles amongst ourselves. I found Brueggemann's analogy [138] of this in-house conflict over Genesis 1 particularly worth repeating: *"As much as any part of the Bible, this text has been caught in the unfortunate battle of 'modernism', so that 'literalists' and 'rationalist' have acted like the two mothers of 1 Kings 3:16-28, nearly ready to have the text destroyed in order to control it."*

As for me, I've just stopped worshipping the Bible, and stopped giving it more authority than it asks for itself. I recently found a popular rhyme --- *"Two men looked out from prison bars, one saw mud, the other stars"* --- which got me thinking about different ways to read the Bible. In my train of thought, that nugget of wisdom became: *"Four men looked into a puddle: one saw the mud, the other saw stars, the third saw his own reflection, and a fourth claimed that the puddle was alive and could speak and had magical powers that could bring riches and healing to anyone who would dip their fingers into it"*. My own rendition is admittedly much more

---

[138] Walter Brueggemann, *Interpretation: A Bible Commentary for Teaching and Preaching.* (John Knox Press, 1982), p. 25

clunky than the pithy original, but my point is that we can use the Bible in four different ways:

> (1) disregard it ... dismiss it as good-for-nothing ... outdated and horribly flawed;

> (2) look into it to see ourselves, warts and all, our heart's motives, thoughts, desires;

> (3) look through it and beyond it to the infinite and see God;

> (4) turn it into a shrine or a god and worship it.

I'd advocate #2 and #3: using the Bible to learn about what we are and what we could be. Reading it through the lens of Jesus Christ and his teachings: *"Love the Lord your God with all your heart and with all your soul and with all your mind ... and love your neighbour as yourself"* (Matthew 22:37) and *"Do to others as you would have them do to you"* (Luke 6:31).

9

What can a modern Christian believe now?

What do I believe now?

Why do I, as a scientist in Western society during the 21st century still leave the life of Jesus 'on the table'?

Are you throwing out the Bible?

How can an all-loving and all-powerful God allow so much suffering in this world?

As I wrote in the introductory chapter, there's a wide spectrum of beliefs between the two extremes of conservative fundamentalist Christianity and secular atheism. In this chapter, I'd like to share where I've landed, after much thinking, asking, investigation, and prayer.

In chapter one of this book, I presented a series of questions that unpacked a complete re-shaping of what I believe. Questions regarding the creation accounts. About the Bible itself. About other world religions. And now when I look back on the journey, I can honestly say I didn't lose my faith, I actually strengthened and deepened it.   In wrestling with the scientific questions, I completely lost any ability to believe that an atheistic worldview can explain everything, and reaffirmed (or re-found?) my belief in God's involvement. At the same time, I've learned I can still remain faithful to scripture even though I take a much less dogmatic stance on it, particularly the concepts of its inerrancy, infallibility, inspiration and authority. In the process, I found a new value for the scriptures, and re-discovered a confidence in sharing what I believe with whomever will listen. So what do I believe now ...

ABOUT THE BIBLE

In my journey through trying to incorporate the book of Genesis into my worldview, I've moved through three distinct camps of thinking.

At first, I was fully a literalist. I took the words at face-value. Whatever the text said must be the way things were. Other YE Christians will here use phrases like *"a plain reading of the text"* and *"a literal reading of scripture"*.

When that became unsatisfactory --- when my beliefs clashed with increasing force against the findings of science and the moral/ethical issues raised by many of its stories --- I completely left the YE view and moved into Concordism, which is a perspective that tries to find agreement or compatibility between the Biblical texts and science. Concordism, which reads our own world-view into the text, was the driving force behind the 'Gap Theory' and the concept of 'apparent age' that I described in the first half of chapter two. It is also behind the much more developed idea that consumed the 2nd half of chapter two, which tried to re-interpret Genesis within Big Bang cosmology and Darwinian Evolution on a verse-by-verse basis. But all of those Concordist paradigms eventually cracked.

Those failed attempts raise some important questions. Why do we presume that God would give us a text that only makes complete sense to 21st century readers? Why do we feel the need to take an ancient document, one written thousands of years before humans had made any scientific discoveries and try to find modern science hidden in that text? If the answer to that question is *"God knows everything and he wrote the Bible"*, then you also have to attribute to God the errors and discrepancies that I've talked about at length in my preceding chapters.

As the scientific evidence pushed with increasing force against my fundamentalist and Concordist thinking, something had to happen. One approach would be to just stiffen my back and harden myself against the opposition, much like how we humans make bulkier buildings to stand up against ever stronger winds and earthquakes, or stiffer piers to stand up to greater tides and wave action. The problem with that approach is that eventually the opposing force is too great and the structure snaps. This is what I see happening when Christians eventually give up their faith when faced with some of the big questions addressed in this book. Too many of my friends and family have given up their faith because their rigid belief system cracked.

A very different approach is the one taken by nature: trees simply bend to the hurricanes and earthquakes that knock down buildings, and sea plants just slosh back and forth in the violent surf that demolishes the boat or the pier. In both cases, they just shrug their shoulders and wait out the destructive forces around them. Some might view this revision of my theology in the new light of understanding from modern science as a defeat. A compromise (again, that word that certain people just can't accept). So be it. I see it instead as a reasonable way to deal with two different sets of truth.

My current view now is that Genesis in particular, and the Bible in general, is not meant to be a science or history textbook. It does not explain the details of origins of the universe and life and people, beyond teaching that God was ultimately behind it all. Chapters 37 and 38 of the book of Job should definitely not be your go-to source for weather-prediction. When Jesus taught that the mustard seed *"is the smallest of all seeds on earth"* (Mark 4:31), he was not speaking as a horticulturalist: there are many, many plants with smaller seeds. (some translations try to circumvent this problem by re-writing the text as *"the smallest of '**your**' seeds"*, but that word 'your' is not in the original Greek … it's an editorial insertion, another one of those human fingerprints on the text).

So now I find myself in a third camp. I've come to reconsider the Bible from a whole different viewpoint. One that can remain faithful to the text as divinely inspired, while at the same time recognizing that humans were involved from start to finish in the writing, copying and distribution processes. Rather than dictate the Bible to get it exactly right, God preferred to work it out with us: a mother could easily make a perfect cake all by herself, but might instead choose to do it with her children, despite the mess and mistakes, in order to make it a shared personal experience. As Peter Enns put it: *"As Christ is both God and human, so is the Bible"* [139]. My current view integrates the Bible with other sets of truth: scientific discoveries of the origins of all things … archaeological findings of religious writings which predate biblical writings … sociological insights into the way humans think and are wired … historical insights from Babylonian, Egyptian, Chinese, and South American civilizations … et cetera. For me, doing this was revolutionary and liberating. A paradigm-shift. Now I could move forward with my faith and share it with others, including non-believers and avowed atheists, and not be embarrassed into silence by

[139] Peter Enns, *Inspiration and Incarnation: evangelicals and the problem of the Old Testament.* (Grand Rapids, Michigan; Baker Academic Press, 3rd printing, 2005), p. 17

certain interpretations and misconceptions of the OT. The truth will set you free! I can read the words describing the creation event and either take the text literally (six days of creation, 6,000 years ago) or figuratively (billions of years, with God using naturalistic processes as his tools). In the same way, I can see the parts of the story of the Garden of Eden and Original Sin as either literal or figurative. The literal interpretation involves an over-the-top response on the part of God, and raises quite a few very difficult, uncomfortable (and indefensible?) questions, whereas the figurative interpretation is consistent with a view of God being infinite love. I don't have to accept a long-standing traditional interpretation of scriptural passages when an alternative interpretation better explains things and still stays true to scripture. It's all about interpretations!

I still think the authors of Genesis fully believed what they were writing was absolutely and literally true and not merely imaginative stories or simply metaphor and allegory. Otherwise, I don't know why they would bother with such precise details as the geographical descriptions of where to find the Garden of Eden: *"A river watering the garden flowed from Eden; from there it was separated into four headwaters. The name of the first is the Pishon; it winds through the entire land of Havilah, where there is gold. (The gold of that land is good; aromatic resin and onyx are also there.) The name of the second river is the Gihon; it winds through the entire land of Cush. The name of the third river is the Tigris; it runs along the east side of Ashur. And the fourth river is the Euphrates."* (Genesis 2:10-14). Notice it doesn't just give the names of some mythical rivers or lands which might have pre-existed the writer, but also says it's the place where the reader can now find good gold and resin and onyx (a beautiful stone with waving bands of color)! Clearly they meant for this text to be taken at face value. But that doesn't mean it has to be true. It's worth pointing out that there's no place on earth where these 4 rivers and lands converge, let alone can be found (some no longer exist). This portion of the text only makes sense from an ancient perspective but not to modern readers (which mirrors the problem I described for Concordism, which imposes onto the text a meaning that is available to __us__ in the 21st century but not to the ancient readers, the original recipients).

Another example I would give that suggests the original writers of Genesis believed the text was absolutely true (yet at the same time undercuts its believability) is the detailed vital statistics they include: the precise ages at which dozens of key people (only males) were born, had sons (occasionally daughters are also mentioned) and died (see Genesis chapters 5, 10 and 11). But just because the authors might believe these details to be true doesn't mean they were true. Today it takes some pretty flexible mental gymnastics to explain not only how these men in Genesis lived for many hundreds of years, but also how they weren't fathering children until they were well beyond 50 or even 100 years of age (Genesis 5), especially since God had already given them the command to *"be fruitful and multiply"* (Genesis 1:28), that *"the daughters of men were beautiful"* (Genesis 6:2), and that there were apparently no laws against any sexual activities (the Mosaic laws wouldn't be introduced for another 2,000 years). Instead, it's worth noting that the authors of Genesis had access to those Mesopotamian texts which listed Sumerian kings with unusually long life-spans (for example, the Sumerian king Alalgat is said to have reigned for 36,000 years) which also decreased to more contemporary standards after a Flood described in their Sumerian records. Perhaps the authors of Genesis were just white-washing those older pagan stories.

For these reasons, and many others, I think the author(s) of Genesis also fully believed that the world was created in six consecutive days, each being the normal 24 hour period by which we all set our clocks even today. This is consistent with the context: the repeated use of the word 'day' together with the repeated mention of evening followed by morning. But that doesn't mean we have to also take it as historically and scientifically accurate, as I'll explain in the next section.

Likewise, I'll agree that many other Biblical authors and leaders seemed to fully believe that the events recorded in the book of Genesis were historically factual. Adam is mentioned by Luke (Luke 3:38), Paul (Romans 5:12-14; 1 Corinthians 15:22 and 45; 1 Timothy 2:13-14), and Jude (Jude 14). The Flood is mentioned by Peter (2 Peter 2:5). But, again, this doesn't prove the historicity of those stories. I've already made the point that these authors were people of their time and culture. They saw the world the way others at that time saw the world. They also believed that heaven is somewhere 'up' in space, and hell is somewhere 'down' in the depths of the earth. That the earth was flat and the sun revolved around the earth. They believed in the existence of Leviathan, which they took to be either a great sea monster (Job 41:1; Psalm 74:13-14; Psalm 104:26; Isaiah 27:1) or a fire-breathing dragon (Job 41:19-20). They held that dietary laws and circumcision were of paramount importance, that animal sacrifices needed to be offered at various times, and that people and things sometimes needed to undergo purification rites. These are all legitimate pre-modern Jewish beliefs and values that most of us don't hold anymore.

Yes, even Jesus refers indirectly to Adam (Mark 10:6), and directly to the Flood (Matthew 24:38-39). But again, he was speaking to a thoroughly Jewish audience, and either stooped to their level of understanding or possibly shared in that limited understanding. Please, before you react too strongly to that statement, consider that the writer of the book of Hebrews does say that Jesus *"... shared in their humanity..."* (2:14) and *"... had to be made like them, fully human in every way..."* (2:17). He did appear to have certain human limitations prior to the Resurrection story. There were things he didn't know (Matthew 24:36 ... about the final day). Things he couldn't do, like ministry in a crowd that didn't have faith in him (Mark 6:5), or be in two places at once. He still walked wherever he taught throughout Judea and Galilee. He still needed to catch a good sleep (Mark 4:38). At times it seems he experienced human emotions like anger (*"He looked around at them in anger and, deeply distressed at their stubborn hearts"*, Mark 3:5; or clearing the temple in John 2:13-17), sadness (*"Jesus wept"*, John 11:35) or extreme sorrow (*"My soul is overwhelmed with sorrow to the point of death"*, Matthew 26:38), possibly even some degree of fear (*"At this, they picked up stones to stone him, but Jesus hid himself, slipping away from the temple grounds"*, John 8:59). He could still suffer, get thirsty and weak, and be killed. All of these verses tell us that prior to the Resurrection event, he was not omniscient, omnipotent nor omnipresent. Contrary to what he is quoted as saying, we know that the mustard seed is not the smallest of seeds (Mark 4:31) and I think we can agree that Hades is not 'down' in the depths of the earth (Matthew 11:23; Luke 16:23). Instead, I think he said those things because his audience thought that and/or because he himself thought that. I would apply the same interpretation when Jesus refers to Adam and to the Flood.

ABOUT THE CREATION STORY

There is probably no end to alternative interpretations of the Creation accounts. Let me present two that seem to be popular right now and which I found interesting for a short while, but eventually set aside, and then I'll describe a third one which is how I see it now.

Henri Blocher re-framed the first chapter of Genesis as an elaborate poetic literary device [140]. He called attention to an apparent parallel structure in the six days of creation: everything begins as *"formless and void"*, then God uses the first three days to create spaces and the next three days to fill those spaces with things ... the 'formless and void' is 'given form and then filled'. It's almost like God is creating a shelf-unit and then putting things into the shelf spaces (which is how I can imagine the Jewish

---

[140] Henri Blocher, *In the Beginning: The Opening Chapters of Genesis* (Intervarsity Press; 1984)

teacher presenting this Creation account to his students and listeners):

Day 0: formless and void

Day 1: light and dark   **Day 4:** celestial bodies

Day 2: waters above/below; sky   **Day 5:** fish; birds

Day 3a: dry ground and seas   **Day 6a:** animals
Day 3b: vegetation   **Day 6b:** humans

Day 7: rest

There is also an appealing parallelism in that days one and four each describe a single creation event, days two and five both describe a single act with two parts, and days three and six both have two creative acts. This proposal is often referred to as the Framework Hypothesis [141] [142]. However, some fundamental flaws in this have been pointed out. For example, the sun which was made on day four is placed in the firmament or sky (day two) not within light (day one). Or the fact that fish, made on day five, belong in the seas (day three) not the waters above the firmament or the waters beneath the earth (day two) [143]. Finally, plants were made on day three and placed on the land which was also created on the third day. So the claim that this literary device is a divine construct fails, as far as I am concerned: it is clearly a flawed product or artefact of either the author(s) or of the interpreter(s).

An alternative version of this Framework Hypothesis uses the Creation account to teach the reader about authority structures. The first three days involve the creation of realms, and the next three days to talk about the rulers of those realms. The sun and moon are said to *"govern the day ... and the night"*. Fish and birds would rule over the seas and sky, respectively, while the animals would rule over the land, and man was then created as God's representative *"so that they may rule over the fish in the sea and the birds in the sky, over the livestock and all the wild animals, and*

---

[141] John H. Walton, "Proposition 12: Other theories of Genesis One either go too far or not far enough" in *The Lost World of Genesis One*, p. 110. (Intervarsity Press, 2009)
[142] Rikk Watts, "Making Sense of Genesis 1", *Stimulus* 12(4):2-12, 2004
[143] I'll explain below how the waters below the firmament might be very different from the seas.

over all the creatures that move along the ground."

A second re-interpretation describes Genesis chapter one as a temple text [144]. It claims that the anecdote is not an explanation of the materialistic origins of things, but rather the assignment of function to pre-existing things as God sets up his temple. Once a temple has been built, what does one do next? Other ancient societies would set up an icon or statue of the god to which that temple belonged, and believed the god ruled over their domain from that temple. Likewise, God sets up humans, 'made in His image', in the middle of the Garden as a co-ruler over creation, with the instruction *"Rule over the fish in the sea and the birds in the sky and over every living creature that moves on the ground"* (Genesis 1:28). One of the main lines of evidence for this re-interpretation by John Walton is the claim that the Hebrew word for 'create' ('bara') is used dozens of times in the OT, but almost never in the context of a material object. He lists these occurrences in a table in his book, and indeed some of them are abstract or non-material things: a pure heart (Psalm 51:10) ... north and south (Psalm 89:12) ... ends of the earth (Isaiah 40:28) ... darkness and disaster (Isaiah 45:7) .... and many others. But surprisingly, and contrary to the author's claim, that table also lists many material things: heavens and earth ... creatures ... people ... rivers ... smoke ... celestial bodies ... cities ... blacksmiths ... kings ... et cetera. I'll leave it to the interested reader to decide what they think of this re-interpretation of Genesis 1.

My present thinking about the Creation accounts is this: the ancient author(s) wrote them from the simple and naïve understanding that everyone at that time had of the way things were, but divine inspiration prompted the Jewish writers to begin to re-interpret that pre-Jewish understanding in a slightly different light. How did everyone at that time see the world and the universe? Take a walk with me and look at the world through eyes that are not informed by any modern scientific understanding whatsoever.

They did not have airplanes or wheeled/motorized ground transport to help them put the lands around them into context or to explore the far reaches of the world and realize it as a globe, and they had very limited boat travel. The vast majority of people at that time never travelled more than a few days' walk from home. So the best that the more adventurous and inquisitive among them could do would be to climb to a nearby mountain top and look around them, and all they would see is an apparently flat earth, at the edges of which were the mountains and the sea (depending on where they were and how far they travelled, the latter would be the Mediterranean Sea, the Red Sea, the Persian Gulf, the Caspian Sea or the Black Sea).

---

[144] John Walton, *The Lost World of Genesis One.* (Intervarsity Press, 2009)

Recall the scriptural references to "*... the four corners of the earth ...*" (Isaiah 11:12; Ezekiel 7:2; Revelation 7:1; Revelation 20:8), "*... the ends of the earth ...*" (Job 37:3; Acts 1:8) and "*... the edge of the earth ...*" (Job 38:13).

And when they looked up, they had no telescopes, binoculars, satellites or any other tool to tell them that the sun, moon and stars were any further away than the birds in the sky. There was no reason for them to think that those objects in the night sky were unfathomably bigger than the earth and millions of light-years away, rather than just lanterns a few miles up at best. They would not know that the sun was 400 times bigger than the moon (to the uninformed person they look like they're almost identical in size, which is why we can experience both a solar eclipse and a lunar eclipse), or that many of the stars were millions of times bigger and hotter than the sun. All of those celestial bodies seemed to move in an arc across the sky, and the ancient star-gazer had no way to explain how lanterns might simply float in mid-air a couple miles up, so they envisioned that those little lights were hanging from a big dome or upside-down bowl placed on top of the flat earth, held up by the mountains and curving down to the sea(s).

When raindrops fell down from the sky, they had no understanding of the water cycle, including the concept of evaporated water condensing 'out of thin air'. The only way for them to comprehend this mysterious water from the sky was to propose that there was a large body of water beyond the dome ("*the waters above*"; which might explain why the sky is blue?) and small holes in the dome which let the water drip through. And when they explored the river systems, they found that water seemed to just continually flow out of the ground ("*the waters below*"): in many cases, this flow seemed to never stop, even when there hadn't been rain for several months and all the surrounding fields had long since dried up. "*Where does all this water keep coming from?*" they might ask. It just kept pouring out from somewhere underneath, so there must be yet another large body of water deep underneath the earth and gushing to the surface.

These simple misinterpreted observations formed the basis of the Hebrew creation story [145]. It's clear from the wording that the ancients saw the dome in the sky (translated in the KJV as 'firmament', in the NIV as 'expanse', and in other translations as 'vault') as something solid. In the book of Job, when describing God's control over various aspects of weather, one of Job's friends says: "*can you join him in spreading out the skies, hard as a mirror of cast bronze?*" (Job 37:18). This solid dome was thought to hold back the waters above (from which the rain trickled out) and separate

---

[145] John Walton, *The Lost World of Genesis One*. (Intervarsity Press, 2009)

those upper waters from the underground waters below the earth (from which the rivers came forth).

So now let's re-read the Genesis account with these ideas of a solid dome holding back the waters above, and another body of water deep under the earth … *"And God said, 'Let there be an **expanse** between the waters to separate water from water.' So God made the **expanse** and separated the water under the **expanse** from the water above it. And it was so. God called the **expanse** 'sky' … And God said, 'Let there be lights in the **expanse** of the sky to separate the day from the night, and let them serve as signs to mark sacred times, and days and years, and let them be lights in the **expanse** of the sky to give light on the earth' … God set them in the **expanse** of the sky to give light on the earth, to govern the day and the night, and to separate light from darkness" … and let birds fly above the earth across the **expanse** of the sky"*. Not only would this dome have holes for the rain and other holes or hooks for the celestial lights (notice that God sets the lights "*in*" the firmament, not "*beyond*" it), but it also had rooms to store the lightning, thunder, hail, snow, wind, et cetera (Job 37 and 38; Psalm 135:7; Jeremiah 51:16). Maybe the ancients also thought it had windows for God and the hosts of heaven to watch us, and to call down from.

The Babylonians, Egyptians and other peoples of the earth also had this understanding of the vault or dome spread over a flat earth, and they had similar stories of creation [146]: stories of who created that dome and those waters, and how they all got there. But they attributed the latter to their own various deities: the sun-god, the moon-god, animal gods, demi-gods (half human, half divine), et cetera. They also describe those deities separating out waters from waters (the Egyptians personified the primordial waters as 'Nun', while the Sumerians personified it as 'Nammu') … separating land from waters … separating light from darkness.

What about the origin of living things? The ancient authors had no understanding of cell biology, DNA, genes, chromosomes, mutations, inheritance patterns, ecological niches, natural selection or biological evolution. But they did know that living things came from other similar living things. As they leaned back on the rocks in the hillside hour after hour watching their sheep, one boy asked *"Papa, where do sheep come from?"* The obvious answer: from their mama sheep. *"But where did the mama sheep come from?"* The answer …. well, you know where this is going. Even these ancient Hebrews could clearly see that their sheep always gave birth only to other sheep, and each generation of sheep came from a previous generation of sheep. As the hours ticked away on that lazy

---

[146] Rikk Watts, "Making Sense of Genesis 1", *Stimulus* 12(4):2-12, 2004

afternoon, the father and son silently envisioned a nearly endless series of generations of sheep going back more years than they could count. But it couldn't go on forever like this: there had to have been a 'first sheep' at some point. And the only thing that made sense was that JHWH made the first sheep, which gave birth to all the other sheep which have existed ever since. Likewise, JHWH made the first cow, which gave birth to more cows. And the same for sparrows, and frogs, and insects and wheat. YHWH made them all, *"each according to their kind."* And much the same for humans, although here the story had to have some interesting twists and unique details because "everyone knows that people are somehow different from animals" (it was that same egocentric streak in humans which gave us the geocentric theory: the idea that the entire universe revolves around the earth). To the authors of scripture, it couldn't have been as undignified an event as the Mesopotamian's version of Aruru pinching off a piece of clay and casting it out into open country, where it becomes a man (of course, in those ancient societies, it **had** to be a man that was created first). Another Egyptian version had the god Khnum making man out of clay on his pottery wheel. But JHWH would not have done it that way.

So Genesis was written in part as a polemic against those alternative and competing religious understandings [147]. It taught that there is only one God, not many. That God created everything in a peaceful benevolent way (speaking it into existence), rather than through acts of violence (the Babylonian version had Marduk creating the world by splitting open the carcass of the goddess Tiamat, whom he had killed in a battle). That humans were created to be co-regents with God over a garden of paradise, rather than as servants or slaves of the Babylonian or Egyptian god(s). That God provided food for people, rather than creating the humans to bring food and sacrifices to the god(s), as the Babylonians believed. That the sun, moon, stars, water, plants, animals – in fact, everything – were all merely created things to be enjoyed, not powerful deities to be feared. Genesis doesn't even give those foreign deities the honor of having names: *"God made two great lights—the greater light to govern the day and the lesser light to govern the night."* (Genesis 1:16). It doesn't use the obvious words 'sun' and 'moon', which would also be the names for those Egyptian and Babylonian gods, but opts instead for 'greater light' and 'lesser light'.

It seems, then, that the Genesis account is very much a human invention, and its purpose is to correct the theology behind the popular understanding of the time. More to my point though: its purpose is not to be

---

[147] Clark H. Pinnock, "Climbing Out of a Swamp: The Evangelical Struggle To Understand the Creation Texts" *Interpretation* 43:143-155 (1989)

God's scientific or historical version of how it all happened. It doesn't seem that God ever found it necessary to use the Biblical texts to correct their thinking about 'the firmament', or the shape of the earth, or the relative sizes of the celestial bodies, or the water cycle, or the correct ordering of when plants and animals appeared on the scene, et cetera. In the same way, he never seemed to find it necessary to correct their thinking about the process of thinking itself: the ancients, including the Israelites, believed that our intelligence, emotions and personality arose from the very center of our body ... from our kidneys, liver and intestines, rather than our brain ... and that is the language that the Hebrew texts used. For example, when David wrote in Psalm 40:8, *"your law is in my heart"*, the text is literally written *"your Torah is in my guts"*. In Philippians 1:8, Paul literally longs for his readers *"in the bowels of Jesus Christ"*. As John Walton put it: *"Through the entire Bible, there is not a single instance in which God revealed to Israel a science beyond their culture. No passage offers a scientific perspective that is not common to the Old World science of antiquity"* [148].

So the Creation account in Genesis is the first step in a demythologization of the cosmos; a leveling of the playing field to dispel any concept of other gods and goddesses. The Israelites didn't need to know exactly how things were created ... the exact mechanism and chronology ... but they did need to know that those things were in fact simply creations like themselves rather than gods to be feared. And as the texts of Genesis 1 and the rest of the Bible continue from there, we find out more and more how humanity revised its thinking as it learned about God. It's our on-going diary, or notebook, of our search for God, rather than his Owner's Manual to us. Once we get past the seriously challenging stories in Genesis 1-10, which have a hugely Mesopotamian resemblance, we come to the physical and spiritual journey made by one family, headed by Abraham, his son Isaac and his grand-son Jacob.   Thomas Cahill gives a great summary [149] of the huge changes in our thinking as this family transitioned from Sumerian polytheists in Babylon (*"We can be certain that Avraham began, like all Sumerians, as a polytheist..."*) to Semitic monotheists in Canaan. Cahill begins with Abraham merely hearing a voice (*"Even in the earliest stages, then, this relationship is different from the relationships of other Sumerians to their patronal gods."*), explores several of the encounters those patriarchs had with God, ends with Jacob's physical wrestling with God, and comes to a conclusion: *"The religious center is no longer what it*

[148] John Walton, *The Lost World of Genesis One*, p.17 (Intervarsity Press, 2009)
[149] Thomas Cahill, T*he Gifts of the Jews: How a Tribe of Desert Nomads Changed the Way Everyone Thinks and Feels."* (Bantam Doubleday Dell Publishing Group, 1998)

had been for the Sumerians and all other ancient cultures — impersonal manipulation by means of ritual prescriptions – but a face-to-face friendship with God". But old habits are hard to break: all three patriarchs still build altars (Genesis 12:7; 26:25; 35:7) and offer sacrifices (there were no Mosaic laws requiring altars or sacrifices at this point in time), Jacob's wife Rachel hangs onto the statues of her father's household gods (Genesis 31:19, 34) and the nation of Israel tries to discern God's will by 'casting dice' (the Urim and Thumim, which are believed to have been small sticks or stones which gave a yes or no answer; Exodus 28:30; Leviticus 8:8; Numbers 27:21; Deuteronomy 33:8; 1 Samuel 14:41; 1 Samuel 28:6; Ezra 2:63; Nehemiah 7:65). But just the same, they opened up a whole new perspective on God, one that didn't exist before they left polytheistic Mesopotamia. And we get novel revelations of God through the eyes of people like Job, Ruth, Rahab, David, Isaiah, and Daniel. As we continue reading, we learn more and more about God, mixed in together with their cultural misunderstandings, eventually coming to the full revelation of God in the person of Jesus Christ. And we're still learning today!

ABOUT CHRISTIANITY, WORLD RELIGIONS AND JESUS CHRIST

It's clear that humans have been on a search for God for at least a couple hundred thousand years. I think many religions may give us some clues about who God is and how to find him. Many people believe they've found God through some of the most bizarre of spiritual journeys, and I can believe that even the parts of the journeys through very non-Christian beliefs actually led them to God.

If I'm lost while journeying through a forest, I can find my way out of a forest using a wide variety of strategies, some more precise or effective than others. I can get a sense of what direction to go if I use the sun and my watch to give me a crude sense of east-west directions ... the proverbial 'moss grows on the north side of a tree' or a night-time sighting of the north star to give me a sense of the north-south axis (or if I'm down under, the Southern Cross can point me to the South Celestial Pole) ... the direction of flow of a stream to tell me which way to find the valley (where civilization is more likely to be found than at higher elevations). Maybe I can listen for certain distant landmarks, like the ocean, a highway, an industrial center. Using those cues, and ignoring red herrings, and possibly a little luck, I may eventually find my way out of that forest, albeit with a lot of meandering and re-tracing of my steps. Or I may end up becoming worm food before getting out. But a map and a GPS unit will tell me exactly where I am, where I want to be, and the shortest and quickest route between the two.

In my opinion, many religions in general, including Christianity, can provide rough clues for our journey through life to find God, but Jesus Christ the person provides the map, compass and GPS co-ordinates. I'm not saying that all religions are the same. Clearly they are different, often contradictory, sometimes even at enmity. But I am saying that many of them have some ring of truth, some more than others, mixed in with some wrong ideas. Even the modern version of the religion referred to as Christianity does not fully follow the life teaching of Jesus. But Jesus is a person, not a religion, and he gives the best example to follow in our search to know God. Other individuals have been put on similar pedestals: Buddha (Siddhartha); Confucius; Mohammad; Ghandi; Mother Theresa; the Dalai Lama; and many others. But when I take a close look at the life stories of even those highly revered individuals, I find that they fall short of the ideal: for some, it's a life of violence, a racist or misogynist attitude, or even activities that today would have them arrested. For others of those human heroes, it's an attitude of indifference to human suffering around them, or of haughty indignation to certain groups of people. This is not the case for Jesus Christ. In the end, I think that he gives us the best example to follow in getting to know God.

Why do I, as a scientist in Western society during the 21st century, having just written over a hundred pages which dismiss much of traditional Christian interpretation, still leave the life of Jesus 'on the table'? I don't think anyone can credibly deny that Jesus Christ lived and died at the hands of an occupying Roman army, and the prompting of a jealous religious establishment, leaving behind an abundance of theological and practical lifestyle teachings. But he was more than just a 'great teacher'. He started something that can't be explained. His closest followers — 'the twelve' — were essentially nobodies. Several were fishermen, one was a tax-collector; we (I at least) don't know the occupations of the others, but they certainly don't seem to have been intellectuals or community leaders (Luke, the writer of one of the gospels, was a doctor, but was not one of the twelve disciples). And during his arrest and trial they all abandoned Jesus. Within days after his death, they went back to being nobodies ... I particularly like how they're portrayed in the Gospel of John a few days after the death of Jesus: "*Simon Peter, Thomas (called Didymus), Nathanael from Cana in Galilee, the sons of Zebedee, and two other disciples were together. "I'm going out to fish," Simon Peter told them, and they said, "We'll go with you." So they went out and got into the boat, but that night they caught nothing.*" (John 21:2-4). I can hear the defeat in Simon's voice when he mutters "*I'm going out to fish*", and it conveys the resignation or even fear which the other disciples now felt. They had run and fled during Jesus' arrest and trial, and now they put that whole experience behind them, hoping to fade away into the woodwork and go back to their old lives (and I wonder if it's just an artistic flourish or comic relief on John's part to add that they caught nothing). Their hopelessness and confusion are also conveyed in the words of another disciple just a day or two later: "*... they crucified him, but we had hoped that he was the one who was going to redeem Israel ...*" (Luke 24:20-21).

But then something happened. They and many other people began reporting having seen Jesus alive again. And not just seeing him, but saying that they'd walked, talked and ate with him. Sounds ludicrous, I know. And, yes, I also know that this certainly wouldn't have been the first time that someone, after having lost a loved one, will claim to have seen that loved one alive. But how often do thousands claim to see the same previously-dead person, sometimes even hundreds of people gathered together in one single sighting (1 Corinthians 15:6), and will they stick to that story if threatened with torture and death? Here's where the story really becomes remarkable, at least to me. The disciples — nobodies who had just demonstrated their cowardice by fleeing as soon as the Romans and the religious leaders started flexing their muscle, and then fading into the background by going back to fishing — abruptly turned around, stood up to those leaders and began preaching a new message ... one about salvation and being restored to God through the life and work and resurrection of Jesus Christ. And these cowards now suddenly exuded an unexplainable and completely new conviction, despite continuous hardship, poverty and opposition. For their efforts, all of them suffered persecution and martyrdom. Simon Peter was crucified up-side-down in Rome. Andrew was whipped severely and then bound, but not nailed, to a cross until he died two days later. James was thrown from a pinnacle of the Temple at Jerusalem, then stoned and beaten with clubs. Thomas was stabbed to death with a spear. There is overall agreement that six of the eight remaining disciples were also martyred, but discrepancies about the final cause(s) of death (which include beheading, being flayed alive, sawn in half, burning, stoning). Only John died of old age, although having previously been boiled in oil during an earlier wave of persecution in Rome (he survived), and later exiled to the Roman prison island of Patmos for a time before finally being freed. And of course, Judas, the one who betrayed Jesus, took his own life

      All that these disciples had to do, even just one of them, was to admit: *"OK, you're right. The story's made up. We all just got together and conspired to push this hoax. But now I give up"*. Instead, they persisted with this story. And for what gain? There was no money or power to be had in doing this; in fact, any possessions or power they might have had could be completely forfeited or confiscated. For its first 300 years, the Christian church was weak, powerless, persecuted, a minority. There was no empire or structural organization for Christians to rule over. For the first several hundred years, the adherents of this new persecuted faith simply met in each other's houses, generally in secret. Why endure such pain and suffering for a hoax? And not just them, but thousands of others who were convinced by what they too saw and experienced. In one anecdote which could have easily been challenged and refuted by Roman or Jewish leaders, 500 people claimed to have seen the risen Jesus (1 Corinthians 15:6). Thousands persisted in this belief, in ever increasing numbers, despite massive persecution campaigns against them led by the same religious leaders who tried to silence the movement by killing Jesus: *"On that day a great persecution broke out against the church in Jerusalem, and all except the apostles were scattered throughout Judea and Samaria. Godly men buried Stephen and mourned deeply for him. But Saul began to destroy the church. Going from house to house, he dragged off men and women and put them in prison."* (Acts 8:1-3; also see Acts 9:1-2 and Acts 22:4-5). They were fed to the lions, made into living torches to light the games in the Coliseum, and other horrific forms of torture, but they remained steadfast in their newfound belief. Once more, for what gain? All they had to do was deny Christ, and stop believing, preaching and spreading their 'good news'. But they persisted, and thousands of others joined them, including highly prominent and successful people like the Roman centurion Cornelius (Acts 10:1). Another influential leader who joined them was the religious leader Saul (later renamed Paul), who had previously hated Christians to the point of hunting them down to bring them bound to Jerusalem to face punishment and death (Acts 9:1-2; Acts 22:4-5). And for centuries more kept joining this faith. Voluntarily. Why?

      All the historical claims of this new movement could have been challenged and refuted by the religious leaders and Roman government who had tried to silence it, but that never happened!? Why not?

---

[150] I make nothing of the discrepancy about how he died, since a very plausible scenario is Judas hanging himself (Matthew's version) and the body left to hang in the hot Mediterranean sun until it was either cut down or rotted off the rope, whereupon the bloated corpse burst open and the innards spilled out (Luke's version, given in the book of Acts).

Another compelling aspect of this abrupt hundred and eighty degree turn in human history is the cultural context in which this took place: a Jewish setting.   The Shema captures the central and defining belief of Judaism: *"Hear, O Israel, the Lord, the Lord your God, is one Lord and you shall worship the Lord your God with your heart, mind, soul and strength, and him only shall you serve"*. Jews heard this command at least once every day of their life, and I was heard at all their religious gatherings. The first two of the ten commandments stipulated that there are no other gods and that nothing physical can be fashioned to represent God.   Anyone and anything that asserted divinity was seen as blasphemous (this was the only charge that carried any traction in the conviction of Jesus during his trial). Almost every member of the early Christian church was Jewish ... was steeped in Jewish tradition ... had deep Jewish roots and powerful Jewish ties. Their relatives, friends, neighbours and business partners were Jewish and would therefore cut them off if they betrayed this central, defining tenet. And yet these very same people had no trouble equating Jesus with God, and worshipping him. This is unfathomable in a Jewish world; nothing at all like people today deciding to become vegan, or to follow the teachings of Ghandi, or even to announce that they've suddenly turned to Buddhism. This kind of decision completely disrupted one's life; it was in part the motivation for Saul of Tarsus to hunt Christians down to imprison or kill them.   But even he ended up embracing Jesus as the Son of God, and became the most powerful advocate of this new religion. How does one explain that?

No, this is something completely different than the mass hallucination of hundreds (thousands?) of people who just desperately wanted to believe that a loved one was still alive. This was something that changed the world, even 2,000 years later. So this is in part why I've looked a little more closely at the life and teachings of Jesus. Even though they might contain gems of wisdom, I can't relate to the Bagavad Gita any more than I can relate to the OT ... to Hinduism any more than I can to Judaism. But the life and teaching of Jesus is clear to me, unimpeachable and something I can aspire to emulate (but fail miserably all too often).

THE REACTION I EXPECT TO GET, PART II

I began this book with a few of the responses I expected to receive (p. 17), and I won't repeat all those thoughts here. But I do want to elaborate a little further on what I expect from certain fellow Christians.

First, I'm not a universalist: that is, someone who teaches that everyone will eventually get to heaven. I do think some can make choices that lead to eternal destruction, but I don't think that such a judgment will be meted out on the basis of how many 'bad things' they've done, or even the severity of some of their sinful acts. And certainly not meted out on the basis of attendance at a Christian church, the quantity of time spent reading the Bible or in prayer, or the sum of money given to the Christian church. Many might be in for a big surprise when they encounter some of the people they'll find on the preferred side of the pearly gates. And maybe more surprised at who won't be there: according to Jesus, *"Not everyone who says to me, 'Lord, Lord,' will enter the kingdom of heaven, but only he who does the will of my Father who is in heaven. Many will say to me on that day, 'Lord, Lord, did we not prophesy in your name, and in your name drive out demons and perform many miracles?' Then I will tell them plainly, 'I never knew you. Away from me, you evil doers!'"* (Matthew 7:21-23).

But even if they stop short of calling me a universalist, some might say I've made the gospel too soft, taken off the edges, made it too easy. My response: why does it have to be hard and harsh? Jesus said: *"... my yoke is easy and my burden is light ..."* (Matthew 11:30). Sure, he also said: *"Take up your cross and follow me"*, and promised struggles and persecution if we follow him (Mark 10:29-31; John 15:18-21), but while the Christian church went long on commandments and dogmatic theology designed to exclude people, Jesus kept it very simple. His overall synopsis of the law was *"Love the Lord your God with all your heart and with all your soul and with all your mind ... and love your neighbour as yourself"* (Matthew 22:37). And with respect to commands: *"A new command I give you: love one another. As I have loved you, so you must love one another."* (John 13:34). *"Do to others as you would have them do to you"* (Luke 6:31).

Third, some might still say I've rejected the Bible. No I haven't. I just don't worship it. And I won't hold the words of the Bible above the words from science, sociology, or history solely on the simple, blind, unquestioned rationale that *"it's the Bible"*. The Bible was handed down to us by humans, and I'm committed to the stance that it's been contaminated by the hands of humans. But I'll also maintain that its writings are inspired, and give us many important insights into a relationship with God through the eyes and lives of previous believers: again, it's our collective notebook or diary. Nonetheless, I still expect that some will accuse me of violating scripture in the same way that the Pharisees accused the disciples of violating the Sabbath by picking heads of grain as they walked through a field. Jesus wasn't concerned: he told them that *"the Sabbath was made for man, not man for the Sabbath"* (Mark 2:27). Neither the Bible nor the

Sabbath were meant to be worshipped by people, but to help in our worship of God. At this point, some will quote Jesus's teaching *"For truly I tell you, until heaven and earth disappear, not the smallest letter, not the least stroke of a pen, will by any means disappear from the Law until everything is accomplished"* (Matthew 5:18). But this teaching of Jesus is not a commandment to us to take the scriptures as historically, scientifically accurate documents, especially on matters like the Creation story, the Flood, the Tower of Babel or the conquest of Canaan. Instead, he's talking about them as theological documents, and himself being a fulfillment of the Law and the Prophets (Matthew 5:17): the final answer to humanity getting right with God. In this same passage, he repeatedly teaches *"You have heard it said ... but now I say ..."* (Matthew 5:27-28, 31-32, 33-34, 38-39 and 43-44). Despite the many dietary laws in the Pentateuch (and there were indeed many), he teaches *"What goes into someone's mouth does not defile them, but what comes out of their mouth, that is what defiles them"* (Matthew 15:11; also see verses 17-20). Concerning divorce: *"Moses permitted you to divorce your wives because your hearts were hard. But it was not this way from the beginning. I tell you that anyone who divorces his wife, except for sexual immorality, and marries another woman commits adultery."* (Matthew 19:8-9). Each time he does this, he's emphasizing that the scriptures may be a good starting point, but we need to take them to a higher, more complete and more accurate understanding. For that reason, I feel justified in calling for a more informed reading of the Bible (but not an outright dismissal of it). We can read that human diary and learn from previous fellow believers, but we don't have to remain at their level of theological thinking or repeat their mistakes (especially when it comes to the scientific, intellectual and ethical questions which are the prime targets of my book).

To some, this less-than-literal reading of the Bible is wrongly perceived as a new, modern movement borne out of the church abandoning its faith and growing cold. Actually, the truth is that the fundamentalist movement which holds every word of the Bible as literally true is itself a very recent phenomenon. Neither the Apostle's Creed nor the Nicean Creed make any mention of the necessity of reading scripture literally (both are specifically intended to summarize the basic, undeniable, bed-rock foundational beliefs that all Christians must hold). All they say about creation is that God was the one who created everything, but make no mention of 'six days' or any details of how he did so. The exact same statement can be made about the *"Rule of Faith"* written by Irenaeus. Another one of the greatest early church fathers Augustine of Hippo (354-450 AD) wrote that he didn't know what to make of some of Genesis, particularly the six days of Creation; in fact, in his book entitled "*The Literal Interpretation of Genesis*", he concludes that everything was created simultaneously in one instant of time, rather than over 6 distinct calendar days (if you take the time to read his book, you'll see he doesn't at all use the word 'literal' in the same way that many YE Creationists do today). Many other great church leaders down through the ages since Augustine were very ambivalent about those and other details of Creation. It was only approximately two hundred years ago that the fundamentalist movement, which demanded a 'literal' reading of Genesis, was born and the church has been further divided on that point ever since.

Fourth, some will wonder or make assumptions about where I stand on the 'work of the cross'. Exactly what Jesus accomplished in his death. I'm still not fully convinced why spilt blood was necessary for some seemingly clean-living individuals – like the little old lady next door who's only ever been kind and generous, or the little kid who died before his fourth birthday – nor why spilt blood was enough to excuse others with a long list of horrendous sinful acts and/or spiritual flaws. Perhaps it just attests to how seriously God takes 'sin'. Perhaps it wasn't to satisfy God, but rather to neutralize any claims that an Accuser might have against us. This book is not the place to start using words like 'penal substitution', 'propitiation', 'expiation', et cetera. But I do acknowledge that even at my best, I am selfish, proud, boastful, angry, vengeful, et cetera. *"If we claim to be without sin, we deceive ourselves and the truth is not in us."* (1 John 1:8). *"All have sinned and fall short of the glory of God"* (Romans 3:23). *"We all, like sheep, have gone astray, each of us has turned to his own way"* (Isaiah 53:6). So in trying to compare myself with God, I find I only fall well short. That kind of realization of 'never quite making the grade' is a familiar one in life ... the more skilled you become at playing the guitar or piano, the more you see how much better you could be if you worked even harder at it ... the more scientists advance knowledge, the more they'll admit how much they still don't know. In the same way, the more familiar you become with God, the more you realize how inadequate you are, and how often and easily you fall short of his ideals. For this reason, everyone needs salvation and redemption. And the key message from the Bible is that God has provided that. In Jesus.

Fifth: Others who have a fear or contempt of knowledge will conclude that all my searching and learning has corrupted my faith. I would say emphatically, once again, that knowledge has indeed changed how I see human interpretations of spiritual things, but has also deepened my core faith in God and liberated me to share with confidence whatever faith I have (whereas previously I was too often embarrassed into silence). Knowledge and learning are not antagonistic of faith. Moses is said to have been schooled in Pharaoh's courts in the Egyptian empire (see Acts 7:21-22). Daniel was schooled in Babylon, the empire of his time (Daniel 1:3-6). Paul the Apostle was taught in all the ways of Judaism by a leading rabbi of his time (Acts 22:3). Luke the writer of the third gospel and the Book of Acts was a doctor (Colossians 4:14), and was therefore trained in Greek thinking. So higher learning and intellectual pursuit are not things for which anyone needs to apologize.

My own searching has given me a new perspective on my beliefs, and I want to share that with others. But there's a fear in doing so. I'm reminded of Plato's allegory of the cave [151]. In the opening line, Plato presents this as a *"parable of education and ignorance"*. I found it perfectly captures the range of emotions I went through as I embarked on this journey of searching for what I truly believe. In his allegory, people are imprisoned in an underground cave, and can only see objects as two-dimensional shadows projected on the wall by light from a fire inside the cave. One person is freed, and because he can now walk around and look at things from different perspectives, he notices in greater detail the real three-dimensional objects which were projecting the two-dimensional shadows which he and his fellow captives were studying: he's just taken the first step toward a new understanding of what had been there all along. But he continues to explore his surroundings and eventually makes his way out of the cave. At first he's blinded and dazzled by the brilliant sunlight: now he's lost any ability to perceive things and feels lost; there is a certain fear in losing grasp of what was previously a firm perception of 'reality'. Eventually his eyes adapt to this new level of illumination and he can once again see: but not just the few things that might have been in the cave, but now everything outside of the cave, even into the heavens. He now has a whole new perspective on reality. And he comes to the realization that if he were to go back into the cave to his fellow captives, he would be acutely aware of the darkness. His eyes would be unaccustomed to seeing from that perspective. And even if he were to wait for his eyesight to once again accommodate to that dim light, he would never again see things the way he used to. He now knows that they are only shadows of a limited number of objects. Later, Plato emphasizes to his listener how it would be wrong for that person to not go back to the prisoners and help them learn the truth about their view of reality, and also how those fellow prisoners would reject and even mock any person who came back to help them. I can relate completely to the same progression of emotions --- being confused, blinded,

---

[151] Plato, *The Republic, Book VII*

fearful, but then enlightened, confident, and finally wanting to help others out of the same confusing predicament, yet fearing their response to the telling of my new understanding.

Finally, one response I do hope to elicit is discussion. This book was never intended to prove one side over the other, but simply to encourage dialogue and critical thinking; to get you to convince yourself of exactly what you believe and why. In the end, I've shown that one doesn't have to let Genesis (nor the Pentateuch, nor even the OT in general) rob you of your faith.

CONCLUSION: WHAT HAVE I STILL HUNG ON TO?

So, after all this questioning of how seriously (or not) I take the book of Genesis and certain other parts of the OT, I thought I should end with a partial declaration of what I could still believe. There are still several loose threads which have the potential to further change my theology. I'm still struggling through those, and it may take a while before I'm done with them: but those loose threads should be the topic of another book, and I don't want to delay the publishing of this one. So here's my theological statement as of the completion of this book.

I'm still fully convinced that there is a God who is not only omniscient, omnipresent and omnipotent, but also all loving. [That statement alone opens up a whole other theological debate that has raged for millennia: how can an all-loving and all-powerful God allow so much suffering in this world? Sorry, that would be the subject of a whole other book.] He is ultimately responsible for the origin of everything in our universe, and possibly many other parallel universes, and has a twinkle in his eye when it comes to humans: made in his own image. He wants to have a relationship with us, and wants us to enjoy a relationship with him, and to enjoy all creation with him. But he's not going to force himself on us. He much more enjoys watching our feeble and inconsistent attempts to understand him, and rewards all serious attempts to find him. *"You will seek me and find me when you seek me with all your heart"* (Jeremiah 29:13); he speaks to us in a still small voice. As much as he wants us to 'walk in the garden' with him, we are limited in so many ways. We're mortal, not eternal. Full of selfish motives and self-destructive desires. We know that people are hurting in so many ways all around us, and we're content to let that go on rather than make a change: this is the sin of Sodom (Ezekiel 16:49-50). And that's in part how we've *"fallen short of the glory of God"* (Romans 3:23). So God has to change us, from the inside. Create a whole new heart and mind ... *"Do not conform any longer to the pattern of this world, but be transformed by the renewing of your mind. Then you will be able to test and approve what God's will is — his good, pleasing and perfect will."* (Romans 12:2). To do this, he sent Jesus to show us the way: complete self-sacrifice; utter commitment to others; an unrelenting effort to make those changes for the better in ourselves and in the world; total passion to commune with God. Of course, all too often we fail on all four accounts. And for those little things (and perhaps some big things) that we've done which leave a stain of guilt and give others valid cause to accuse us and demand a penalty, he's chosen to take the blame himself and pay whatever price it takes to restore fellowship, even if that price is his own death. *"For God so loved the world that he gave his one and only Son, that whoever believes in him shall not perish but have eternal life."* (John 3:16). And once we've come to realize the extent of his love for us and have accepted his free gift of forgiveness and restoration, he sends us back out to continue the work of restoring the world back to himself. Not just preaching a message, but also getting our hands dirty and cleaning up the mess and fixing the brokenness all around us. [As an aside, I feel this is part of the answer to that last question I raised in the paragraph above: when we scream at God *"how can you allow all this suffering in the world?"*, his answer back to us is *"how can **you** allow all this suffering in the world? Let's work together to change that."*] We can continue on our own self-absorbed way, concerned more and more about making our own life happy and comfortable, even while people around us suffer, sometimes as a result of our selfish pursuit of personal comfort; in the end, we ourselves become responsible for creating hell on earth. Or we can choose to collaborate with God in making it all new again.

ABOUT THE AUTHOR

The author is a Professor in the Department of Medicine of a leading Canadian university, holds three advanced degrees, and has published over 135 research articles and book chapters in scientific journals. He has also served for over 30 years in various church ministries: these have included service on an elder's board, leadership of youth groups and young adult groups, teaching in Sunday school classes (children, youth, young adult and adult classes), and numerous ministries of service. He blogs regularly at http:/ http://lukejjanssen.wordpress.com/

INDEX

Damadian
  Raymond, 87
Daniel, 105, 167, 193, 201
Darwin, 69, 74, 75, 80, 81, 91
David, 22, 105, 106, 107, 108,
  114, 120, 122, 123, 138,
  165, 175, 178, 192, 193
Dawkins
  Richard, 25, 81, 93, 129,
    132, 152
Dead Sea scrolls, 138
Descartes
  René, 87
Diamond
  Jared, 85, 104, 108, 153
Eden, 51, 52, 53, 54, 55, 56,
  104, 114, 125, 126, 127,
  131, 134, 135, 177, 184
Egyptian, 22, 92, 109, 113,
  139, 142, 153, 154, 166,
  167, 168, 183, 191, 201
Einstein
  Albert, 87
Enns
  Peter, 154, 168, 169, 172,
    173, 183
expanse, 33, 34, 189, 190
Ezekiel, 31, 48, 151, 189, 202
Faraday
  Michael, 87
fine-tuning, 89, 90
flagellum, 70
flat earth, 48, 188, 189, 190
Flatland, 7, 67, 68
Flood, 6, 55, 136, 137, 138,
  139, 140, 141, 142, 145,
  146, 153, 164, 165, 168,
  171, 175, 185, 199

Framework Hypothesis, 187
Francis Bacon, 23
Galen, 45
Galileo, 46, 87
Gap Theory, 30, 182
geocentric, 45, 48, 176, 191
Gilgamesh, 138, 145, 146
God-of-the-gaps, 5, 66, 74, 85,
  86, 87, 88, 98
Gosse
  Henry Philip, 24
Gould
  Stephen Jay, 80, 81
Hartle
  James, 64
Harvey
  William, 87
Hawking
  Stephen, 64
Heisenberg
  Werner, 87
hominid, 23, 99, 100, 116
Homo sapiens, 5, 100, 107,
  108, 148
Hosseini
  Khaled, 11, 128
hydrothermal vent, 71
incest, 38, 59, 60, 117, 177
inerrancy, 6, 18, 35, 124, 156,
  162, 164, 165, 170, 171,
  172, 173, 174, 181
infallibility, 18, 110, 124, 156,
  164, 170, 171, 172, 173, 174
inspiration, 6, 35, 156, 157,
  161, 162, 163, 164, 165,
  166, 169, 172, 181, 188
Intelligent Design, 5, 18, 19,
  74, 80, 91, 98

Made in the USA
Charleston, SC
12 December 2014